IND CIRC 951.9042373 M657H
Mills, Randy Keith, 1951-
"Honoring those who paid the
M 312230 04/17/12
New Albany-Floyd Co. Library

"Honoring Those Who Paid the Price":
Forgotten Voices from the Korean War

"HONORING THOSE WHO PAID THE PRICE":
FORGOTTEN VOICES FROM THE KOREAN WAR

RANDY K. MILLS

Indiana Historical Society Press
Indianapolis 2002

© 2002 Indiana Historical Society Press. All rights reserved
Printed in the United States of America

This book is a publication of the
Indiana Historical Society Press
450 West Ohio Street
Indianapolis, Indiana 46202-3269 USA
www.indianahistory.org
Telephone orders   1-800-447-1830
Fax orders   317-234-0562
Orders by E-mail   shop.indianahistory.org

The paper in this publication meets the minimum requirements of American National Standard for Information Sciences—Permanence of Paper for Printed Library Materials, ANSI Z39.48–1984. ∞

Library of Congress Cataloging-in-Publication Data

Mills, Randy Keith, 1951-
   Honoring those who paid the price : forgotten voices from the Korean War / Randy K. Mills
      p.   cm.
   Includes bibliographical references and index.
   ISBN 0-87195-162-2 (alk. paper)
     1. Korean War, 1950-1953—Participation, American. 2. Korean War,
   1950-1953—Indiana. 3. Korean War, 1950-1953—Personal narratives, American. 4.
   Soldiers—Indiana—Biography. 5. Indiana—Biography. I. Title.

DS919 .M555 2002
951.904'2373—dc21

                                                    2002068877

No part of this publication may be reproduced, stored in or introduced into a retrieval system, or transmitted, in any form or by any means (electronic, mechanical, photocopying, recording, or otherwise), without the prior written permission of the copyright owner.

In November 2000 my wife, Roxanne, and I made a journey to Indianapolis to visit the state's Korean War memorial, which lists the names of all those Hoosiers who gave their lives in the Korean struggle. We gently touched the names cut into the stone of those whose stories are told in this book—Harold "Sonny" Bender, Donald Faith, Jr., Charles Garrigus, Jr., Everett Wayne Leffler, Robert "Bud" Fitch, Donald Hamilton, Karl Bowling, Martin Craig Brizius, and Kenneth Ray Cox. Many others not chronicled in this work have their names carved into the granite as well. To all of these brave young Hoosiers, this book is respectfully dedicated.

Contents

Acknowledgments ix
Introduction xiii
Chapter One 3
ILLUSIONS OF PEACE
Chapter Two 37
THE STORM BREAKS
Chapter Three 81
ILLUSIONS OF VICTORY
Chapter Four 113
BITTER RETREAT
Chapter Five 153
THE IMPERFECT WAR
Chapter Six 197
THE HOOSIER HOME FRONT
Chapter Seven 233
AFTERMATH
Appendix 243
Notes 245
Bibliography 259
Index 263

ACKNOWLEDGMENTS

Foremost I wish to thank my wife, Roxanne, for her editing work on this project. Her efforts were of primary importance in bringing the book to its final form.

I would like to thank Andy Jacobs, Jr., for his permission to quote freely from his book *The 1600 Killers: A Wake-up Call for Congress*. Also I wish to thank the Indiana Historical Society and especially the late Robert M. Taylor, Jr., director of the education division, for the support of a Clio Grant. The grant was an essential part of making this book possible.

Thanks also goes to those who took the time to be interviewed for this work and for those who shared letters, photos, and other materials from Korean War veterans. Their contributions make up the heart of this project. Those who gave interviews and/or provided other materials include: William Barnard, Beau Barnett and the Barnett/Leffler families, Delores Beeson, Alan Bender, Marvin Boeglin, Ronald Burton, Thomas Chappell, William Chappell, Alan Cork, Charlene Cox, Dexter Crane, Herbert Crowe, William Cunningham, Robert Doane, Kenneth Dougan, Jackie Brizius Ellis and the Brizius family, William Etheridge, June Ettensohn, Gordon Fitch, Joseph Grappo, Marynelle Greene, Sidney Greenwood, David Graham, Joseph Haag, William Hasselbrinck, William Hyde, Andy Jacobs, Jr., John K. Koehler, Lois Livingston, William Marshall, Donald Mayville, Paul McDaniel, Raleigh McGary, Samuel Muncy, Ira Neal, Stanley Nelson, Henry Orth, Jr., Betty Ann Risley, Carl Spencer, Ralph Steele, Howard Suttmiller,

Paul Torian, Jess Thurman, Peggy Warnsman, Robert Whitehouse, and Hobert Young.

For their typing contributions I wish to thank Elizabeth House, Emily Nelson, Erin Oxendine, and Andy Mills.

For his important assistance in helping to find Hoosier newspaper articles, I wish to thank John Selch at the Indiana State Library, Indianapolis, Indiana.

One of the significant episodes covered in this work, the call-up of marine reserves during the early part of the Korean War, is given detailed treatment in my wife Roxanne's and my book *Unexpected Journey: The Story of a Marine Reserve Company in Korea*, published by the Naval Institute Press in 2000. Also, the incredible and tragic stories of Francisco, Indiana's Charles Garrigus, Jr., and Washington, Indiana's Lt. Col. Donald Faith, Jr., can be found in a shorter version in a December 2000 article "His Valorous Conduct: The Story of a Hoosier Hero in the Korean War" in the *Indiana Magazine of History*, written by Roxanne and myself. Another shorter piece I wrote, detailing the call-up of the Evansville marine reserve group, can be found in the summer 2000 issue of *Traces of Indiana and Midwestern History*.

Sing in me muse and through me tell the story
Of that man skilled in all ways of contending
The wanderer, harried for years on end,
After he plundered the stronghold
on the broad height of Troy.

Opening lines of Homer's *The Odyssey*,
translated by Robert Fitzgerald

INTRODUCTION

Indiana, at the very demographic heart of the country in the late 1940s and early 1950s, stands as a particularly important case study of the effects of the Korean War upon the American people. In 1996 Indiana officially recognized the sacrifices of its citizens who gave their lives in the Korean War. At the Korean War memorial dedication service in Indianapolis in May of that year, Indiana governor Evan Bayh declared, "We live in an uncertain and dangerous world. And if future generations of Americans are called upon to protect the freedom that we savor today, I also pray that they will answer the call as the men and women we honor here today so bravely did. . . . And let them know beyond any doubt that here in Indiana we are always, always honoring those who have paid the price."[1] This book is written in the same spirit of Governor Bayh's words and pays homage to all Hoosiers who served during the Korean conflict. The road to completion of this work, however, was not always smooth. Often seemingly good leads regarding prospective interviews failed to materialize. Sadly, in some instances, potential interviewees passed away before they could tell their stories, their memories of the war lost forever. In a few cases a Hoosier veteran would initially be excited about telling his story only to contact me later and apologize, but explain that in the process of remembering his experiences, difficult and painful memories dredged up from the past caused him to be unable to talk about the war.

While not every Hoosier veteran could be interviewed for this book, I hope that the stories selected will convey a realistic picture of how the war affected Indiana and its citizens. Those interviewed all possessed a vivid memory, and the details they recalled were often connected to powerful emotions as well.

This work also relied upon personal letters and national media sources of the day, along with definitive historical studies of the war, to serve as a kind of quality control. Hoosier newspaper accounts also served as vital sources for conveying the larger context of those trying days that fell upon Hoosier fighting men, their families, and the state throughout the conflict. Letters were especially useful in re-creating the thoughts and feelings Indiana men possessed at particular moments of dramatic and personal confrontations. The voice of Robert "Bud" Fitch, for example, is one that is rather somber for an eighteen year old, and there are hints in his last few letters that the young man knew he might not return to Indiana alive. Two weeks before his death Fitch wrote his mother, "You know you are supposed to regret that you played around and didn't study back in high school but I don't feel that way at all."[2] More than three hundred letters were examined for this work.

Several previously published books relate the larger story of the Korean War. The specific ones used as references for this volume are recommended for anyone who wishes to gain a better understanding of this difficult and complex period in United States history. These works include: *South to the Naktong, North to the Yalu* and *East of Chosin: Entrapment and Breakout in Korea, 1950*, by Roy E. Appleman; Bevin Alexander's *Korea: The First War We Lost*; John Toland's *In Mortal Combat: Korea, 1950–1953*; Eric Hammel, *Chosin: Heroic Ordeal of the Korean War*; S. L. A. Marshall, *The River and the Gauntlet*; Joseph C. Goulden, *Korea: The Untold Story*; and what I believe to be the definitive work on the subject, Clay Blair's *The Forgotten War: America in Korea*. However, many other works on the Korean War not listed here may also serve to enlighten.

For most of its history the United States has proudly proclaimed its many successes in war. Korea, however, fails to fit easily into the category of triumph. This complex struggle has long raised questions regarding its necessity and our troops' ultimate accomplishments on the battlefield. One unfortunate result of these complexities has been the diminution of the Korean conflict to the status of a forgotten war. The unfairness of this standing is underscored by the fact that more than fifty-four thousand Americans were killed during this intense and bitter struggle.[3] The war's intensity can be seen by comparing the number of deaths from this three-year conflict to our much longer struggle in Vietnam; Korean casualties were just a few thousand shy of the Vietnam War's twelve-year total. Yet despite several dramatic battles and events in Korea, few today can name a single major episode or personality of the war. Typically Korean veterans returned home and tended not to talk about their experiences so that years later family, friends, and neighbors were surprised to discover one of their own fought there.

Indiana, like the rest of the nation, had many casualties. Inscribed upon the state's Korean War memorial are the names of 927 Hoosiers killed during the conflict. Unrecorded are the actions of Hoosiers who served and of their families who gave up their loved ones for the duration of the war. This book seeks to call attention to the sacrifices of Hoosier servicemen and their families who endured the Korean struggle.

It is ironic, given the forgotten stature of the war today, that the Korean conflict began on such a dramatic note and included so many events that quickly stole the stage of public interest at that time. Many of the battles fought in Korea loom as the fiercest ever engaged in by American forces and in some instances took place under the most difficult environmental circumstances ever experienced by our military.[4] One such military engagement occurred at the Chosin Reservoir in December 1950. While marines on the west side made an epic escape from that icy, mountainous wasteland, two regiments of the army's Seventh Division were all but wiped out to the east of the reservoir. "It would be hard to find a more nearly hopeless or more tragic story in American military history," noted one major historian of the war about the Seventh's debacle.⁵ A number of Hoosiers fought on both sides of the Chosin, and two, Lt. Col. Donald C. Faith, Jr., born in Washington, Indiana, and Sgt. Charles Garrigus, Jr., born near Terre Haute, received the Congressional Medal of Honor and the Distinguished Service Cross, respectively, for their valorous actions east of the Chosin. Both medals were awarded posthumously. The stories of their sacrifices are told here. Later, Hoosiers would serve at the pivotal battle of Chipyong-ni in February 1951, during the massive Chinese offensive in April of the same year, and in most of the war's other major engagements.

Unbelievable weather conditions loomed as a potential deadly enemy of Hoosier troops fighting in Korea. Larry Zellers, a civilian prisoner of war, noted that "no non-Korean has ever been heard to say a good word about [Korea's] weather."⁶ Summers there are dominated by monsoons and are hot, rainy, and humid. Temperatures during the summer season can reach 100 degrees or higher, with humidity approaching 90 percent. Climbing Korea's steep hills with full gear was hazardous for Hoosier GIs. "This sun is scorching and it is only the first of May," complained an Indiana soldier serving in the army's Second Division.⁷ During one summer an Indiana marine reported that "the mornings are nice and cool but hot as hell by the late afternoon."⁸ Another letter complained of the unbelievable amount of summer precipitation, noting, "It has been raining heavily, as usual, and here we are set up in a rice paddy . . . built to hold water!"⁹

Winters were worse. In Korea the winter winds seem to come straight from the heart of the Arctic. Hoosier letters almost always carried complaints about Korea's extreme winter climate. One teenager wrote his mother, "Boy it sure is getting cold here. The ground is freezing and the wind really blows down from Siberia."¹⁰ Another complaint at that same time read, "I'm sitting in our tent wrapped around our oil stove freezing to death . . . the weather around here isn't like anything I've ever seen."¹¹ Many Korean War veterans continued to have nightmares about the weather even after being home for many years. Zellers related in this regard, "It must have imprinted itself somewhere inside of me because even now, my friends laugh at me in the wintertime for overdressing when I go out. In [the Korean] prison I came to terms with hunger, but I never got used to being cold."[12] Perhaps no other fighting man in Korea summed up the reality of the bitter cold better than the Hoosier teenager who wrote home explaining to his parents, "It's hard to write with mittens on."[13]

Then there was the terrain. "It is *impossible*," wrote one Indiana lad, "to advance more than 3–5 miles during one day through this terrain, even if you don't meet any resistance. We will be standing on a ridge and way below is a valley you can hardly see. We got all the way down and all the way up the other side. It takes all day. And you haven't even gone a mile by map." The young man added, "If someone would have told me a month ago I would be walking the distance I have with the loads I have carried, I would have told them they were crazy."[14] Harold "Sonny" Bender, a southern Indiana native, described the Korean landscape as "nothing but mountains, high ones too, higher up north than our Rocky Mountains. Back here where we are they are not so high, but up where the front lines are they reach up above the clouds. Every time we go up to dig our fox holes they make us pick out the highest mountain and there we go lugging 50 lbs of ammunition up the mountain side."[15]

Hoosiers could be brutally honest in their opinions of fighting a war in such a place. Most Indiana natives, accustomed to the highest standard of living in the world, had difficulty adjusting to an underdeveloped culture. One Hoosier wrote home declaring, "This is the dirtiest place I ever saw. The people look awful, go nude on the street, and the place smells terrible."[16] A Greene County man wrote his mother, "You said that *Life* magazine said the Korean people were very clean. Well they are the dirtiest, lowest grade of people I have ever seen."[17] A Boonville man wrote back to his mother telling her, "After I got one look at this filthy place I decided for my money the communists can have it. We are now quartered in tents here in Korea, which is sure a far cry from the luxuries of Japan!"[18] Another Hoosier wrote home relating his own disgust regarding Korea when he first landed there: "We arrived here yesterday afternoon but didn't disembark until 4:30 this morning. When I said Japan was not as clean as our standards I didn't realize how filthily people could live. No place can compare to how bad conditions are here in Pusan, a city of 200,000 which doesn't cover as much area as Goshen. There are shacks and shops here that are far dirtier than any chicken coop, and a coop smells like a perfume bath compared to these living quarters. Why anyone would want to fight for this place is beyond me. If we leveled this place the damage wouldn't amount to $500." Ironically, in another letter by the same Hoosier, written just two months later, the writer offered a much softer description of the Asian countryside: "It's been snowing almost every day since Thanksgiving. There are about 4 or 5 inches on the ground now, and it has turned out quite a bit colder. It looks nice out though, like today with snow covered peaks jutting up into a clear, dark blue sky. I don't see what the newspaperman meant by a dull drab country."[19] There were other kind assessments as well. Marine reservist Fitch of Oakland City wrote of his first view of the country: "We were lying in the harbor. Korea is a beautiful country to look at with lots of mountains with snow on them."[20]

In a more exotic judgment, one Indiana soldier described Korean households in this manner: "Their homes are small mud and stick affairs with grass roofs and tiny rooms. The biggest rooms measure about 6' by 6' and are only about 5' 9" or 10" high. I know because I have to bend my neck to stand up. The Koreans all sit around in these rooms on grass mats with little tables in front of them and eat a meal subsisting almost entirely of rice; even their bread is made of rice and it tastes like sawdust. Almost all the clothes they wear are white. The trousers are made like quilts and are real big and baggy, fitting tightly at the ankles, with tiny sneaker like shoes that the toes curl up on."[21] But despite the extreme weather, the impossible terrain, and the culture, Hoosier fighting men gave a total effort in Korea, as we shall see.

INTRODUCTION

An understanding of the overall context of the war is essential in grasping the story of Hoosiers participating in the Korean conflict. The struggle evolved through three stages. The first phase included the abrupt shock of the war's beginning and America's woeful lack of preparation. It is during this stage that our undertrained troops, rushed mostly from Japan, where they were part of a post–World War II occupation force, held a tiny, shrinking perimeter around the southeast Korean seaport of Pusan. At this time many Americans believed that this action heralded the beginning of World War III with the Soviet Union. A vast number of Americans, including many Hoosiers, pleaded for the use of atomic weapons to save our beleaguered troops surrounded at Pusan, while news media accounts often mention the phrase Dunkirk to capture the desperation of the Pusan defense.

Stage two began with Gen. Douglas MacArthur's brilliantly conceived landing at Inchon behind North Korean lines in September 1950. Cut off from their supply lines, enemy troops fled north across the thirty-eighth parallel with United Nations forces in hot pursuit. At this juncture it looked as if the war was all but over. MacArthur even announced that American troops fighting in Korea would be home by Christmas. However, as UN forces approached the Yalu River on the borders of North Korea and Manchuria, the Chinese suddenly hurled a half a million troops into the war, forcing the Americans to beat a hasty retreat south. It was during this time that the First Marine Division and a portion of the Eighth Army's Seventh Division found themselves in incredibly savage weather conditions and trapped at the Chosin Reservoir. Only one narrow mountain trail was available both to supply the threatened troops and allow for their escape. For a short period it looked as if these Americans would be annihilated. Again there was talk of using atomic weapons. The marines, in what many consider their finest hour, fought their way out of the trap in a two-week campaign. Units of the Seventh Division were not nearly as fortunate and less than half of that group survived. Many Hoosiers were among these gallant marines and GIs.

Stage three of the war involved UN forces finally stopping the Chinese juggernaut along the thirty-eighth parallel. By July 1951 the war became static, reminiscent of World War I. Although both sides sought peace at the negotiating table, the conflict would drag out for two more weary years, finally ending in July 1953 in an unsatisfying truce. It is likely that during this last phase the war became a forgotten struggle in the minds of most Americans.

Like most other narratives of the Korean War, the greater part of this account focuses upon the more dramatic early portion of the war, that part of the struggle which occurred before fall 1951. After this time the conflict, as previously noted, evolved into a stagnant affair. The trench-like fighting that followed was, according to historian John Toland, exactly what the Chinese leadership wanted. They conceived that such a strategy "would force the Americans to join the kind of positional warfare where bloody fights were waged with little exchange of land as in the first world war."[22] In the absence of large set-piece battles, encounters involved mainly heavy artillery barrages and sharp, deadly patrol skirmishes.

"Honoring Those Who Paid the Price": Forgotten Voices from the Korean War examines each phase of the war by relating significant examples of Hoosier involvement during each period. While not a definitive book on the subject, this work does seek to give the reader an overall picture of those difficult times as they affected citizens of the state. More than just a retelling of war stories, the book also includes an examination of the Hoosier home front, along with the story of the complex circumstances of African-American Hoosiers who served in Korea. Built around oral interviews, personal letters, newspaper articles and editorials, and other firsthand accounts from the era, each report is blended into a narrative that places it in its historical context. It is hoped that these verbal snapshots of the war in turn convey a larger picture—a rich collage of Indiana and her citizens during the Korean War.

"HOOSIER BUSINESS [GROWTH],
BOOSTED BY RISING PRICES
AND INCREASED OUTPUT,
IS AT AN ALL-TIME HIGH."

June 1950 report of the *Indiana Business Review*

"[WE] HOPE THAT THE NATIONS WILL
COME TO THEIR SENSES
AND MAKE WAR IMPOSSIBLE."

Excerpt from an *Evansville Courier* editorial
two days before the Korean War broke

"GARRISON DUTY IN JAPAN
WAS SIMPLY GREAT."

Interview with a Hoosier GI stationed in Japan in June 1950

Chapter One

Illusions of Peace

World War II profoundly reshaped America. The war "mobilized millions of men and women who otherwise would have never left their home towns or met a single foreigner. . . . Another twenty million Americans left their homes to find work in war industries."[1] The latter event would be "the largest internal immigration in American history."[2] Some Indiana communities, such as Evansville, would be forever changed by the war's boom times. A case could be made that this southwestern Hoosier city experienced more changes for a community its size during the war than any other city in America. The city's Chrysler-Plymouth plant and Sunbeam Electric Company were quickly converted to make small-arms ammunition, producing, by the end of the conflict, the majority of that item used for the war effort. Republic Aviation Corporation also came to Evansville to produce P-47 fighter planes. By far the most profound change to Evansville, however, came with the LST (landing ship, tank) shipyard, which evolved into the world's largest inland ship works. At the peak of production, approximately sixty thousand people labored in the city during the war, roughly half of Evansville's population, with many of the workers moving in from the rural South.[3] Most of the workers came to stay.

Other Hoosier cities, such as Indianapolis, also witnessed a revival of the manufacturing sector during the war. The state's capital, for example, saw a reopening of factories abandoned earlier by departing automakers.[4] But despite the massive economic expansion wrought by the war, most Americans, especially Hoosiers, wished to forget the great changes caused by the war or the changes that continued in the postwar years. By the late 1940s Americans found themselves primarily longing for peace and prosperity and whatever progress that insured the latter. A decade of depression followed by almost half a decade of global war had left citizens with a feeling they somehow deserved better and more secure times. The early portion of 1950, on the eve of the Korean War, seemed to offer just such a comforting possibility. Almost every national news magazine carried special features in their January 1950 issues anticipating the economic stability on the horizon. *U.S. News and World Report*, ordinarily one of the more conservative media venues, optimistically predicted circumstances would "be more nearly normal in 1950 than at any other time in 10 years" with most Americans being "better off than ever before."[5] *Newsweek*, after surveying a panel of "45 leading experts," strongly agreed, foretelling "a prosperous year for 1950."[6] Sources also agreed the chances of war were remote.

Indiana was also experiencing prosperous times. A Lafayette paper touted, "The annual report by the Indiana department of the state revenue, forthcoming at the end of the fiscal year June 30, reveals that Hoosierdom continues in a strong and enviable position. People of Indiana have done well during the past year.... The increased revenue, besides speaking eloquently for the well-being of Hoosiers, should go far toward easing some of the state's pressing financial problems."[7] Just a few days before the unexpected beginning of war in Korea, the *Indianapolis Star* reported that "Hoosier business [growth], boosted by rising prices and increased output, is at an all-time high." The state's business index had risen more that 7 percent in May according to the *Indiana Business Review*. New building projects led the prosperity charge in the state's capital with 561 new building permits issued in May.[8] Other topics, but none to do with potential war, also occupied Hoosier newspapers in spring 1950. On a less pleasant subject, Indianapolis also fretted over a rise in juvenile delinquency in the form of violence among children of prosperous north-side residents. The *Star* noted this rise "bears out a police maxim that poor kids steal, but rich kids destroy."[9] Meanwhile, the capital, often at the center of the state's political intrigue, watched as one local resident eyed a possible run for a Senate seat in the November election. Democratic congressman Andy Jacobs, Sr., had the support of Gov. Henry F. Schricker for this endeavor.[10] Jacobs declared his intention to run for the Senate seat held by Republican Homer Capehart on 4 June 1950.[11]

In the state's northeast corner, the *Fort Wayne Journal-Gazette* reported on 11 June 1950 that given the present situation, a peacetime draft act seemed all but doomed. Fort Wayne also struggled with the problem of delinquency in those weeks before war came. Mayor Henry E. Branning, Jr., warned "that parents must take a genuine interest in the activities of their children if delinquency is to be controlled during the Summer months."[12] On the international scene, the Fort Wayne paper, in a somewhat prophetic editorial two days before the war broke out, noted Americans must "shed the old shell of isolationism. . . . America is already learning to live in a dangerous world without her heart being always in her throat." The editorial, titled "Uncle Sam on a New Job," ended by declaring, "the evolution of the world toward unity may be moving faster than we imagine."[13]

In Bloomington, Indiana University's *Indiana Daily Student* made an insightful observation in early May 1950 on the fifth anniversary of the end of the fighting in Europe. In an editorial titled "Peace Begins at Home," the student paper noted, "Five years ago today the streets of American cities and towns were filled with cheering people. The war against Germany was over. Some persons didn't participate in wild celebrations, but paused either in thought or prayer as they realized the battle for peace was still ahead. . . . Just as we won a shooting war we cannot afford to lose the peace. Scientists, statesmen, and the public in general agree that our present civilization cannot withstand another major war. Campaign for victory against our worst enemy—war."[14] Just a week before the war's outbreak, the student newspaper emphasized the joys of summer and encouraged male students attending the university for the summer session to join an intramural softball team. "Why not take advantage of this recreational opportunity? The increase in participation, which was outstanding last year, should be repeated, or, if possible, excelled. For the greatest possible enjoyment of this Summer on campus, and a sorely-needed relief from studies, get a team together and register at the intra-mural office by tomorrow."[15]

On a more academic, as well as ironic, note, the paper reported of the visit of American ambassador-at-large Philip C. Jessup, who came to Bloomington to head a conference on world peace. Specifically, Jessup told a large audience, "I am optimistic for peace because I have confidence that the American people and the other peoples of the free world will respond successfully to the challenge with which they are now confronted." The conference aside, the *Daily Student* seemed more concerned with sports matters than world affairs in those innocent days before the storm broke in Korea. In one editorial, for example, the paper noted, "The new era which seems to be dawning on Indiana University now appears destined to have added impetus from the Athletic Department. . . . Our football teams have already embarked under an extensive rebuilding program under Coach Clyde Smith that it is hoped will carry the Crimson squad to the top of the national football picture. Coach Branch McCracken's basketball team was one of the finest in the country last year, and the material at McCracken's command indicates that the team will uphold its position for years to come."[16]

In the remote southwest corner of the state that late spring, Evansville residents enjoyed watching their Class B baseball team continue its winning ways. A sports headline in the *Evansville Courier* on 22 June 1950 bragged, "Evansville Whips Cedar Rapids in Double Header."[17] Both the *Courier* and the *Evansville Press* also carried daily reports on the area's oil boom in a column entitled

"Oil Drilling, Developments in Tri-State Field." Joining in the growing optimism of other state newspapers, the 23 June edition of the *Courier* carried an editorial entitled "Hope On, Hope Ever!" in which the editor called for all nations to "come to their senses and make war impossible."[18]

The *Indianapolis Recorder,* chief newspaper for the state capital's African-American population, often conveyed a less optimistic view of Indiana's condition, especially regarding the social, political, and economic conditions of Hoosier African Americans. In April 1950 an editorial charged state leaders with failure to observe and enforce the Indiana Fair Employment Practice Act. Specifically, the paper noted a disturbing instance of job discrimination by the Indiana Girl's School. "The party to the complaint, Miss Dorothy Crossland, is an upstate young woman of appreciable attainment. Over the state she is well known in musical, church, civic, fraternal and organized labor activities. . . . The young woman charges she was invited to appear at the school for an interview on making an application for the post supervisor." Although the job involved the supervision of African-American girls, the director of the school stated, "she did not realize that the applicant was 'colored.'" The article further reported that the policy at the state-operated school "has been . . . to employ whites only."[19]

Complaints of injustice were also leveled by the *Recorder* in June 1950 when it became apparent that a popular summer amusement park would once again ban African Americans. Under the headline "The Shame of Indianapolis" the paper pointed out, "Riverside Amusement Park this season is continuing its hate-inspired and illegal policy of exclusion of Negroes. It seems almost unbelievable that in this year of 1950—five years after the end of World War II—a Northern city could exhibit this shameful spectacle, fully worthy of the late Adolf Hitler." The *Recorder* went on to assert that "the Negro war veteran; the internationally famed Negro scientist; the Negro mother and the Negro workingman who supports the economy of Indianapolis, alike are stigmatized and insulted by this Nazi-style policy. We do not know whether the signs 'Patronage Whites Only Solicited' still confront the little children who go to enjoy the rides and concessions. We do know that these signs and this policy inject the vile poison of racialism into the innocent minds of children. We do know that this is an affront to God and man."[20]

Writing of the laws that already existed on the state books, the *Recorder* lamented, "it is also an affront to the laws of the State of Indiana, which provide that 'all persons within the jurisdiction of said state shall be entitled to the full and equal enjoyment of the accommodations, advantages, facilities and privileges of . . . places of public accommodation and amusement.'" Regarding discrimination practices, the newspaper also chastised Indianapolis city leaders. "The city government has an interest—and a responsibility—in the question because the park is situated on ground leased from the city. We declare it is high time that this barbaric practice be ended once and for all. And we ask: Is there not in our city some official, private person or organization that is big enough to lift this loathsome weight off our backs—so we can go ahead building decent neighborliness, if not brotherly love?"[21]

Several other pieces in the *Recorder* in early 1950 suggest the difficult circumstances that confronted African-American Hoosiers. African Americans who served in the armed forces in Korea faced yet another level of racial hardships. In training and later in combat situations, African Americans had the added burden of the awareness of discrimination back home along with the discrimination they often experienced fighting for their country. The racial prejudices many white Hoosiers carried into the armed forces at this time can be readily seen in a 1950 letter one Hoosier recruit wrote to a teenage friend back home. "For ass-chewing we have a mixture of Gooks, Hawaiians, Mexicans, and Negroes in our company. The Gooks are stupid, the Hawaiians are gung ho, Mexicans lazy as hell and the Negroes are sick bay commandos."[22] Despite the prejudices working against African-American Hoosiers, however, they still managed to carry out the tasks they were sent to do. In instances where black troops did fail, their failures were no more or less than those of white American soldiers.

Other sources also indicated Indiana experienced great ambivalences during the post–World War II era. The state, for example, somewhat reluctantly jumped on the national bandwagon of seeking prosperity and progress as its primary goals. In this regard, Hoosier journalist John Bartlow Martin claimed that the state's citizens in the late1940s simply wished for a return to a more innocent time, noting how every Hoosier small town had once wanted to be called a city, "but now every city wants to pose as a small town, as if to get back to simpler days." Indiana, Martin went on to assert, was very much "conscious of its past greatness."[23] Indiana's two Republican senators, Homer Capehart and William Jenner, certainly seemed to possess the reactionary tendencies that Martin observed in his study of the state. Wealthy farmer and businessman Capehart once declared he was "sick and tired of the New Deal and intend[ed] doing something about it."[24] Senator Jenner loomed as even more conservative than Capehart. "One of the more rabid of the right-wing Republicans," Jenner attempted to call the nation's attentions to what he believed to be wholesale Communist conspiracies and subversions taking place in the nation under the very noses of its citizens.[25] Later, Joseph McCarthy stole Jenner's thunder.

The state's fear of change in the postwar era can be further illustrated by some Hoosier citizens' strong aversion to Progressive presidential candidate Henry Wallace in 1948. Fear of Wallace's pro-Soviet stance generated violent protest in many parts of Indiana. A professor was dismissed from Evansville College for serving as the leader of the county's Elect Wallace Chapter. The school was later condemned by the American Association of University Professors for "failure to understand and support the principle of academic freedom." Most Evansville citizens probably applauded the firing.[26] However, if Martin is correct, not many Hoosiers took interest in any criticism of their state. The tendency to look backward seemed to have a powerful pull in Indiana, one not easily redirected. Most Hoosiers were happy with the isolationist rhetoric flaming forth from Jenner and the rural homilies espoused by Capehart, who won his 1950 reelection campaign in a landslide.

One thing the Hoosier State did share with the rest of the country was a warm patriotic afterglow, which continued to linger for several years after World War II ended. The war had united the nation and the state like nothing else before or since. Oakland City native William Marshall recalled how "most everyone had large wall maps in their homes of the battlefronts, and people talked about each battle's outcome like it was a game in the state's basketball tournament. The war seemed to be the daily topic of almost every conversation."[27] Years later, Hoosiers still remembered those times—the "Good War"—in positive ways. By the late 1940s many young Hoosiers found themselves joining either a regular or reserve component of the armed forces. Enlisting was not a difficult choice for many, as serving in the armed forces still made a strong and positive impression in Indiana; members of the armed forces received admiring glances when walking down a Hoosier street while in uniform.

The U. S. Army in particular launched a strong recruiting effort in the late 1940s to try and bring in young men who were worried about their financial and vocational futures. It helped the army's cause that many young men often had difficulty finding decent work at this time. One full-page advertisement in a popular national magazine in May 1950 declared, "The young man of today who wants to get ahead can continue his education and start building a career at the same time, in the new U.S. Army. Each man's abilities are charted, to place him where he should develop rapidly. . . . Today's U.S. Army," the ad went on to proclaim, "is providing career opportunities for America's finest young men."[28] Eighteen-year-old Hobert Young of Oakland City was perhaps typical of many young men in their late teens who were attracted to the army because of the economic opportunities that branch of the service offered. Coupled with Young's desire to enlist was his

ILLUSIONS OF PEACE 11

Hobert Young of Oakland City with the orphan Korean boy his squad adopted. The young boy was killed shortly after the photo was taken.

tendency not to back down from a dare. Young vividly recalled how these two circumstances brought him into the army: "I was working construction around February of 1950. Because of the bad weather, work had dropped off so there wasn't much to do. One evening a few of us guys who worked together were out drinking when someone made a dare that we all go up to Indianapolis and join the army. I was eighteen at the time and didn't really know what I wanted to do with my life, but I was never one to back down from a challenge. The funny thing was the guy who made the dare to begin with never passed his exam, while I ended up in Korea." Young took his basic training at Fort Knox, Kentucky, where he found "training tough. It certainly wasn't the life I thought it was going to be when I joined up. Of course at the time, I or no one else around me had any idea there would be a war. After basic I went to Okinawa in April and joined the 29th Regiment. Everyone there was doing a lot of drinking—wasn't much else to do. It was just the way things were in the Army over there."[29] Young's boredom soon came to an abrupt end.

Other young Hoosiers were driven by financial pressures to seek a life in the army. In the rural hills of Greene County near Solsberry, Kenneth "Ray" Cox struggled with trying to make it in an area where good jobs were hard to find. Still, the young man had a wealth of friends. When Cox entered the Newark Common School at six years of age he met and befriended Robert Doane and Doane's two older brothers. These young boys grew to be inseparable companions, sharing the adventures available to rural Indiana youth at that time. When Cox moved next door to the Doane family, the friends "practically lived together . . . there were few things that we did not do," Bob Doane recalled. High school did not appeal to Cox, and he quit school at sixteen to work in a Terre Haute bowling alley, setting pins. Unsatisfied with this menial labor, Cox joined the army. He took his basic training at Fort Hood, Texas, and became a tanker, assigned to the Seventy-second Tank Battalion of the Second Infantry Division. Although his financial state seemed more secure, he missed his boyhood friends.

Bob Doane was especially proud of his childhood pal. "He was the first of my generation in our community to serve in the military after World War II," said Doane.[30] The *Bloomfield Evening World* noted on 3 May 1949 that "Recruit Kenneth Cox, son of Mr. and Mrs. Lennie Cox of Solsberry, has just reported to the famous 'Hell on Wheels' 2nd Armored Division at Fort Hood after completing his individual basic training at Camp Breckenridge, Ky."

Similar to Young and Cox, Samuel Muncy of Anderson was motivated to join the army because of financial need. Muncy liked the culture of army life. "I joined the army in 1947 when I was seventeen years old. The best job you could get where I was at only paid about a dollar an hour. Dad and mom had two other kids besides myself, and my folks were struggling to make it, so I joined the army to help them out." Muncy went to Fort Jackson, South Carolina, for basic training, then to PLS—Potential Leadership School. In 1948 he was sent to Korea as part of an occupation force. "The worse part of that time was that the North Koreans, who controlled all the power plants, kept shutting the power off to the South. We'd have a poker game going and we'd end up having to finish it by candlelight—once they shut it off when we were bouncing dice off the wall so that one guy had to hold a candle over the dice so we could see what had been rolled. Weekends there wasn't much to do—most places were still off limits in Korea; it wasn't like Japan. In Korea, you either played cards, slept, or ran to the P.X. I think a lot of the off limits situation was because Koreans had been so isolated from non-Asians, and our officers didn't want us out interacting with the general Korean population and getting in trouble. The Japanese, I suppose, had done a pretty good job too of making the Koreans distrust foreigners."

Later Muncy saw patrol duty along the thirty-eighth parallel. "I got stationed along with three other guys, to patrol the thirty-eighth parallel. You could see a lot of movement across the line. We had binoculars on them and they on us. Once in a while we'd spot one and we'd wave and he'd wave back. It was just a bunch of kids having fun or so it seemed at the time." In fall 1949, U.S. troops were withdrawn except for a small force of American advisers, and Muncy and his unit were sent to Japan. This included the Thirty-first, Thirty-second, and the Seventeenth Regiments of the Seventh Division. Muncy remembered his peacetime service in Japan as being especially comfortable. "Garrison duty in Japan was simply great. I was with a special platoon—I & R—Intelligence and Reconnaissance. On top of that, our whole division was away from all the brass most of the time. There were a lot of places to go—a lot to do in Japan as well. Once in a while the general would come in to see how we were doing, but he wasn't there for long then he'd leave."

Muncy was especially proud of his regiment and of the special work assigned to his platoon. "The Thirty-first Regiment was a great outfit, and I & R was a special platoon. We got special training like ranger school—everything but jumping out of planes. Also, I & R platoon underwent training to prepare us to go out on patrols behind enemy lines, so that we ended up having had more training than most of the GIs in Japan when the war started. We were also Colonel Miller's pets. We were allowed to wear white shoelaces in our combat boots and blue scarves in the summertime with open shirts. We got a big brass plaque made that said 'I & R Platoon, 31st Infantry Regiment' and placed the plaque on the front of our barracks. Every Friday night the whole platoon would move all the bunks to the end of the barracks and get down on our hands and knees and use shoe polish to shine the floor."

The special treatment given to Muncy's I & R group, however, soon led to trouble. Muncy remembered, "Eventually our special treatment created some friction between our group and the other fellows in the regiment. For example, some other GIs had taken to wearing the white shoe laces and blue scarves until Colonel Miller sent down orders saying only the I & R outfit was allowed to do this. Pretty soon after that we started hearing people say, 'Here come the Colonel's babies.' Of course when the war started all this came back the other way because of our training. Then I & R got sent into some pretty bad stuff."[31]

Stanley Nelson of Winslow, experiencing difficult financial circumstances, joined the army in the late 1940s. Nelson left school in the eighth grade and began working as a carpenter when he was just barely a teenager. The work was not especially steady, but Nelson found he enjoyed the job. However, a new situation soon forced Nelson to make other plans, "My mother and father were divorced and my father was unable to support us. To make matters worse I was unable to work steadily due to local employment conditions. I thought I could contribute more to the support of my mother and my younger brother and sister if I was in the army." Nelson joined the army in 1949, at the age of seventeen, and took basic training at Fort Knox, Kentucky, which consisted of close-order drill, marching, and practicing on the rifle and grenade range. "We also had a week of bivouac in the mountains. Because of the intensity of this training, I felt I was prepared for anything. I had developed a great ego and thought I was pretty tough. After basic training, I was stationed at Camp Drake, Japan, in March of 1950 serving with the Eighth Engineering Combat Battalion, First Cavalry Division, where I was a company carpenter. Garrison duty was easy, and I was getting very comfortable when the war broke out. Because of the relaxed conditions in Japan, none of us were prepared for a real shooting war."[32]

Stanley Nelson of Winslow (right) joined the army in 1949 because he was unable to find steady work as a carpenter.

Still another young man who joined the regular army because of economic hard times was Charles Garrigus, Jr. Like the fictitious Joad family who struggled so desperately to survive during the Great Depression in John Steinbeck's *The Grapes of Wrath*, the Garrigus clan pulled up roots and moved in an attempt to better their lives. In 1937, at the height of the depression, they journeyed southward from Yeddo, near Terre Haute, to Francisco, where Charles Garrigus, Sr., a lanky man who stood well over six feet tall, took on the grinding and often dangerous task of working in the nearby King's coal mine. The Garrigus sons labored as hired hands for local farmers, who in the national economic emergency paid the brothers in produce as often as money. Gladys Garrigus and her daughters cooked, cleaned, and washed daily for a large family in a world void of modern conveniences. The children found it especially tough going; the difficult environment in which they lived often demanded adult work from their small and tender hands. One of the younger Garrigus girls, Delores, recalled how her parents taught them to carry out both traditionally male and female tasks. "Times were so hard back then that you had to be prepared to do most any job," she noted. On the other hand, she remembered, "families and communities were always ready to help one another out. There existed a real loyalty to pitch in and take care of community problems."[33]

Just eleven years old when his family came to rural Gibson County in 1937, Charles Garrigus, Jr., discovered some pleasures in spite of those hard times. The boy, whom his sisters teasingly called June Bug, possessed a shy Huck Finn smile and loved to spend his free time tinkering with engines or driving farm vehicles down the dusty lanes that crisscrossed the Hoosier countryside. Schoolwork often interfered with Charles's desire to work with mechanical problems, and he dropped out of school before receiving a high school diploma. By the end of his teenage years, Charles was laboring on a farm, contently working on and driving the farm vehicles whose engines so fascinated him as a child. World War II, however, changed Garrigus's life forever.

Serving in the armed forces during World War II brought many young men who grew up in the harsh poverty of the depression a stability they had not known before. At the war's end, most of these young men returned to a relatively unstable world. When Garrigus was honorably discharged in November 1946 "by reason of demobilization," the twenty-two-year-old Hoosier traveled north to Gary, where he tried his hand as a heavy-equipment operator. Civilian life, however, lacked the predictability he had come to know in the army, and he reenlisted.[34] The now strapping six footer looked forward to a career in the army, working with trucks and heavy equipment. When North Korea launched a savage and completely unexpected attack on South Korea in June 1950, Garrigus was serving as an assistant motor pool sergeant in Japan in the Seventh Division's Thirty-second Regiment. The regiment was commanded by Hoosier-born Lt. Col. Donald C. Faith, Jr.

Faith was born in summer 1918 in Washington, where the Faith family lived scattered out in Daviess and Pike Counties. Faith's father was career military, attaining the rank of a brigadier general, and Donald attended schools at a number of military bases around the world. Donald hoped to attend West Point but was turned down because of a dental disqualification. Shortly before World War II, the same condition caused him to be turned down when he tried to enlist in the army. On an appeal, however, the persistent youth received permission to join, and he quickly rose through the ranks. "Considered one of the army's most promising officers," Faith was given command of the First Battalion of the Thirty-second Infantry in 1949.[35] By then the thirty-two-year-old Hoosier stood an athletic six feet and wore his hair in a military crew cut. He quickly established a reputation for being "friendly, forceful, and charismatic."[36] In spite of Faith's qualifications and abilities, however, he had never commanded any kind of military group in combat—a situation Faith abhorred. Faith later gained that experience in an arena of unbelievably savage conditions.

Donald Mayville was an uncertain teenager in the late 1940s who joined the army to escape a near poverty situation. Although not a Hoosier, Mayville fought alongside Faith and Garrigus and interacted with both men at the epic struggle at the Chosin Reservoir in the early part of the war. Young Mayville's reasons for joining the army in 1948 were typical of so many others who enlisted at that time.

> I was born and brought up in Michigan on a small chicken farm in Farmington. My father was sick much of the time but we were allowed to live free on some company property. When my father couldn't work anymore we moved to the inner city of Detroit. There I worked at Kroger's and Western Union. At that time my mother was taking 20 dollars out of my 28 dollars a week I made at the Supermarket.
> My mother was a dominating woman. I couldn't do anything without her telling me no, even when I was seventeen. So I joined the Army to get out from under her thumb. I should have stayed in school, because I would have graduated in 1952, long after the Chosin. I took my basic training at Fort Riley, Kansas. After basic I went to Japan and joined the 7th. Army Division where I was stationed on Hokkaido at Camp Crawford. Two weeks after arriving I was sent south to Eta Jima to Morse Code Radio School. The school was in the same buildings that Admiral Yamamoto took his training for the Navy. I remember they had a head chopping block on the parade field for the Japanese students that failed the course. I was in the six month course for three months when North Korea started the war.[37]

Ira Neal, an African American, also found his life forever changed by the war. Raised in Memphis, Tennessee, Neal, because of the Korean conflict, eventually came to Evansville, where he spent the balance of his vocational career as a school administrator. In the late 1940s, however, Neal, similar to so many young men his age, faced a world fraught with economic woes. This was even

Ira Neal of Evansville. Neal's Korean War experiences sharpened his defiance of segregation practices when he returned to the United States.

more true for African-American youth. "In November of my junior year [1947] a bunch of us quit school to join the air force. I was sixteen years old, but I lied about my age. Dropping out of school was not all that unusual back then," Neal recalled. "There wasn't a lot of work. I went down to the recruiting station and took some tests. This was the first time I remembered having a white person take a real interest in me." At the recruiting office the officer in charge noticed Neal's high scores and encouraged the young man to finish school. "I didn't have any interest in that," Neal said. "My buddies and I were wanting to see the world."

Neal's group trained at an air force base in Mississippi where they stayed for about a month doing close-order drills and waiting for orders. "We were finally told the air force had its quota of blacks. Back then the armed forces only took 10 percent of blacks for each branch of the service. We were given the option of joining the army." Neal and most of his group joined the army and were transported to Fort Dix, New Jersey. "It was like going from heaven to hell as far as the weather," Neal recalled. The military world that Neal entered was almost completely segregated. "We had just a few white commanding officers. We got thirteen weeks of basic training, and then I was shipped to Japan to an all-black unit," he said.

Neal experienced the ugly dehumanizing practice of segregation even while in uniform. "Most of our transportation in the U.S. was by train, and when we were taken to chow we had to go to the snack car and stand there while the white troops came by to go to the dining room," he said. "We all had the same meal tickets, but the blacks weren't allowed into the dining cars."

In Japan, Neal recalled, "I was in the Seventy-sixth AAA—an antiaircraft unit. But most blacks there were in a sweat battalion—transportation units, unloading at docks, that kind of thing. These guys really worked extra hard." Despite prejudicial treatment, Neal discovered that at the all-black base and in the general surrounding area, "the black man was king: We had everything—the clubs, the good times." Outside the area, however, "you might as well have been in Mississippi." In Tokyo there were many places a black man could not go, Neal recalled. "Once I remember being on a trolley and a Japanese woman asking me in broken English if I was a spook," he said. "She had heard all the talk from the white soldiers." But there were also positive aspects for African Americans serving in the armed forces. Neal, for example, completed his General Equivalency Diploma (GED) while in Japan. "Later I was able to get my high school diploma by presenting my GED scores to the high school board of education back home," he noted.[38]

Herbert Crowe, an African-American Hoosier from Boonville, went into the army in late 1950 and took basic training at Fort Knox, Kentucky, in an all-black unit. Crowe also experienced prejudice even while in uniform. "In Boonville whites and blacks got along pretty well, so I had a harder time away from home," he said.

"You just tried to get used to it." Crowe, however, longed to get away from Indiana at the time "to see the world."[39]

Eighteen-year-old Donald Hamilton of Solsberry wrote home often from his garrison stay in Japan. His correspondence conveys much about what life was like for Hoosiers in Japan in the months before the war. In one letter written in the early part of 1950 Hamilton told his parents, "I didn't get my mail room inspected yesterday; I guess they forgot about it or something, at least it didn't bother me, because they didn't inspect it." In true Hoosier spirit the Greene County native also expressed his dislike of privilege: "The commander of the 7th army [Division], which the 32nd is part of, was up here to look this outpost over. He has a special train which he travels over Japan in. It is really nice, but I wouldn't care if it jumped the track or something, because I don't think there should be that much difference between men in the army." In another letter Hamilton spoke of the excitement of payday. "Well here it is finally—pay day! I began to think it was never going to come around," he wrote. "I am sending one hundred dollars home. I drew one

Donald Hamilton of Greene County. Hamilton was an army medic and chose to return and aid some wounded comrades rather than join his unit's retreat. He was declared missing in action in December 1950, and his body was never recovered.

hundred and sixty six dollars for two months, but I had to pay back some debts and get a few things that I needed. I kept thirty five dollars, but don't suppose I use over ten of it. I still have some money coming for the month of June, but I don't know how much." The Hoosier teenager shared his thoughts about his future with his father, Oval Hamilton. "You were asking if I was going to reenlist," said Hamilton. "Well, I don't think I will unless the army is the only place I can make a living for myself. You were asking if I would like the Dobson place. Well, I would like it, but I don't know how long it would take me to pay for it. As you know, I already owe about four hundred dollars. However, if you think it can be arranged I would like to have it."

In June 1950 Hamilton's letters to his father indicated how much he looked forward to getting out of the army and returning to the farm in the fall, touching upon what he might do for a living once he returned to Indiana: "I suppose that you have got the biggest part of your corn and things out by this time. I guess that I will get back just in time to shuck the corn this fall, but I will miss the most dreaded part of the work this year; I think you know what it is that I always hate. You were telling about those little red foxes that you seen over along the road the other day, why didn't you catch one of them for a pet? I sure hope that I can get on one of the jobs around there either as an aid man or safety man with one of the construction companies. That would be a real job if I can manage to get a job like that."

In a letter, two days before the North Koreans invaded the south, Hamilton was making plans for coming home. "I guess you know that I left the states one year ago yesterday morning at 11:15. It sure doesn't seem like it has been that long," he wrote. I haven't written any letters since Monday because I was on pass over my birthday. I sure had a good time too. . . . I don't know whether I ever told you or not but I have a Bendix combination radio and phonograph with about 50 records, but I guess I will have to sell it before I leave because it is too big to bother with, but it sure is nice. I would like to have it at home but it would get busted before it got there. . . . I figured up the other day that I will get about two hundred and eighty dollars when I get discharged, plus one hundred and fifty dollars travel money, and it won't cost over seventy five dollars to pay for my way home, so I should have a nice little pile of money when I get out. Just a little more than I had in the bank when I came in; I guess I am just about breaking even these last two years."[40] Hoosiers such as Hamilton who served in Japan in the late spring of 1950 had no way of knowing their plans for coming home would soon be crushed.

Unlike their happy-go-lucky counterparts in Japan, Hoosiers in the army's Second Division, stationed at Ft. Lewis, Washington, were less content about their environment. One teenage Hoosier, Everett Wayne Leffler of Monroe City, sent his family a poem that captured the negative attitudes of most GIs who served stateside on the eve of the war:

> Fort Lewis, Washington
>
> Below the Canadian border,
> Fort Lewis is the spot,
> Where we are doomed to serve our time,
> In the land that God forgot.
>
> Up with the snakes and lizards,
> In a place where a man gets so blue,
> Right on the edge of nowhere,
> Three thousand miles from you.
>
> We cuss and fuss and we freeze,
> It's more than we can stand,
> For we are not convicts at all,
> We are defenders of our land.
> We are soldiers of the Infantry,
> Earning our measly pay,
> Guarding the people with millions,
> For just two fifty a day.
>
> Living only with memories,
> Waiting to see our gals,
> Hoping that when we get home,
> They haven't married our pals.

> No one knows we are living,
> And no one gives a Damn,
> Back home we are forgotten,
> We're nephews of Uncle Sam.
>
> The best time of our lives we've missed,
> The time we spent in the Army,
> Fellows: if the draft don't get you,
> For God's sake don't enlist.
>
> Now when our work is finished,
> We go to a place known so well,
> Old St. Peter then will say,
> "Enter you men from Fort Lewis,
> You've served your time in Hell."[41]

Many Hoosiers also joined reserve components in the post–World War II era. News media of the day especially touted the advantages of joining reserve components, aiming its advertising primarily at World War II veterans and young men who needed a little extra cash. One such ad declared that "America's large citizen army [is] . . . a pleasant way to maintain old friendships! Rewarding too—for under the new Reserve Program [a person] draws full pay of his grade for each training assembly, builds retirement credits, [and] equips himself for further advancement."[42] Huntingburg native Thomas Chappell joined the army reserve upon his discharge from Fort Knox, Kentucky, following his service in World War II, where he had participated in heavy fighting in France and Germany. "I was foolish for enlisting in the reserve," Chappell recalled, "but the officer in charge promised me 'you will not go if a conflict occurs.' I have never forgotten those words." Unfortunately, the recruiter's promise was typical of those made to veterans leaving the service after World War II. Chappell, like other veterans, was anxious to return home and forget the war. He traveled back to his native Huntingburg and soon landed a job at the same furniture factory where his father worked. He married a young lady from Jasper, and by 1950 the couple had two children. Because of the distance to travel to reserve meetings, Chappell

Hoosiers who served with the Second Division just before the war started were stationed at Fort Lewis, Washington. The photo shows a group of artillery men of Fort Lewis including Monroe City native Everett Wayne Leffler, Jr. The Hoosier is in the fourth row and eighth from the left.

attended only a single meeting and was placed on inactive service, a status that he believed protected him from any possible call-up.[43] Chappell and thousands of others in reserve components soon received a shock.

Chappell's younger brother William, impressed by his older sibling's uniform and war stories, longed to escape Huntingburg and see the world. In 1949 the seventeen year old joined the navy. "My older brother was kind of a hero to me, and, along with the influence of a neighbor who had been in the war, John Stillwell, I joined the navy," said William. "I was really excited about the travel and adventure that branch of the service offered." As it turned out, the navy provided William with many experiences he could never have gotten back home. "I remember one time our captain had allowed us a party on a beach in Saudi Arabia. While we were there we saw the plane we carried catapult off the deck. For some reason, the plane went straight down into the water. The captain decided to give the plane to the Saudies if they would salvage it. A little later we saw a caravan of camels pull up to the beach. The Saudies had slaughtered a whole mess of goats and were giving them to our ship out of gratitude for the plane. The meat was wrapped in sacks and smelled terrible. Of course we couldn't refuse the gift. As soon as we could though we dumped the stuff in the ocean."[44]

Another opportunity of service for Hoosiers in the late 1940s was the Marine Corps Reserve. The story of the marine reserves' inception is unique and deserves some attention here. The nation's armed forces was greatly reduced following World War II. The end of the war found Americans demanding that the boys be brought home and the nation get on with peacetime living. President Harry S. Truman, combating the twin dangers of inflation and unemployment, was forced to cut military spending rather than social programs.[45] In order to keep some psychological sense of military preparedness during the demobilization frenzy, the nation's leaders turned to technology rather than a large and expensive standing army. The nation's confidence in employing technology as a means of meeting any military threat or emergency can be seen clearly two weeks before the war came in Korea. Secretary of the Army Frank Pace, Jr., speaking at West Point, declared that U.S. forces must "be prepared to meet . . . masses of heavily mechanized [enemy] ground forces with smaller numbers of highly scientific ground troops equipped with revolutionary new weapons." More specifically, Pace listed "guided missiles and rockets, target-seeking equipment and the possibilities of tactical use of atomic weapons," as examples of such revolutionary safeguards.[46] Thus, shortly after the end of World War II, the United States possessed no long-range plans for a war requiring a substantial number of well-trained ground troops.

The dangerous situation of demobilization confronted the U.S. Marine Corps more profoundly than the other branches of the service. The postwar mission of the Marine Corps was to provide a trained force "to meet the requirements . . . in time of war or national emergency."[47] Numbering 480,000 strong before 1948, the Marine Corps was slashed to 86,000 under the Truman administration. A plan, however, was soon devised to alleviate this dangerous situation. Having had great success during World War II with a reserve system, the Marine Corps decided to re-create a strong non-regular component that would serve to bring the marines up to full strength in an emergency.[48] Consequently, a major portion of the postwar Marine Corps defense budget was allotted to training reserve units. More than 120 cities across the nation eventually became sites for new Marine Corps Reserve companies. Indiana had four of these sites: Indianapolis, Evansville, Fort Wayne, and an inactive unit at South Bend.

The balance of Hoosier reservists and their counterparts across the nation were teenagers who joined the reserves for extra money, the travel and adventure the duty offered, and the glory that came with wearing a marine uniform. Inspired by the patriotic afterglow that followed World War II and by movies, such as the 1949 release *Sands of Iwo Jima*, these teenagers desired to play marines in the worst way. Many of them were underage but convinced a parent or guardian to sign for them. For their part, parents likely believed their sons safe from actual harm since reservists of that time did not have to undergo the rigors of Marine Corps boot camp. In addition, as with the army reserves, enlistees in the Marine Corps Reserve across the nation were promised they could quit anytime they wanted. What was rarely stressed, however, was that this promise was null and void in the event of a national emergency. Most, of course, could not possibly have imagined that any such emergency would occur. Joining seemed to offer adventure for the teenagers and a little extra money for the older, more practical reservists.

Leaders of the Evansville reserve unit created a unique way to fill their roster. In 1947 four high schools—Central, Bosse, Memorial, and Reitz—dotted the city. Maj. Paul Torian, the company's commander, quickly asked coaches in each school who were marine veterans to recruit high school players. "There are four platoons in a rifle company, and I hit upon the idea of having a platoon to represent each high school in the city," Torian recalled. The coaches felt they were doing their players a favor by encouraging them to join the reserve and believed that the experience would be of great benefit to the boys in the future.[49]

Another successful recruitment tool for the unit came through the exploits of the company's softball team, which won Evansville's competitive industrial league in 1949. Sports, however, were not the only drawing card for reserve units across the state. Ralph Steele was a junior at Elkhart High School when he came to join a marine reserve unit at South Bend for reasons other than sports. Remembering that day, Steele recalled: "Elkhart High School was having a Career Day during my junior year in 1948. I had not been an athlete in school, was not handsome or popular, hadn't made good grades. In fact high school had been a mostly bad experience. At the time we had Career Day I was very unsure about my future. I didn't think of myself as college material, so I ended up with a dozen or so other guys listening to the Marine Corps pitch from a salty marine in those recruit blues. He looked pretty sharp, and I was thinking how the girls would go for a guy in a uniform like that."

Steele was unsure about joining the regular marines, but then he and his group were told of another possibility. "We were told if we didn't want to join the regular marines, they had this new thing called the Marine Corps Reserve. It turns out a reserve company was starting up in nearby South Bend. This reserve thing sounded a lot better than the regular service since we'd only have to go to weekly training meetings if we wanted. There was also a volunteer two-week summer camp at a marine base that sounded like it might be fun." Many underage teenagers, such as Steele, who were being lured by the reserve pitch, soon realized that a parent would have to sign a release form. "The only problem was my parents. I was their youngest, and they'd already sent my brothers to World War II, and I guess this made them pretty protective of me," he said. "They hadn't let me play football for example. My mother, in particular, wasn't going to sign a release for me to join. (I was underage at the time.) As it turned out, this was one of the few times my father bucked the system. He stood up for me and told my mother, 'Let the boy be a marine.' So my dad ended up signing the release form for me to join. A few weeks later I get this little red card in the mail saying I'm in the reserves." It turned out, however, that the South Bend company never had a meeting, so Steele and others in the South Bend group never went to anything connected with the reserves. "All I had was this card saying I was in the reserves. It was almost like belonging to a 'Terry and the Pirates Club' like I had belonged to when I was a kid. After a while I assumed, since I hadn't gone to any of the training sessions, that I was no longer in the reserves. This notion, I was to discover, was sorely incorrect."[50]

Many of the members who joined Hoosier reserve units in 1948, 1949, and 1950 were still in high school or recently graduated. David Graham, a Bosse High School student when he joined the group, was perhaps typical of the many Evansville teenagers who soon made up a large portion of the local marine unit there. Graham recalled how he was a seventeen-year-old student when "the recruiters came to Bosse in full uniform and made their pitch." The glory of wearing a Marine Corps uniform, along with

Andy Jacobs, Jr., of Indianapolis with his father, who was then an Indiana congressman. Andy Jr. was one of more than one thousand Hoosier marine reservists called up in the early part of the war.

the extra money from attending weekly drills and summer camp, acted as a powerful magnet to teenagers such as Graham.[51] Henry Orth, Jr., another Evansville native, dropped out of high school at sixteen to work and discovered the reserves offered some solace for not having finished schooling. Orth recalled going to a few of the meetings at first and "playing soldier," but the hard-working Evansville man soon grew tired of the routine at the reserve headquarters and mostly stopped attending meetings. Still, Orth recalled there were perks when he did show up. "The best thing about the deal was you could go into a tavern and be served as long as you were in uniform—underage or not. We'd go to Bert Lehr's [a local tavern] or pick up girls while we still had our uniforms on."[52]

Indianapolis teenager Andy Jacobs, Jr., came into the Marine Corps reserves in much the same fashion as other teenagers in the state and across the nation. "I finished Shortridge High School in '49 when I was still seventeen. A good friend who belonged to the local reserve unit told me the slogan for that summer was 'Set your sights on summer camp.' The reserve camp was at Little Creek, Virginia, that summer and my friend reasoned we could get a free ride to the East Coast. When we finished the two weeks, we could hitchhike to New York City and have the adventures of young men. Consequently, we saw New York as it existed in 1949. Of course that world's gone now."

Jacobs also remembered how, "being a reservist was a good way to get a date on Thursday night after a meeting while you were still in uniform. People were still goo-goo about the Second World War, and everyone gave veterans special treatment. Wearing a uniform, even as a reservist, got you some attention. It was also good to know the job was certainly no longer a dangerous occupation, so it was safe to be courageous, as they say. Although it was peacetime, the uniform looked the same." Jacobs also had to talk a parent into signing a release form. "My father, Andy Jacobs, Sr., who was in Congress at the time, signed for me since I was underage. Oddly, he cast a vote against aid to Korea in early 1950 as well as against aid to the French in Indochina. He stated in the *Congressional Record* that if we sent the arms our sons would follow."[53]

Howard Suttmiller, a veteran of savage combat in the Pacific during World War II, joined the Indianapolis reserve because he wanted to stay in contact with the corps and make a little extra money. Suttmiller recalled, "I got out in '45 after thirty-two months overseas. I fought on Tawara, Saipan, Okinawa, and served occupation duty in Japan at Nagasaki. When I got back to Indy I went to school at Butler and decided to pick up a little extra money by joining the reserves."[54]

Because so many reservists joined for every reason under the sun other than training to be a marine, it was not unusual for reserve companies all across the nation to battle with the problem of low attendance at meetings. The Evansville unit apparently was struggling with this problem by the spring of 1950, for the company's monthly monogram declared at that time, "members of 'C' Company should keep the goals for the Organized Marine Corps Reserve in mind, and, regardless of their own reasons for joining . . . make every effort to accomplish its goals. That means starting here in 'C' Company with better attendance, more cooperation, and better military bearing."[55] Another problem for reserve leaders was the lack of training time. "In just two hours a week, it was difficult to get much training done," one Hoosier officer recalled. "On top of that, the emphasis, of course, had to be on making it interesting and fun because the young enlistees could quit anytime."[56]

But if the weekly volunteer meetings failed to prepare reservists for handling weapons and for eventual combat, it was hoped by Marine Corps top brass that the two-week volunteer summer camps would fill the void. Indeed, the national director of the reserves declared in 1948 that the military efficiency of the reserve as a potential fighting force "increased 100 percent over 1947" because of summer camp training.[57] Contrary to this assessment, summer camp participation fell off from 54 percent in 1948 to 47 percent in the summer of 1949.[58] Still, those camps were exciting events for Hoosier reservists. A letter written by Oakland City's Gordon Greene to his mother from a marine camp in 1949 suggests the discomfort along with the lure of adventure these camps represented for teenage Hoosier reservists:

Dear Mother,
   We arrived here Sunday afternoon about 5:30 o'clock. Our trip was marred by rain and fog. The Pullman we came over on was an old dilapidated one. There was no air conditioning but only two small fans in each end. Coal dust was continually coming in and as a result all the seats and bunks were covered with soot. The train was late in Evansville,

and we got a late start, leaving about 4:00 o'clock. We went through Eastern Kentucky, West Virginia, and Virginia. A small passenger boat took us from New Port News to Norfolk. There are 184 men in our battalion consisting of 2 rifle platoons, 1 30 cal. Machine gun platoon, and the 60 mil. mortar section that I am in.

I saw about 20 aircraft carriers in the harbor and many Navy and Marine Corps planes. Today, Monday, we practiced on embarking and disembarking from a troopship into the landing crafts and from there to the shore. I will spend most of tomorrow working in the mess hall. Next week we will spend in or on board a troopship for several days off the coast of Virginia. I think maybe I will go to Richmond, Virginia, the week end with Barney to meet Tom Buyher who will arrive there on a train from Washington D.C. We will leave here probably Saturday, July 1, and reach Evansville the next day, Sunday.

See you later,
Gordon[59]

Despite the excitement and feeling of adventure these camps generated for teenage enlistees, both weekly sessions and summer camps failed to prepare reservists for the rigors of actual combat. As one historian of the Marine Corps noted, "once-a-week nighttime drills inhibited training, and summer camps were not well attended. More significantly, new recruits did not attend boot camp or receive advance training." The reservists were "largely untrained and many [had] joined for social and athletic reasons." The result of these circumstances was a "reserve unprepared for war."[60] Some reservists' experiences in the training process led them to believe that the drills and camps were a monumental waste of time as well. Said one disgruntled reservist of his experiences, "I witnessed nothing but confusion, disorder, overspending, . . . and everything but sound constructive training."[61] All of this, of course, would not have mattered had it not been for the outbreak of the Korean War.

"The news hit the United States like lightning from a clear sky."

Newsweek, 3 July 1950

"Where's Korea?"

Comment of one Hoosier marine reservist upon hearing war had broken out in Korea

Could this be the "beginning of World War III?"

Time, 10 July 1950

CHAPTER TWO

THE STORM BREAKS

The degree of shock generated by the Korean War can be best understood by looking at the nation's perceptions regarding global problems just prior to the conflict's beginning. One national magazine reported that despite some global tensions "worries are largely domestic everywhere." The magazine further noted that "war fears, and war talk are dying out in much of the world. People find out there are other things to worry about in 1950." In light of budding domestic concerns and growing prosperity, the article ended by declaring "war now seems remote."[1] When war did begin, many thought Korea heralded the first engagements of World War III. *Newsweek* reported, for example, that "Americans had been assured that Soviet Russia wouldn't be ready for a showdown before 1952 at the earliest.... Yet dispatches from Korea seemed to say that the time of Russian readiness could be now."[2] *Time* asked grimly, "Could Armageddon begin with so feeble a fanfare as the muffled Battle of Korea? Could the push-button war of the physicists start among the grass roofs of a land where men had hardly caught up with Galileo?" In closing, the author queried darkly, "If this was the beginning of World War III?"[3] One national article even hinted that America might strike the first blow in an atomic war: "The big question still was: Where would the Reds strike next? Moscow held the initiative ... unless ... the U.S. decided to strike back with all-out atomic war."[4]

The specifics of the war's beginning were this: North Korea unleashed a motivated, highly trained, and well-equipped army of 135,000 men, supported by more than one hundred Soviet-built T-34 tanks, two hundred bombers and fighter planes, and hundreds of heavy artillery pieces on South Korea in the early morning hours of 25 June 1950. South Korea was woefully unprepared for this onslaught. Because the United States feared that South Korea would attack North Korea in an attempt to reunify the country, South Korea had been allowed to maintain only a lightly armed 65,000-man constabulary force that existed primarily to keep peace in the volatile country. Surprisingly, the United States responded quickly to North Korean aggression. When President Harry S. Truman made the final commitment of sending ground troops into Korea three days after the invasion, it would be under the banner of the United Nations. Gen. Douglas MacArthur was given command of the UN forces. The United States, however, provided by far the greatest amount of matériel and men for the struggle.

American forces at the time of the invasion were as woefully unprepared for a ground war as the South Koreans. Military historian William Breuer noted, "As a result of Truman's determination to achieve the first peacetime 'economy budget' in ten years, he had ordered Secretary of Defense [Louis A.] Johnson to 'cut away the fat' in the armed forces. Johnson complied. But he also hacked off bone and sinew along with the blubber. Now the U.S. Army had been pruned to only 592,000 poorly trained men armed largely with weapons that were relics from World War II." Breuer further noted, "In the face of the Cold War tension and Communist saber-rattling around the world, the army's strength was less than half what it had been nine years earlier at the time of an epic American disaster—Pearl Harbor." When the first American troops landed in Korea, the units "were at only 70 percent strength and armed with World War II–era rifles, tommy guns, carbines, and machine guns. Most of these weapons were unfit for combat. Mortar mounts were broken; there were no spare barrels for automatic weapons; shells and grenades had corroded from age. Communications radios were in short supply, and many of those available would not function."⁵ Perhaps those most surprised by the suddenness of the war were the members of America's armed forces. Samuel Muncy, serving with the Seventh Division on garrison duty in Japan, recalled how the shattering news came to him.

"It was Sunday morning, and I was lounging around on my bunk when I saw the sergeant hurrying over from one cadre leader to another, so I knew something was up. I was due to leave for the states the next day—my overseas time was up, and I was thinking something must be going on the way the sergeant was running around to the different squad leaders. I just figured the higher ups had gotten mad about something and were giving us some kind of extra duty, but I wasn't too worried myself, since I was about to leave. I had already turned in my stuff. I didn't even have a rifle— just two sheets and a pillow. The next morning I was supposed to get on a ship at Yokohama and go home. Whatever was going on, I'd not be a part of, or so I thought."

"I was curious. I got dressed real quick and went to the front door so I could get nose to nose with the CQ [charge of quarters]. 'Hey,' I told him, 'I'm going home tomorrow, so just tell them you couldn't find me.' He glanced downward and then looked back up at me and said, 'I can't do that—this is bad.' That made me hurry down to the headquarters. When I got there I saw these maps spread out all over the place—some said Chosen, some said Korea. All the officers and noncoms were huddled around them. Then our captain said, 'Fellows we are at war—the North Koreans went across the parallel this morning.' The first hand that went up after he said that was mine. 'Captain,' I told him, 'I'm on orders to go home.' The officer didn't bat an eye. He just looked at me real steady and said 'Your orders have been canceled. You are with us for the duration.' I thought at that moment, man if the North Koreans had just waited another week, I'd been back in the States."⁶

Greene County native Donald Hamilton, a medic in the Seventh Division's Thirty-second Regiment, tried to speculate what the invasion might mean for him and his unit. On 26 June he wrote his parents: "I suppose that by this time you have heard the news. Really sounds good, doesn't it? They called all the men in from pass, last night, that is the men of the 865 anti aircraft Battery and put them on alert, so it really looks bad. As of yet they haven't put us on an alert, but I look for them before long." In typical Hoosier fashion the young farmer still worried mostly about the crops back home. "Oval, have you got all your corn out by now?," wrote Hamilton. "I guess you have because it is almost the last of June and almost time to start putting up the hay. It just doesn't seem like it should be this late in the season, but I guess it is." Hamilton ended the letter by speculating on his chances of getting his discharge as soon as it was supposed to come in: "I have my time down to about three months now. It may not do me any good because if this trouble keeps up they wouldn't think of discharging anyone. They could declare an emergency and keep every man until it is settled. They say that they could move us out of here in 24 hours." A day later the teenager wrote, "The news doesn't sound so good today as I hoped for. The U.S. is giving Southern Korea planes and ammunition, so I look for this to start something big, but I hope not. . . . There is news that comes on the radio at 11:00 at night and almost everyone in the barracks does not go to bed until they hear the news."[7]

Stanley Nelson, on garrison duty in Japan with the army's First Cavalry Division, recalled what was going on in his life when he heard the news. "I was on guard, pulling CQ duty, listening to the *Amos and Andy Show*, when a news flash came over the radio and stated that North Korea had invaded South Korea," said Nelson. "Even after the news broke, no one thought it was serious. Many of us weren't even sure where Korea was."[8]

When the war came, Kenneth Ray Cox was home on leave with his family and friends up in the hills of Greene County. The nineteen-year-old man spent most of his time with his best friend Bob Doane. Doane remembered those last few days of his friend's stay. "We squirrel hunted, double-dated, and other things that teenage boys would do. On one squirrel-hunting trip, with me and my brother Bill, Ray was using his dad's double-barreled twelve-gauge shotgun. He was holding the butt of the stock against his stomach and while cocking the two hammers the gun discharged. I think it would have hurt an ordinary person, but not Ray, . . . he was that tough." The long, hot days of summer were filled with other adventures for Cox and the Doane brothers. Finally, however, the time came for Cox to go back to his base. Bob Doane remembered that final day: "The last day I saw Ray, we were standing in the front yard at my house when we spotted a big black car coming toward us. Ray realized it was Sheriff Bill Branstetter. Ray jumped down on his hands and tiptoes and in a sideways motion skipped down into the woods. The sheriff stopped and casually asked me, 'Is this where Ray Cox lives?' I quickly said, 'No, he lives right down the road in the next house.' I had unwittingly helped Ray avoid capture. We stood in the yard and watched the sheriff go up to Ray's house and enter. It was then that I learned a new term: AWOL. Ray said, 'He knows I am here somewhere because my ID card and billfold are there on the table.' He then went on to tell me that he had sort of overstayed his leave time. He had been using Bill's [Doane] single-barreled shotgun, so he asked me after the sheriff left to walk down with him and get it. I did, and when I walked away from his house, I casually said, 'I'll see you around,' and he said 'OK,' never thinking that we would never see each other again. He was caught hitchhiking and returned to Texas. From there was sent to rejoin his outfit on their way to Korea."[9]

Hoosier marine reservists were also shocked by the abruptness of the war, but two weeks later came much more disturbing news; marine reserve units were being activated. Under these circumstances, no one was allowed to quit. Evansville reservist David Graham recalled coming to a reserve meeting on the eve of their summer camp departure in 1950: "We met as usual down at the headquarters, and they called us into formation to read a letter. I thought the letter was going to be about where we were going to summer camp." Maj. Paul Torian began to read in his deep somber voice, and Graham could not believe what he was hearing.

"Our order for summer camp had been canceled, and we were being activated. They gave us a few weeks to get ready . . . talk to our bosses and so forth."[10] More than a few members of the unit's roster had neglected to come to a single meeting and, consequently, believed they were no longer in the reserves. Nevertheless, those men received notices.

Indianapolis marine reservist Andy Jacobs, Jr., had started working that summer delivering concrete blocks to construction projects "and unloading each block by gloved hand. When I read about the war starting, I failed to see any connection between that event and my future. I just went on hauling blocks." Then in early August, Jacobs, on his way with still another load of blocks, read about the call-up of his unit. "Usually someone with a year of college could have gotten a deferment, but I was already in the reserves and could not get out. Those eight-inch concrete blocks sure got heavier when I realized this," he said.[11]

Evansville marine reservists boarding a train in August 1950. Four Indiana cities had marine reserve units called up in the early portion of the war.

The South Bend unit, which had never met, was activated a little later than the ones at Indianapolis, Evansville, and Fort Wayne. Being called up later, however, was just as shocking. Ralph Steele remembered both the beginning of the war and his activation notice: "One day in the summer of 1950, I drove down with some friends to Syracuse, Indiana, to meet some girls. While I'm there, I go over to the newsstand and pick up a paper and read that North Korea had invaded the South. At the time I didn't connect it to the marine reserve. I didn't even think I belonged to the reserve since I had not attended a single meeting." By October 1950 it looked to Steele as if the war was all but over. "I even bought a new car—a Chevy for $1,976," he said. "Then in November I came home from work. I was still living with my parents, and mom showed me this thick letter from the Twelfth Naval District. The letter said to report to Cleveland for my physical. It also stated that I had extended duty for an excess of thirty days. At the time I misread the letter. I thought to myself, 'I can stand anything for thirty days.'"[12]

Some Hoosier parents scrambled to try and keep their underage sons out of the war or at least postpone combat duty until their training had been completed. William Marshall of Oakland City had secretly gotten his grandfather to sign for him in spring 1950 before the war began. All together he and ten other teenagers in that small town had joined the Evansville reserve company. Now Marshall's family desperately wrote several letters to congressional leaders to try and keep the high school senior in school. One letter was written by Marshall's aunt, Mrs. Homer McAtee, to Sen. Margaret Chase Smith of Maine, whom McAtee thought would be a sympathetic ally. The letter said:

Dear Mrs. Smith:
    I am writing you asking that you use your influence to keep these half-trained (in some cases "no" trained) boys from being sent overseas to be slaughtered. Ten boys from our community, which is only about thirty miles from Evansville, Indiana, were sent with the Marine reserves August 28th to Camp Pendleton, California. My seventeen-year old nephew was among them. He persuaded my father who is old, sick and a paralytic to sign the papers giving consent for him to join. Other high school boys were going to Marine meetings four hours each week, and he thought the two weeks training each summer would be fun. They

were told if they grew tired of coming to the Marine base just "turn in their suits." But when this boy's mother came home (she teaches in the northern part of our state to support several children) and tried to explain that my father had no legal right to give his consent and that he was sick and had not even read the papers which he signed—do you think she could get this boy out? NO! She could not even get him deferred to finish high school.

One of the boys who went with my nephew was considered "combat ready" as soon as he got there and is expected to go overseas any time. My nephew, with three other boys who are very young and who have had absolutely no training, are supposed to go to boot training. How long that will take I have no idea. The other five boys will have four weeks of combat training and will be shipped out. The last mentioned boys have had no real training either.

Mrs. Smith, are our leaders in this country going mad? Surely I am not the only one who wonders. I read your speech of a few weeks ago and I thought it was the most sensible thing I had read for some time. I do not know whether or not you have children but I give you credit for having enough imagination to know what a terrible thing they are doing to these boys. I have helped rear two of my sister's children, and this nephew has taken the place of my son who died. I know in writing people in public offices one is considered a "crack brain" but there are a great many parents and relatives who like myself are not blessed with the gift of words and we would appreciate it so much if you will help with your influence. It may be too late to help my boy, but there will be others just as dear to someone's heart. My sister said she saw another boy much smaller than ours who was leaving with the Reserves also and he had been crying.

I just hope those of you who have influence can get these facts before the American people—maybe public opinion will have some effect on those in charge of these things. If there is any way you can help these boys by bringing their cases before the public more forcefully, I know all of us having sons or relatives in the Reserves will be very grateful. I am sure many parents are like myself not blessed with the gift for words and we are hoping someone like you will help us.[13]

The McAtee letter brought quick responses from Senator Smith as well as from Indiana's two senators. Sen. William Jenner replied to the Marshall family that he could do nothing to stop the process. "Your letter relative to deferment of the 17-year old reservists has been received," wrote Jenner. "I have discussed the matter at length with officials in the Department of the Army. The attitude is, these boys are reservists and are subject to call the same as other reserve units." Jenner did point out that "if the boy is in school, by applying for deferment, he will be permitted to finish his school year." The conservative senator added, "It is unfortunate this situation exists, and I only wish there might be something I could do. However, all authority is in the hands of the Department of Defense and the Selective Service Board, over which I have no jurisdiction. I agree with you this matter of taking young boys and sacrificing them on a battlefield to cover up the bungling foreign policy we are shouldered with, is a blot in our history, and you may be sure if there is anything I can do to change the situation, I shall do it."[14]

Ultimately correspondence from the Marshall family and others failed to change the minds of the Marine Corps leadership. As the commandant of the Marine Corps, Gen. Clifton B. Cates explained in a letter to the Marshall family's congressman, Edward Noland, "a very large number of Marine reservists are in the high school age group. It becomes apparent that should all of these young men be deferred, the strength of the Reserves available for active duty would be considerably reduced."[15] William Marshall boarded a train to Camp Pendleton on about the same day he was supposed to have begun his senior year in high school.

Democratic congressman Andy Jacobs, Sr., father of Indianapolis reservist Andy Jacobs, Jr., did not attempt to get his son out of combat, although some national political leaders whose sons served in the reserves did so. The Indiana congressman did, however, publicly call for the firing of Secretary of Defense Johnson and suggested his replacement be Gen. Dwight D. Eisenhower. Jacobs also urged Truman to follow through on his intention to appoint Republicans to high executive positions, stating that "it would have a solidifying effect on the country."[16]

As Hoosiers struggled to come to grips with the departures of their sons, the war situation continued to worsen. The 135,000 heavily armed and well-trained North Korean soldiers quickly routed the undertrained paramilitary armies of South Korea and rapidly advanced southward. On 1 July Truman, under the flag of the United Nations, had ordered the first U.S. ground troops in to fight. Many of those came from Japan's garrison duty units; the majority barely knew how to handle a weapon and were woefully out of shape. By middle and late July these troops were holding a small and precarious perimeter around the southeast seaport of Pusan.

The first American ground troops arrived in Korea in the form of Task Force Smith and included 406 men from the First Battalion of the Twenty-first Regiment of the Twenty-fourth Infantry Division. Each man carried 120 rounds of .30-caliber rifle ammo and two days of C rations. The task force also had two recoilless guns and a few bazookas; most of the latter, however, could not stop the Russian-made tanks employed by North Korean troops.[17] Out of shape and with little training, the Smith group incurred heavy losses in its first encounter with the enemy. Shortly following the Task Force Smith debacle came units of the army's First Cavalry Division, Stanley Nelson's outfit. Nelson recalled: "We made an amphibious landing on July 18, 1950, and met no resistance. Some of us had doubts that there really was a war going on as we had not been told anything or heard stories from the front. Even if there was, I thought the North Koreans would take one look at us and run. Was I ever wrong."[18] Nelson's naïve observations upon landing were echoed in a *Time* article that compared the beginning of the First Cavalry's voyage from Japan to "the festivity of a luxury liner's departure from a 30-day pleasure cruise of the Mediterranean.... Three days after the fleet left Japan, it dropped anchor.... Not a shot was fired." Most of the men, the magazine reported, "came ashore without even getting their feet wet."[19] The ease of the landing was terribly misleading for the First Cavalry. Soon after disembarking, Nelson had his initial combat experience: "Our battalion was sent to the front to support the infantry, and my first night out it rained the entire evening. My foxhole soon filled with water, and I did not have a dry thread left on me. However, that was not my greatest concern. We had watched thousands of North Korean soldiers march into the mountains all day, and we knew some time that night they would probably attack. The Air Force had bombed and napalmed the North Koreans most of the day; however, at night we were on our own. Even the artillery could not help much."

Nelson's group had just settled in when the enemy launched a furious attack: "The first wave came in the early morning hours. I heard loud yelling and whistles; with the main force charging on my right about one hundred yards away. As it turned out, the U.S. troops to our right had already bugged out and moved into our forward holes. As soon as our officers found out what had happened, they ordered those troops back and sent a few others and myself to go with them. We retook those positions and spent the rest of the night there. Unfortunately, we did not know that there were a large number of North Koreans about one hundred yards in front of us. When daylight broke, it was very still, and we were unaware of the fact that the enemy was so close. We were all tired of being cramped in the foxholes, so we started to stretch our bodies. That's when one North Korean saw us and immediately began to fire our way. We took fire the rest of that day."

The night brought new horrors to Nelson and his comrades: "When night fell, we were charged by the North Koreans and were forced to withdraw. They had outflanked us and were firing at us from the front and the rear. My lieutenant, a younger fellow himself with no combat experience, was uneasy about giving an order to withdraw so he asked our squad leader, who was a World War II veteran, what he should do. The vet's reply was 'get the hell out of here.' So we started to withdraw which, within a few minutes, turned into another major bugout. Leaving machine guns, ammo, and equipment behind, we were under heavy fire from both flanks. When we reached the main road, we were in a cul-de-sac. The North Koreans were still in front and on both flanks. Many wounded Americans were left behind, as most of us were just trying to save ourselves."

Nelson's experiences during those first few days of fighting reflected the harsh reality of the early war for American troops in Korea. The term bugout became a popular term and practice for the first raw undertrained Americans as they struggled to survive. Nelson's particular struggles, however, were far from over. He noted: "After reaching the road, we headed south for about one-half mile. At this time officers were trying to separate troops into their companies and squads. Then some new replacements and ROKs [Republic of Korea troops] arrived, and they were well armed. However, most of them had never fired an M1 rifle or a .30-caliber machine gun. Our platoon sergeant took one of the machine guns from a ROK soldier and gave it to me and warned me that I had better not lose it. That night we went back into the mountains to try and take back some of our former positions. As we reached the top of the first ridge, we met heavy resistance. It was not raining at this time and the North Koreans could see us. Suddenly we began receiving heavy fire, probably a captured .50-caliber machine gun. I advanced forward to a large rock to gain cover and fired almost all of my ammo so the wounded could be removed and the others get to better positions. Then we withdrew again. A few hundred yards away we dug in and it began to rain." It was during this time that Nelson was almost killed. "Just before daylight a North Korean soldier was wandering through our positions and almost stepped in my hole. He raised his weapon and as he did I grabbed my machine gun and started to fire at him, but only one round would fire. The webbing had become wet and the machine gun would not function. Luckily one shot was all I needed."

There were many other dangers and discomforts for GIs such as Nelson, who struggled to survive in those early, brutal days of the war. Nelson recalled, "As the day wore on, we were running very low on water, ammo, and food. I volunteered to go back to the rear to get more water. It was a long trip carrying two full five-gallon cans, along with my rifle and ammo. Fortunately, while at the water point, I got all the water I could drink and was able to get a few cans of C rations out of the back pack of a dead GI. When I returned with the water and the few C rations, we had taken some POWs. Things were so tense that the oldest sergeant in our platoon had become delirious and said he could not take it anymore. Up until that time, he had been a good soldier. We had to tie him up in a poncho. After a while, however, he became more rational and we untied him."[20]

By late July 1950, American troops were so threatened by their inability to stop North Korean advances that two battalions of the Twenty-ninth Regiment were quickly rushed to Korea from Okinawa. Without time to zero in and test fire their weapons, these raw troops were expected to stop a highly trained enemy. One of the more tragic episodes in the first weeks of the war involved the Third Battalion of the Twenty-ninth Infantry. One historian of the Korean War, Joseph Goulden, believed the near annihilation of this battalion offered "stomach-turning evidence of what can happen when sending untrained, ill-armed soldiers into combat." Consisting primarily of troops who performed clerical and security duty, many of these young men knew little about their weapons or fighting tactics. Nevertheless, these green GIs were sent almost immediately to try and stop the North Korean onslaught. One survivor told how the North Koreans "hunted us down like they were shooting rabbits fleeing a brush fire."[21]

Oakland City resident Hobert Young remembered those hectic and trying days the Twenty-ninth endured. "Our barracks in

Okinawa had intercoms in them and one night, about 5 p.m. or so, an announcement came over the speakers that we were to be in full pack and ready to leave by 6 a.m. the next morning," said Young. "We were told we would be airlifted to Korea but that was all. The next day an officer told some of us it was unclear if we'd ever be able to land in Korea, things were so bad there."

Young's company of about two hundred men flew in a single plane and soon landed in Korea. "We had all our gear—weapons, packs, ammo—everything with us, so it was very crowded, and we were all pretty shaken and scared as we flew," he remembered. "We landed in Korea, near Pusan, around two in the afternoon, and they had us loading up in personnel carriers as soon as we got off and walked out onto the field. We were packed pretty tight, too, about sixteen of us on each vehicle, which was a lot more than they were supposed to carry." The Twenty-ninth Battalion's baptism of fire came quickly. "It didn't seem very long until we got to the front lines sometime in the late afternoon," said Young. "As it turned out, we didn't even have time to dig a foxhole down in the valley where we stopped before we got hit. All hell just broke loose. We weren't able to hold, things were just so chaotic around us. It didn't make matters any better that our original commander had stayed in Okinawa. We didn't even know the new guy all that well, actually never knew him at all until we got to Korea."

Savagely attacked, Young and his fellow GIs scrambled to escape. Young said: "Our retreat back was pretty disorganized, actually a panic. I remember stepping over several bodies of our guys. Luckily, the North Koreans didn't pursue us. We got back a ways and dug in for the night but most of us were out of ammunition before the night was over. That's one thing I remember well about those first weeks in Korea. We didn't really have enough of anything—ammo, food, the right kind of weapons. You could really tell our country wasn't ready for that war."

That first night in Korea for Young was horrible. "No one slept a wink. The ground was so rocky, you couldn't dig a decent foxhole, you just had to hunch down real far to get any sense of protection," he said. "I suppose this was the first combat for most of us that night. At three o'clock that morning they really came at us, but we had our machine guns set up and were able to stop the attack cold."

The next few days the Twenty-ninth received supplies and more ammo and were able to take back the hill that stood over the valley where they had first been hit. "We advanced further, about another mile. Things slowed down there for a few days," said Young. "It was then I discovered I had to work through the bad feelings I had about shooting a weapon at another human being. It was a lot harder than you might imagine. I mean you could actually see the man you were firing at going down. Anyway, it surprised me at the time how much this bothered me in those few days we had before the fighting got bad again. Once things heated up though, I didn't have time to think about it."

The physical environment was another difficulty for Hoosiers fighting in Korea. Young recalled, "The terrain was another reality I had trouble adjusting to. Korea, where I was at anyway, was just so mountainous and rocky, and there weren't any paved roads. It always seemed like it was either too hot or too cold—a very hostile land. But for me the worse problem was the smell of those rice paddies where the Koreans dumped human waste. The smell would literally make you sick, and then if you were being shot at you'd find yourself having to fall to the ground in all that muck. You really never got used to that; at least I didn't."

Young, however, did find that some problems had rather simple solutions. "One thing I did learn real quick was that the carbines we were supposed to use weren't very good over long distances. I soon picked up a M1 rifle. In my opinion a person might as well thrown a rock as to try to hit someone any distance away with one of those damn carbines."

About three weeks after the Twenty-ninth's landing in Korea, their luck ran out. "One afternoon we got hit about three o'clock, and you could tell this attack was more fierce than any of the others we'd been in. We were strung out on a ridge and down into a valley and then over another hill—strung out pretty thin," Young said. "When the North Koreans attacked, there were so many of them, and we got hit so hard that we were quickly overrun. Our commander got killed, and the sergeant in charge told us, 'Boys let's get the hell out of here, we don't stand a chance.' The sergeant wasn't a coward either, but he saw the situation was hopeless, so we cut out and literally ran for our lives." Young and about a dozen others in his party were able to escape. The great majority of American troops did not. "The Twenty-ninth Regiment got it so bad in that engagement that they placed us survivors in the Twenty-seventh Regiment. The Twenty-ninth, the group I'd come over with, was just disbanded. In my group there had originally been over two hundred. Now there were only nineteen of us left to go to the Twenty-seventh. God must have been looking after me. With the exception of sore feet, I hadn't received a wound yet. Mostly though, in those first several weeks, everything happened so quickly and with such intensity and destruction that you didn't have time to think, you just trudged on and tried to survive."[22]

Young might have found some cheer in the fact that his hometown paper, the *Oakland City Journal,* carried a piece about the important work American infantrymen such as Young were doing in Korea. "The role of the foot soldier has again been all important," the paper noted. "Despite all the new and revolutionary concepts yet uttered, the 'poor, bloody infantry' has been the queen of battles in Korea."[23]

Another U.S. division hastily thrown into the war to save the Pusan perimeter was the Second Infantry Division under Maj. Gen. Laurence Keiser. Neither Keiser nor the three regimental commanders had ever led troops in battle. The division staff itself had been quickly assembled and was woefully short of experienced officers and NCOs (noncommissioned officers).[24] Serving in the Seventy-second Tank Battalion of the Second was Solsberry native Ray Cox. In late July Cox had written his sister Lois, telling her he was not able to identify where he was serving in Korea but that he was "alright as of yet."

In early September 1950 Cox and his Second Division comrades found themselves at the focal point of the battle to save the perimeter. On 10 September, less than a week before he perished in battle, Cox wrote his sister, telling in more detail about his difficult life as a tank gunner. "Well, everything over here is just about the same, only once in a while I get too hot," Cox wrote. "I have destroyed a lot of equipment of the North Koreans, being I am a gunner on a tank. . . . I am staying up all night and sleeping in the daytime [since nighttime is] when the enemy likes to fight." Cox added his thoughts about the North Koreans' tendency to fight once the sun had set as "sort of funny in one way, and in another way it isn't." Cox also took time to write his childhood friend Bob Doane. Doane recalled Cox writing him how he had "really made the machine guns on my tank talk that day. The enemy came in waves and I just kept mowing them down." At the letter's conclusion Cox wrote, "It's getting dark so I will have to sign off. Your Pal, Ray." Cox's tank was hit the next day, and the nineteen year old was mortally wounded.[25]

Hoosier Carl Spencer was also a member of the Second Division. He came from a large extended family that lived in the Scottsburg area. Unable to find a good job and needing money to help feed his family, Spencer had gone into the army as an eighteen year old in 1949. On 8 August 1950 he landed with the Second Division at Pusan to help maintain the perimeter. "The weapons we had were from World War II and much of it wore out. The little bazookas we used wouldn't even faze the North Korean tanks." Many accounts told how the American shells just bounced off the enemy tanks like Ping-Pong balls. "We were told the North Koreans were shelling very close to the coast, so just after we landed we were sent north very quickly to help take an important hill," Spencer said.

One of the sights Spencer saw on his way up to his first combat was a convoy of twelve trucks: "We had to stop to let these trucks drive by. The smell was awful. It was the odor of decay from the dead bodies of our boys. I remember body fluid was just rolling out

Carl Spencer of Lexington. Spencer endured the epic battle of Chipyong-ni in February 1951.

from the backs of the trucks. We found out later they were bringing men out from the First Cavalry. There must have been fifteen or twenty in each vehicle. This I saw before I'd even fired a shot."

The summer was agonizingly hot. Spencer remembered, in one instance, the temperature rising to more than one hundred degrees and how he "dug a hole and buried my face to get some relief. What had happened was that we had gotten down in this dry creek bed and been pinned down. It was so hot there that you couldn't touch any of the big boulders without burning your hands, and here we were trapped down there. Our first lieutenant said to us 'we have to get out of here or we'll suffocate.' He said 'let's die fighting.' They pulled us back to Hill 189, and that was my first big fight." At Hill 189 Spencer saw "an awful lot of killing and destruction. I was up on some pretty high elevations and was able to watch our planes strafe and napalm the North Koreans. We fought there for about five days."[26]

The poor performance of the troops caused them to be dubbed "tourists from Japan."[27] Stories related to American civilian POWs by military POWs told of poor weapon performance. "Some of the prisoners stated that they had gone into combat with their M-1's still covered in the heavy grease that was applied to such weapons prior to shipment to prevent saltwater corrosion. Others indicated that their personal weapons were clean and should have worked properly but did not. Stories were told of firing the M-1, then hammering the breach mechanism open with a trench shovel, and then firing again. 'We could have done better with slingshots,' one man said in disgust." Another complaint concerned a lack of adequate intelligence. One civilian POW reported, "Major [John] Dunn said that in his intelligence briefing in Japan, just prior to being sent to Korea, he was informed that he might confront a few obsolete tanks. Then he told of lying in a ditch by the side of the road at night in South Korea counting some thirty to forty modern T-34 tanks as they moved past him. I heard the same comments from many of the others: 'The tanks just keep coming; we never had anything that could stop them.' One GI said bluntly, 'Our bazookas wouldn't even knock the paint off those North Korean tanks.'"[28]

The concerns of Hoosiers stationed in Japan in early July are powerfully reflected in a number of letters sent home by Solsberry's Hamilton. In a letter written just as the war was heating up, Hamilton told his parents, "One year ago tonight I got into the Yokohama Bay, I think it was about 2-o-clock that we got there. I am sure glad that it was a year ago instead of this year because if nothing serious happens in this part of the world, I may get to come back in two months but I don't look to come home for some time yet, so don't count on me being there in October because I don't know what is going to happen." More specifically, Hamilton noted the serious turn of the war. "We were on alert again yesterday but went off of it today about ten-o-clock so I guess that there will be no passes tonight," he wrote. "No one could leave the post last night."

Hamilton continued, "There is a big shipment of men leaving here tomorrow, I don't know for sure where they are going but they say that they are going to the 24th Division to help build up their strength. There was one medical officer left here yesterday, and I think that they said that he was headed for Korea but it might be only talk." Hamilton also told of how those departing unprepared troops were coping with their situation. "You should see the biggest part of the boys going over today. I bet there isn't over 15 or 20 in the Company but what is drinking or already had all they can hold."

The next day Hamilton wrote his parents, relating more bad news. "I suppose that you heard about the 24th Division being in Korea by this time. There was also a big shipment of men left here today to join the 24th, so I guess that they will be going to Korea with them. I don't know what is going to happen to us [the Seventh Division] yet but I am afraid that it won't be too good. They are setting up emergency hospital tents today in case that there would be an air raid. I think that they are going to start censoring our letters that we write so you may not get much of a letter when you do get one. If they are censored, be sure to look for underlined letters or anything else that I could tell you something with."

In mid-July Hamilton reported to his parents that his unit, the Thirty-second, had "moved out this week to an unknown destination, so you can imagine where they are or where they are going." Luckily Hamilton was still in Japan undergoing minor surgery. He next attempted to be transferred to an army hospital. "I went up to see the detachment commander at the hospital here to see about a transfer," wrote Hamilton. "He called Regiment up at Camp, and they won't release me. He told me I am trained as a medic for combat." Hamilton added somberly, "you know what this means." He also quipped, "I may get the G.I. Bill after all, but I don't believe I want it now." More seriously, the Solsberry native told his parents, "I have just about quit counting on getting to come home." While recovering from his surgery, Hamilton continued to fret over going to Korea but always with Hoosier-style humor. "I still don't know when I will get to come home or not but I am still hoping," he told his parents. "One good thing about being here is that if Russia gets into the fight I won't have to worry about being sent overseas because I am already here."

On 17 July, less than a month after the war came, Hamilton told his family the bad news along with a story that indicated what they might expect if he went into combat. "It looks like the 32nd is headed for Korea after all because they are down in the southern part of Japan getting re-organized, and they are building it up to combat strength. And this can only mean one thing and I suppose you know what. I guess I have about three more weeks to go here in the Hospital, but I would sure like to get out and get my things straightened out and rejoin the outfit. There are two Sgt's that I know who have been wounded in Korea. One got his hand shot off by machine gun fire and the other got hit in the stomach and is almost dead from the last that was heard from him. This is hitting a little too close to home to suit me."

Hamilton's father, Oval, tried to reassure his son about his chances, but the son wrote back stating otherwise: "Oval, you said that you felt better about the war, well, I don't because it looks like all hell is going to break loose all over the world from the way the *Stars and Stripes* talk. You were also a little off by thinking I would still be home in October. Well I guess you weren't altogether wrong because if nothing happens I will get out in October [1951]. It sure looks like that the squirrels and game wardens will get one more year's rest." Hamilton's letter also conveyed his continued thoughts of his Indiana home and his concern regarding his own chances of returning. "Oval, you said that you would keep my cow calf this year and I would have a nice bunch when I got back," wrote Hamilton. "Well, do as you want to but don't make too many plans because no one knows what will happen in the next year. I don't even look ahead a year anymore because with the luck I have, there just isn't any need to."

Hamilton's sense of duty along with his Hoosier pride also surfaced in a letter home. "I guess the boys back home are sweating the army out," he said. "Well, I am glad that I got in before it started because I wouldn't want to have the name of being drafted. I guess I must be crazy but I don't like the idea of being made to go to the army." In late July Hamilton wrote his mother asking her to send him "a dagger type knife with about a four inch blade on it . . . send it just as soon and fast as possible."

Hamilton also expressed his disgust over hearing how some of his male acquaintances back home in Indiana were joining the service in order to teach the Communists in Korea a lesson. "What is the matter with Harold and Ralph?," he asked. "Are they crazy or do they just think they are tough. I sure wish they could be over here for just one month. I think that they would be cooled off by that time. Over here everyone is just about half mad at having to stay and will fight at the drop of a hat. You sure do have to hold up for yourself or you will get the devil beat out of you. This is one reason I have been boxing a little over here, but I have quit until I get my teeth fixed which will begin tomorrow morning. I got hit in the mouth yesterday and cut my lip where the edge of the teeth are, but it just bled a little, so I am quitting until I get a mouth piece."

Just before Hamilton went to Korea as a part of the Inchon invasion in September, he wrote these grave lines to his parents: "I imagine that you have the hay all put up by this time. I was looking to be back to help with it next year but it doesn't look like I will make it. I don't like to put up hay, but I believe I like it better than dodging lead. Oval, you were talking about people being mad about sending troops to Korea not prepared, well from the way the boys talk that were back in the hospital, it was nothing but a death sentence to the 24 and 25 Divisions. There isn't over 15% of the old men left in these outfits."[29]

The deteriorating circumstances of the war were reflected in the emergency activation of reserve components. Thomas Chappell of Huntingburg was one of the unlucky army reservists who, having served faithfully in World War II, now abruptly found himself called back into action. To make matters worse, Chappell, as most older reservists, now had a good job and a wife and children to support. Unfortunately, because the war came in such shocking fashion, the American military found itself short of trained infantry. Consequently, army reservists such as Chappell were called into service for their country and sent to Korea with little notice or training. The Huntingburg man faced combat more quickly than he could have ever imagined. "I was called for active duty in August 1950 and boarded a train in Huntingburg headed for Camp Hood, Texas. I had been stationed there with the tank destroyers during

The Storm Breaks

World War II and hated it," said Chappell. "Anyway, I was issued new clothing, had all eleven shots and vaccinations and then loaded back on a troop train headed for Camp Stoneman, California. From there I went to a troop ship headed to Korea. Eleven days from the time I left home I was landing in Pusan harbor. We unloaded and were marched to a troop train with all our belongings in a duffle bag. It was a long cold ride, and we had no idea where we were going. My MOS [military occupational specialty] was rifleman in the infantry, so I knew I'd soon be seeing combat action."[30]

Hoosier marine reservists called up in July also worried about being sent overseas without proper training. Reservists who lacked combat-ready training were supposed to receive adequate instruction before being sent into action. Furthermore, according to official policy, any reservist "who believed he needed more training was removed, without prejudice from consideration for immediate assignment to combat duty."[31] The reality of the circumstances

Eight Hoosier men at an Indiana train station, headed to war. Left to right: Forrest Miller, Robert "Bud" Fitch, Gordon Greene, William Marshall, Charles "Barney" Barnard, Albert Dickson, Donald Corn, and Garold Sheetz.

forced the marines to abandon the policy. Members of C Company, Sixteenth Infantry Battalion, of Evansville, for example, were promised six months of combat instruction before going into battle.[32] The first man killed from that unit, however, perished thirty-four days after leaving Evansville by train for Camp Pendleton. He had received only two weeks of combat preparation. In a rather bitter note following the reservist's death, Charles "Barney" Barnard noted, "one of the boys who came over from Evansville stepped on a mine the first day he was on the line. The boy's name was [John] Elliott. They just didn't give Elliott and the others [who were initially killed] enough training to protect themselves."[33]

Teenage reservist David Graham, who also found himself classified as combat ready after only two weeks of training, held grave concerns about going to Korea so quickly. "When we were getting ready to leave California for Korea, I went down to see an officer to tell him we didn't have enough training—haven't even had boot camp," said Graham. "The officer agreed this was so, but added there was nothing he could do about the situation." The colonel informed Graham, "We need people over there; we need them right now and you're the best we've got." The colonel, however, promised Graham "all the boot camp you want," upon Graham's return from Korea.[34] Elkhart teenager Ralph Steele, in a letter to his family, described the desperation of the Marine Corps call-up: "Well, I guess I'm in. The physicals weren't much at Cleveland. They have a lot of recruits coming in every day so I guess they need men pretty bad! I don't imagine they'll give me a medical discharge on account of my teeth. There are some here with missing fingers, so they're taking about everybody."[35]

The problem created by using undertrained Hoosier reservists sometimes took on a humorous side as one of Graham's recollections demonstrate:

> During my time in Korea we spent about 2 or 3 weeks aboard ship going up and down the coast in preparation for an amphibious landing [at Wonsan]. We had to go up and

down the coast as where we were landing was heavily mined. They had minesweepers in there clearing out the mines.

During this time aboard ship, I was assigned guard duty. While manning my post the officer of the day came around to inspect. As he approached I came to attention and saluted him. He stood there a minute and then he barked, "Report your post." Since I was a reservist and had little or no training in Marine Corps decorum, I didn't know what he was talking about and so I said—"Everything is okay."

He then really swelled up and chewed me out up one side and down the other. "Don't you know the proper way to report your post?" he demanded. "No Sir." I said. He told me that was the first thing I should have learned in boot camp. I responded, "I never went to boot camp Sir."

This really angered the officer. He continued to chew me out and he said, "Son, I am going to teach you how to report your post." He instructed me to come and see him in his quarters when I got off guard duty. I went down to see him and he told me to write this down. "PFC Graham reports post number (whatever number was assigned) all secure. Post and orders remain the same Sir." If your orders have been changed, you state, "Post and orders have been changed Sir." Then he, the officer, inquires what changes have been made and you tell him.

He told me to go and write this 1000 times. Well, we were aboard ship and we did not have anything. I could not find any paper to write on. I got whatever I could find, waste paper in a waste basket, news bulletins off the bulletin board, toilet paper, anything I could find. I finally finished it and took it back to him and he looked at it and said, "Hell, boy this is not numbered. Take it back and number it."

Now I want to tell you exactly what all enlisted marines call this, "Chicken Shit!"[36]

The plight of reservists such as Chappell, Steele, and Graham did not go unnoticed in the national press. A sympathetic *U.S. News and World Report* noted how many reservists were "already behind competitors in business. They'll never catch up with some who stayed home.... Brushing the old uniforms again, [they] are beginning to wonder what they did to deserve it."[37] In another article about the different circumstances of reservists, the magazine pointed out that "reservists already are the forgotten men of this mobilization period." Most reservists who were in the volunteer portion of the program and who had received no pay "thought they were signing up as a patriotic duty for call in time of big war." What really angered the veterans in this group was that they had already served in World War II and were now going to Korea before "18-year-old's, short service veterans, and men with wives but no military record."[38]

Hoosiers also quickly complained about the reserves being called up. One concerned Indianapolis mother wrote a letter to the *Indianapolis Star* lamenting what she perceived to be the unfair call-up of army reservists such as her two sons. "We have two sons, both in reserves, who will probably soon be called to war again though our President says it is not war. They did their part in World War II and finally finishing college and getting jobs to support their families deserved a full and happy life."[39] Another Hoosier mother from Wabash also penned a letter to the *Star* declaring that American "reservists are entitled to a better deal." In the letter the woman explained:

> I'm a mother who is daily getting more and more worked up over the unfair way in which the Reservists have been called back to active duty.
> Perhaps I wouldn't feel so bitter if our boys had been told the truth when they enlisted in the Reserves after they had served in World War 2. Everything has been a misrepresentation from start to finish. If our sons come home from this war, there will have to be something else besides

"Reserves." They will be afraid to join anything, for their faith and trust is gone now.

It's deplorable when you consider these boys are to be our future citizens and should have the utmost respect and faith in their government. Our son enlisted in World War 2 at the age of 17 and served overseas. He entered college when he came home, was married, and had a comfortable home. His 3-year enlistment in the Reserves ended last August, but nevertheless he was recalled to active duty the following October.

He was in his senior year at college, but it didn't make any difference. He wasn't permitted to finish the semester, although, in some of his classes were boys in the draft who were single and had never been in service. These boys were given deferments, and some were just entering college.

I do not think these Reservists should be sent overseas again. They were willing soldiers in World War 2, but in this war, which our President says is only a "police" war, they are unwilling, unhappy and bitter soldiers. The west coast is full of reservists that apparently are not needed. Those with specialized training they are using, but so many others are just waiting, waiting—for what? They sit out there and think of their careers unfinished; their wives and babies; jobs where they were making good living for their families, and bitterness grows in their hearts, for from their high school days they have never been free from the government's grasp.

Ironically enough, these boys with families back home to support have received $20 in pay in two months time. Bitter? What do you think?[40]

Another Indianapolis resident, a father of an army reservist who fought in World War II, wrote of his grave concerns about the lack of combat preparation given to reservists. "It's high time the public should know the facts. The Army's brass in Washington has been cold blooded and ruthless in their method of calling Inactive Reserve Army Officers back into service. Here is what happened to my son. A physical? Blood pressure reading and chest X-ray, nothing more. Past medical records including disability—ignored. Refresher courses, physical toughening or hardening for combat? None. He got that in the Bulge almost six years ago. Fire five rounds on your carbine, lieutenant, to zero in the sight. You're ready. Twenty-five days from a civilian in Indianapolis to the combat zone in Korea. What a speed record." The angry Hoosier father continued, "I understand there are hundreds of others, both enlisted men and officers, that got the same raw deal. Why should any American deserve that kind of treatment? Many letters have gone to Washington seeking the answer. Replies? Sure. Referred here or there, the old brush-off and run around. Any red-blooded American will serve his country in time of peril. But that country should prepare him to do a good job. In this instance the country has failed the man. Why? Congress should appoint a committee to make a thorough investigation."[41]

The *Star* itself soon waded into the fray regarding the lack of employment protection for active reservists. The paper called for "An Even Break for Reservists." Specifically the editor pointed out how "National Guardsmen and other reservists deserve far better of their country than to be made victims of employer discrimination. Such discrimination is grossly unfair to individuals whose patriotism entitles them to extra consideration if anything, rather than a kicking around. Furthermore it damages the nation's military program by causing men to shy away from reserve service." The article went on to assert, "Some employers refuse to hire men who stand a chance of being called into the armed forces in a short time. In certain cases an employer may be justified in such a policy, especially when the hiring and training of service-vulnerable men would slow defense production. But in most instances there is no excuse other than plain selfishness. Everybody on the home front should be willing and eager to bend over backward a little to help men who a few months from now may be fighting for the interests of all on a distant battlefield." The article ended by declaring that "in cases where the law doesn't cover employer discrimination against potential servicemen it is to be hoped that public opinion will exact harsh punishment."[42]

In less kind circles, American and Hoosier reserve officers and noncoms, who served in World War II and were now being recalled to fight in those early dark days of the Korean War, were dubbed "retreads" and "two-time losers." One military historian noted about their cruel situation, "It was obvious to everyone that it was unfair to call men who had already served to serve again, while most adult males who had never served were either safely deferred from the renewed draft or over the draft-age limit." This would not be the case for the retreads: "There were thousands of veteran officers and noncoms in their thirties, and many in their forties, who were wrenched out of their civilian careers and flung into their second war. Many of these men died. Yet as a group, the retreads gave a quality of professionalism and competence that never could have been attained so quickly by training new men."[43]

College student William Hasselbrinck of Francisco faced a problem typical of many Indiana males who were going to college full time when the war started. A sophomore at Indiana State University, Hasselbrinck was encouraged by the university to sign up for a college deferment in order to avoid the draft. When he had not completed the form, the dean of students called Hasselbrinck into his office and strongly advised him to sign. Hasselbrinck refused and was quickly drafted, his sense of duty overcoming his sense of survival.[44] Harold "Sonny" Bender of Boonville had already served almost a year in the Marine Corps in the 1940s when a military cutback caused him to be released early. A college student when the Korean War broke out, Bender did not seek a deferment and was drafted.

Hoosier parents of sons who were of draft age likely would not have been excited about the kinds of choices Hasselbrinck and Bender had made. One Hoosier mother from Spencer, in a letter to an Indiana newspaper, noted, "I am the mother of four sons

Seven Hoosier marine reservists at a farewell party in the early portion of the war. Left to right: William Marshall, Albert Dickson, Gordon Greene, Robert "Bud" Fitch, Forrest Miller, William Cunningham, and Garold Sheetz.

(no daughters). I have had a service flag in my window for almost five years (which is long enough for any mother). My second son is an honor student at I.U. The third one is a promising young artist; The fourth one is still in high school. This is what I have to say to them: 'Don't get too patriotic!'"[45]

Some Hoosiers, especially teenagers, seemed to look forward to the war and the chance to achieve the glory their big brothers had gained in World War II. Marine reservist Gordon Greene, for example, early in his training in September 1950 wrote his mother telling her, "there is talk we will form into a raider battalion." In another letter he boldly asserted, "while we are in Korea we should show these communists where they belong." After several months of ferocious combat, however, Greene would take a very different view of the war, eventually writing his mother, "this new cease fire plan sounds promising. . . . We're all praying that something is settled. It would sure be wonderful if it actually would come through."[46]

The nation's lack of preparedness to fight a war brought forth a barrage of criticisms from Hoosier Republicans. Two days after the war began, Senator Jenner charged that the situation in Korea "reminds us that the same sellout to Stalin's statesmen who turned Russia loose are still in the saddle riding herd on the American people." In the Senate, Jenner stood and shouted, "The time has come when we no longer can entrust our future to those who have betrayed the past. The front paging of the present plight of Korea is a grim reminder that the Russian is sprawled out across the Eurasian continent."[47] Sen. Homer Capehart more delicately attacked the Truman administration for what the Hoosier senator termed "terrible blunders." Capehart argued that the "Truman administration . . . has so badly bungled our program in the Orient that nothing short of a general house cleaning . . . will give us the bold leadership we need now."[48] Republican congressional candidate William McCray, in a speech at Boonville, attacked his democratic opponent Winfield Denton, along with other democratic congressmen, for failing to keep the nation prepared for war. "Americans," declared McCray, "demand that the American leadership be changed so that never again will America be caught in such a miserable state of unpreparedness."[49]

Most Hoosier newspapers, in atypical fashion, quickly put politics aside and got behind the war effort, while at the same time noting the great dangers that now loomed before the nation. The *Star* warned in an editorial, "Korea can become the starting point of World War III." The outcome, the *Star* asserted, "depends on the determination and the strength of the United States. . . . We must insist that the UN stand against this act of aggression . . . we must bring the showdown now."[50] When the first American combat troops disembarked in Korea, the *Star*'s editor wrote, "Rifle-toting American infantrymen and other ground troops have been ordered into battle again less than five years after GI Joe sheathed his bayonet, doffed his heavy helmet and looked forward to a lifetime of enjoying the peace he had done so much to win." The article went on to say that Hoosiers "were hoping for an 'easy' war. But it hasn't turned out that way. . . . The South Korean troops are no match for the well-planned tank assault of the Russian puppets." The editorial ended by proclaiming, "May God be with them—every one of those stout-hearted sons of America on whose young shoulders have fallen the task of seeing our blundering nation through another historic crisis. And may we at home try to be worthy of their sacrifices."[51]

When the war continued to deteriorate in July and August, the *Star* demanded the country "Take the offensive! The total loss of Korea," the *Star* asserted "will be the evil fruit of the confused, paralyzing defensive psychology which has dominated this nation's leadership ever since World War II drew toward its end. . . . While the finger of blame should be pointed, however, victory will require a far more positive response to the Korean debacle. First, we must abandon, once and for all, the Maginot complex. In its place we must develop a psychology of counterattack—diplomatic, and military. Stalin has a world-wide timetable for aggression. This nation must develop a timetable of its own!"[52]

Other Hoosier papers waded in on the subject as well. In a bold front-page editorial, the *Lafayette Journal and Courier* called for a clear-cut policy in Korea. In part the Hoosier paper declared, "People of the United States need to be told, honestly and frankly, of the dangers which confront them in Korea and around the world. No further time dare be lost in adopting and following a definite, clear-cut and positive foreign policy, which will safeguard the nation's interests and those of all free peoples and which will merit and invite the loyal and staunch support of all citizens." The article argued that "the government must dedicate itself wholly to the main task confronting it, directing all its energies and resources to bringing about a quick and victorious conclusion of the war in Korea, for war it is. This means that economies must be effected in all other fields so that our national defense may promptly reach its maximum and most effective strength. . . . It is best for our people to know what difficulties are being faced. Ignorance led at first to unrealistic expectations. If developments are not too favorable at once, continued ignorance is bound to lead to unrealistic depression. The American people can take bad news. They ought to know what the score is. They need to know the facts. After learning the truth, there is need for assurance that something is being done about it."[53]

The *Evansville Courier* also declared itself in favor of the sudden war effort but warned, "Let no one delude himself. There is only one nation with sufficient forces nearby to stop communist aggression in Korea. That is the United States. Britain, with some troops in Singapore, could help a little. France is tied up in the Indo-China struggle. There are no other forces worth mentioning in that part of the world that might be called upon by the UN."[54] The *Evansville Press,* in an editorial titled "United We Stand," gave especially strong endorsement of Truman's call for U.S. involvement in stopping the North Korean invasion. "President Truman has given the world's peace machinery real meaning by throwing the full weight of American military power behind the United Nations' efforts to restore law and order in the Far East. His courageous action may have averted a third world war," the newspaper said. "The attack upon Korea made it plain beyond all doubt, as the President said, that Communism has passed beyond use of subversion to conquer independent nations and now is using armed invasion and war. That challenge had to be met by force, if it was to be met at all. For nothing less would serve." However, the same editorial went on to warn, "Mr. Truman's policy involves a calculated risk. He is taking police action against an armed mob. The mob may fight back. If it does, there may be casualties."[55]

In early July, when the war looked almost hopeless, in an issue of the *Evansville Sunday Courier and Press,* the editor asked readers to "Let the Past Wait." Putting unity before politics the *Press*'s editor declared, "The world's eyes are on Washington because of the tremendous responsibilities America has assumed in a grave international crisis. National unity is a compelling need. . . . The Evansville Press frequently has disagreed with Mr. [Dean] Acheson, particularly on Far East policy. But the secretary of state has declared himself in complete accord with the measures

President Truman is taking in the Korean crisis, and that is the overriding issue now. . . . This is a time to close ranks, for win we must if the world's hope for peace is to be realized. This is a time to put politics and personalities aside."[56]

The *Fort Wayne Journal-Gazette* also came out in strong support of the nation's involvement in Korea. In an editorial titled "The Answer to Aggression," the paper explained its stand. "The United States Government has taken immediate, firm and courageous action to halt and roll back the wilful aggression of Communist North Korea against its sovereign neighbor, South Korea," said the *Journal-Gazette*. "American air and sea forces have been ordered into the fight. It was the only decision which could be made under all of the circumstances."[57]

Jasper's daily paper, the *Dubois County Daily Herald,* carried two editorials in the war's early days. In "Korean Problem Up to U.N.," the editor argued, "It is all but unanimously agreed by party leaders and the rank and file of citizens of the United States that the interference of this country with its armed forces in the South Korean invasion by the Reds is justified. The only argument seems to be the degree or extent of the resistance to be put up by America, with the viewpoint varying even in the ranks of the party in power as well as the opposition."[58] In late July another front-page editorial in the *Daily Herald* related the sudden seriousness of National Guard training for Dubois County men: "Realism will keynote 1950 summer training for the Indiana National Guard's 38th Infantry Division, Guard officials announced today. The Division, including Dubois County's Heavy Mortar Company, went to Camp Atterbury for two weeks yesterday. . . . In view of the Korean and World situation, this year's encampment takes on additional significance, since it may be the initial training period for active military training, in case the guard is sworn in for national service."[59]

The *Terre Haute Tribune* carried a number of articles and editorials during the early days of the war. One day after the war broke, an Associated Press story on the front page spoke of the fear that the Korean War would bring about World War III. "A shudder of apprehension ran through the western world today that the conflict which erupted in Korea Sunday between communist and anticommunist forces might be the spark that would set off a new world war," the newspaper declared.[60] Then, on its editorial page, the *Tribune* proclaimed that "probably the explosion in Korea portends no outbreak of a new world war. Peace-loving nations and peoples of the world will certainly hope so. From Moscow's standpoint it appears merely a corrective maneuver. But it does bring the Far Eastern situation into sharper focus."[61] Two days later the paper added, "Americans are still conditioned by Pearl Harbor. When they awoke Sunday to find that communist North Koreans had invaded South Korea many instantly thought that this was another Pearl Harbor and the big war with Russia was on. There was, of course, a chance that it might be so. But there were many more chances against it. It is well to keep cool under the blows of such incidents. There have been several before and doubtless there will be others."[62]

On 29 June 1950 the *Tribune* attempted to answer the question of why America was fighting in Korea. "The decision to take an active part in the defense of the Korean republic with air and naval forces seems to have been the only practical one to make in the situation, and it was at the moment about the only answer which could be offered to the question of 'Why?' which arose as soon as war broke out there," the *Tribune* said. "How did the United States permit this thing to happen? We faced at once the familiar accusation that we gave 'too little and too late' in previous aid to the republic. The matter is not quite so simple as that, but obviously there was not time to debate it. We had to abandon Korea to its own devices, or jump in and help."[63]

One day later the paper asserted, correctly as it turned out, that "there was no hope today for a quick and easy end to the Korean fighting. . . . The burden of land fighting—if any—probably would be ours, with token troops from other United Nations members making it an international operation. President Truman met late yesterday with his top military and civilian advisers. They separated close mouthed, admitting only that they had been informing each other and Mr. Truman of the Korean situation. A decision on use of American foot soldiers and tanks shortly will have to be made."[64]

In early July the Terre Haute paper's editor, apparently realizing the magnitude of the Korean situation, noted, "United States intervention in Korea has been running up against disconcerting obstacles, as witness the trapping of that American Infantry position by North Korean Red troops in the Osan area, and the large-scale retreat of South Korean troops. These setbacks cause considerable concern here at home, and naturally, too, they cause public anxiety as to just how well our rescue operations are getting along. . . . As the cards lie, America and the other nations responding to the U.N. appeal are likely in due course to be facing more than just North Korean fighting men." Interestingly, the editorial predicted, "We may expect to see Manchurian and Chinese communist troops pouring down through North Korea into the south if the operation is continued for long. That is something which time will disclose, but, if you have to bet, put your money on our side."[65]

The *Indiana Daily Student*'s responses to the outbreak of war are significant because of the fact that so many of the school's male students would quickly face a draft if the war escalated. The paper optimistically reported at the war's start that "I.U. authorities doubt Korean War means U.S. entry." In the same issue an editorial noted, "Philip C. Jessup, American Ambassador-at-large, told an Auditorium audience last Thursday night that the United States' role in world affairs was to keep the peace. It begins to appear that the U.S. is to have an opportunity to do just that—and much sooner than she apparently thought she would. . . . It appears that sooner or later Russia is going to have to be convinced that her tactics will not be tolerated. If the U.N. cannot convince her, it seems that the U.S. will be elected to do it, and now seems to be as good a time as any in the future."[66] A day later a much stronger editorial in favor of U.S. involvement appeared. "The line is drawn. It's a non-existent line called the 38th parallel. At this line, two forces meet. They do not represent only the conflicting forces of the North and South Korea. They represent the conflicting forces of democracy and communism. . . . The United States policy of intervention seems to narrow down to this idea: past this line you shall not pass. . . . Yes, the line is drawn. We are prepared to fight for what we think is right. The world looks to us for leadership. We cannot back down now."[67]

Perhaps because of the university's sensitivity to the possibility of its students being called to serve, the paper often seemed more critical of the country's war efforts than other Hoosier media. In one issue the paper glumly noted that the war was likely to last longer than anyone had at first believed. "How long is the war in Korea going to last? . . . The man in the street, after whole-heartedly agreeing with the President's policy of sending U.S. troops into Korea, apparently believed that North Korean resistance would dissipate upon the arrival of our troops. That has not proved to be the case. In fact, the Communist-trained North Koreans have continued to advance farther into the South Korean Republic's territory. Now the man in the street has begun to wonder how long the U.S., which is fighting under the United Nations' flag, is going to permit the present situation to exist." The article further assessed the grim expense of continuing the war: "Perhaps the United States intends to send more than the present token force into Korea. Let us hope that, if the North Koreans continue to advance, a force large enough and well enough equipped to restore the status quo is dispatched to the war front. War is terrible in any case, but a long small war can be fully as destructive as a slightly larger war of shorter duration."[68]

A week later the student paper complained, "The Korean war moves into its nineteenth day today. For eighteen days Americans have been getting killed—and as yet they have not been told why. For eighteen days there has been quite a bit of blood and quite a few tears expended—but not much sweat. The only persons who seem to be doing any sweating are the Yanks who are slogging through the Korean mud and getting killed." The piece blamed the quagmire in Korea on the American people themselves. "The American people have yet to get excited about the war in Korea," said the newspaper. "Many of them have the same attitude that prevailed at the beginning of our part in World War II. At that time it was thought that we could defeat the Japanese in about six months. But it was more than six times six months before we were able to lay down our guns. And maybe we laid them down too soon. Maybe we should have carried a bigger stick a little longer in Asia. Because the fact remains that we have a war on our hands. A real, live, shooting war."[69] Almost two weeks later the *Daily Student* predicted, "This country is going to mobilize. The change is evident. No longer are we trusting to the wills of men against war. Now we shall put our trust in a fighting force capable of facing any aggressor."[70]

As the war continued to go badly for UN forces in late July, *Daily Student* editorials continued to voice grave concerns. "What's happening in Korea? The American people want to know," noted a piece on 18 July.[71] On 22 July an editorial again blasted American apathy.

> The awakening has not yet come. The average American—shall we say Joe Smith—does not yet realize that we are at war. Listen to Joe, or talk to him, and you will quickly see that this is true.
>
> Again, no bombs have been dropped on our cities. No great destruction has been wrought in our own country, so Joe thinks we are not at war.
>
> Well, declaration or no declaration, we are at war. Men are being killed. They are not dropping off into a peaceful dream-sleep as the poets would have it. They are dying in agony and pain. They are Americans.
>
> Our leaders are moving slowly. They are being careful, for they say they do not want war. They can not be blamed for this. But what else is it when men take guns and shoot at each other, and kill.
>
> Joe says no. He says it cannot be for he was in the service and it was terrible. He does not want to go back in. As the boys said in the last war, "I'll hide in the hills first."

But Joe is wrong. It does not have to be patriotism. It can be a plain, unadorned struggle for survival. They are killing the boys in Korea and soon, if they are not stopped, they will kill Joe. If necessary they will come over here and kill Joe, for this war may not be fought in one spot or be limited in scope.

It is time for Joe to realize how serious this matter is. It is time for Joe to realize that this is a war, complete with the trimmings of war; death, poverty, misery and destruction.

It is time for this country to do everything that it can in its power to bring the quickest end possible to what has been little short of a massacre so far. Joe may want to be left alone, but he may once again have to fight for peace.[72]

Of particular interest in the early days of the conflict were the responses by the *Indianapolis Recorder,* an African-American weekly. On 22 July the *Recorder* carried a story from London on its front page titled, "Korean War Styled Clash between Dark, White Races."[73] While not the primary opinion of whites or blacks in Indiana, the article hinted at the irony of black men fighting to protect a culture that had discriminated against them. *Recorder* editor Andrew W. Ramsey wrestled with the profound problem in an 8 July piece:

> Our nation is now in the grip of the hysteria that may be the prelude to World War III at the same time as it enters the period of mud-slinging do-nothing political campaigns.
>
> Forgotten are the promises of the Four Freedoms used as bait during the late conflict against the Hitler fascists and neglected is the program to bring the better life to more Americans and to the backward peoples of the earth.
>
> More and more Americans are subscribing to the belief that communism and socialism can be defeated by repressive measures and military might. They either doubt the ability of democracy to make itself the dominant political

force in the world by example or they are afraid of the democracy that they advocate.

Having lost ground in the Orient through the racism that has characterized all of his actions on the continent, the Western white man thinks that by defeating in a hot war the forces of Communism, he can win the peoples of Asia into his camp. He fails to realize that those people did not choose between democracy and communism because of the coercion of the Soviet Union or of the intrinsic superiority of the latter over the former.

The growth of communism was easy in Asia, because the Asiatic peoples never saw democracy in practice. . . . Your columnist does not hold as Paul Robeson reportedly does, that the Negro would refuse to fight against the Soviet Union. The American Negro is as American as any other segment of the population and will fight for HIS AMERICA whenever it is in danger, but his enthusiasm in any future war will be substantially less if he feels that he is being asked to fight for the retention of second-class citizenship.[74]

Nevertheless, the *Recorder*, as did other Hoosier newspapers, quickly got behind early war endeavors. In an article titled "Tan Yanks Hit Korean Reds," the paper related the story of African Americans' first efforts in combat, proudly noting that black GIs won the "first big U.S. 'tilt' in Korea."[75] The article celebrated the victory of the all-black Twenty-fourth regimental combat team. Eager to disprove the common notion that blacks could not fight, this group pushed forward through heavy enemy fire and stood off a ferocious charge by North Korean troops. This action led national news media to declare that black U.S. troops had accomplished the first sizable American ground victory in the Korean War. Unfortunately, this feat was soon overshadowed by several inaccurately reported incidents later in the war. As the war progressed, the *Recorder* constantly echoed the theme that African-American participation in the Korean War should be a stimulus to American political leaders to strive for greater civil rights at home. As Ramsey argued, "In dealing with the colored people of Asia, nothing helps us more than evidence we're ending discrimination in America."[76]

The Hoosier State soon became an important place for the national media to try and gauge the country's feelings and thoughts on the war, especially during the exceptionally long dark days of July and August 1950. *Time,* for example, carried an article titled, "The War in Cicero, Indiana." In this piece Hoosier opinions regarding the use of atomic weapons to save the American troops surrounded at Pusan was the primary focus. One Indiana minister stated, "I'm not in favor of the atom bomb. But I think that . . . our military should drop an atom bomb on Russia and get it over with." High school teacher Bernard Scott declared, "What's the use of having these atom bombs if they're not to be used? It's just like having a new car in the garage and letting it be idle. What we ought to do is to notify the Russians that if they don't get back north of the 38th parallel by a certain date, we'll drop the bomb on them."[77]

In a front-page editorial, the *Lafayette Journal and Courier* clamored for using atomic weapons. "United States leadership in the field of atomic energy is the greatest present deterrent, perhaps the only one, against the outbreak of another world war. Use of several A-bombs now should prove effective and lasting discouragement to new Red aggressions everywhere and stop the present one NOW. WHY WAIT LONGER?"[78] Many Hoosiers, however, disagreed about employing nuclear weapons. Edward F. Maddox of Indianapolis penned a letter to the *Indianapolis Star* calling for less talk about quick fixes to end the war and more realistic action. "Appropriation for hydrogen bombs will not help in Korea! Boastful headlines will not help our boys on the battle front! They need guns and planes and tanks and ammunition and reinforcements," wrote Maddox.[79]

Whatever the opinions of Hoosier newspaper editors and Indiana citizens regarding the deplorable performance of American troops of the early part of the war, one thing stood out as powerfully true; Hoosiers such as Hobert Young, Stanley Nelson, Carl Spencer, Ray Cox, and Thomas Chappell had helped save the Pusan perimeter while American military leaders worked to develop a strategy that might turn the war around. Their suffering was great. Fighting day after endless day as "battles violently surged back and forth . . . and hills changed hands with maddening monotony," these men found themselves being pushed to the limits of human endurance. Clay Blair, in his study of the war, noted, "The early September heat was dreadful. No one dared sleep. Very few men got a decent meal; even drinking water was scarce." Worse still, "the American casualties were ghastly: by September 15, total Eighth Army casualties had climbed to 18,165: 4,599 killed or mortally wounded; 12,377 wounded; the rest missing. Truly it was a 'savage sacrifice' of 'beef cattle in the slaughterhouse.' Worse, there were few or no replacements." And yet as Blair related, our troops "hung on magnificently. . . . The defense of the Pusan Perimeter was truly a great victory."[80]

The Inchon landing was conceived to end the war. Incredibly, this strategy was so successful that by October many, including the commander of UN forces Gen. Douglas MacArthur, were saying the war would be over by Christmas. Tragically, for many Hoosiers and other American fighting men, the worse was yet to come.

"By the latest news I have heard, this Korean situation is almost over."

Hoosier marine in a letter to his mother, 21 October 1950

"The way everything is going, it will all be over before long."

Hoosier GI in a letter to his father shortly after the Inchon landing

CHAPTER THREE

ILLUSIONS OF VICTORY

July through December 1950 witnessed America's fortunes in Korea shifting from dismal losses to sure victory to bitter retreat. Many Hoosiers fought during this wild, roller-coaster portion of the war. A large number of Indiana marines, for example, participated in one of the Marine Corps's finest hours at the Chosin Reservoir. But all of them, whether marines, army, navy, or air force, would drink the stinging cup of defeat when the Chinese unexpectedly hurled more than 350,000 troops into the war in late 1950.

The actions of two Hoosiers at this time stand as ultimate examples of courage and valor in combat. Both men, Sgt. Charles Garrigus, Jr., and Lt. Col. Donald C. Faith, Jr., died in the winter of 1950 in one of the United States most brutal catastrophes. The swift and overwhelming nature of the debacle left no time for detailed official records to be taken down, and this, coupled with the death of so many officers and noncommissioned officers in the action, caused much of the story of this event to be lost forever. Roy E. Appleman, whose work, *East of Chosin: Entrapment and Breakout in Korea, 1950,* gives an excellent overall picture of the battle, discovered that "no operational journals, [or] unit histories of those who fought East of the Chosin" existed. Luckily, Appleman did discover the notes of a few survivors taken immediately after the action. These notes included several short narratives written a day or two after the few survivors had escaped the Chinese trap. The most important of these narratives was a four-page typed report by Maj. Robert E. Jones, which tells much about the heroic efforts of Faith and Garrigus. The deeds of Garrigus are also detailed in a manuscript written by Maj. Cosby Miller.[1] To better appreciate the story of Garrigus's and Faith's sacrifices, as well as those of other Hoosiers who served in this difficult phase of the war, one must examine the larger context of the Korean struggle at this juncture.

Despite the bleakness of the Pusan perimeter situation in July and August 1950, the war had, in fact, begun to swing back in favor of the UN forces by late August and early September. The perimeter was, if barely, holding. Conversely, the North Koreans' only realistic hope for victory involved the ability of their forces to deliver a solid knockout punch that would drive UN forces off the peninsula. This had seemed possible in the early stages of the war. By late August, however, American supply lines had shortened, while the North Korean army's stretched many hundreds of miles. Further, American forces, pushed back to the coast, had nowhere to go and a much smaller, more focused, area to defend. By late August both armies were locked together like two desperate fighters, each trying to deal a final blow.

While the perimeter was holding, Gen. Douglas MacArthur hatched a plan to strike behind North Korean lines. The American forces would launch a surprise amphibious landing at Inchon Harbor, on the west side of the country near the South Korean capital of Seoul, and bring a sudden and dramatic end to the war. MacArthur's bold resolve, however, called for the use of a full marine division, requiring the call-up of the Marine Corps Reserve to bring the division to full strength. A smaller contingent of marines had already landed in Korea in August to help hold the Pusan perimeter. For the first time since the war began, Americans had a sudden brush of hope when these marine units arrived. With the call-up of the reserves, more marines would soon be entering Korea. Most Hoosiers and Americans, however, did not understand how unprepared many of these reservists were. The *Indiana Daily Student,* for example, noted about the use of marines in Korea, "The First Marine Division owns one of the most enviable of all World War II records, having been the first ashore at Guadalcanal and Tulagi. If ever they were needed, it's now. With American forces determined to keep what's left of their foothold in South Korea, the Marines may well add another chapter to an already glorious history."² For Hoosier reservists and the communities from which they came, the unexpected activation of the reserves was shocking; no one had anticipated this abrupt change in events.

In July a Fort Wayne newspaper carried a front-page story about the surprise call-up of that community's reserve company, noting, "Some 225 members of Fort Wayne's Company B, 18th Infantry Battalion, U.S. Marine Corps Reserve, yesterday were ordered to report for active duty as a unit at Camp Pendleton, Oceanside, Calif., by August 19. The Marine Reserve company will be the first reserve unit ordered to active duty from the Fort Wayne area. Capt. R. H. Hensel, commanding officer of the unit, said technically it was the first time in the history of the country that a Marine Reserve unit had been ordered to duty in peacetime. . . . Company B, organized here in April, 1948, is comprised mostly of young high school graduates and a nucleus of veterans. The company was alerted July 20 that a two-week Summer camp training period scheduled to begin last Saturday was cancelled."³ Because the call-up came in time of national emergency, reservists who had been promised they could quit at their own choosing were now unable to do so. A later article in the same paper related just how shocking the call-up was to the Fort Wayne community. "For most of the boys in Company B, local Marine Reserve unit, the fighting in Korea seemed far off—until now. Now they're getting ready to kiss the girls goodbye, store their civilian garb, cut the ties of civilian employment and leave their homes for whatever lies ahead. . . . They range in age from 17 to 36. About 20 per cent of the company's personnel are veterans," the newspaper reported.⁴

Many of the Fort Wayne men had mixed feelings about the call-up, as a newspaper's interviews revealed. "'There isn't anything you can do about it,' says Pvt. Paul R. O'Connor, 226 Killea Street. Paul is 17. He joined the company four months ago. Pfc. Warren C. Reynolds, 20, of Decatur said, 'I'm not too happy about it but I'm going.' Cpl. James B. Roop, 22, also of Decatur, has been with the company two and a half years, participated in two Summer camp training periods. 'We have to go and get it over with,' he said. Pfc. Bill Davis of 1216 Kitch Street is 22. He shrugged his shoulders when asked how he felt about leaving. Bill has two brothers who served in the Army during the last war. Pfc. Laurel Flaugher of 1216 Orchard Street stood in the same line, his black hair protruding around a green fatigue cap. He's 18, laughs easily, 'I picked the Marines because my girl friend likes 'em,' he commented. 'She's not too happy now, though.' Pfc. Clifford Falls, 21, of 401 Cherry Street said, 'We might as well go now as ever.' Hairy-chested Sgt. Lawrence Strait, 654 Fifth Street, is 29. He has four children. A veteran with four years service in the Marines during World War II, Sgt. Strait in civilian life was an automobile body and fender repairman. 'The boys need a lota training,' he said."[5]

When the train carrying the Fort Wayne group pulled out of the city, the local newspaper carried a somber and sympathetic story of the company's departure: "The Korean war came to Fort Wayne last night. And a lot of people tried to keep from crying and not many did. No one was ashamed of tears. At 8:12 p.m. 2,500 persons were jammed around the Nickel Plate Railroad Station to see some 225 United States Marines, Company B, 18th Infantry Battalion, leave for Camp Pendleton, Calif. It was the first mass troop departure from Fort Wayne since World War II. Most of the Marines were boys. About 25 per cent of them went through the Pacific campaigns in the last war, but most of them haven't been out of school more than a couple of years. They have no combat experience. And that's what they'll get in California. For the next month or so they'll undergo intensive combat training."[6] The article added that the reservists were given a parade led by a band from the local American Legion post.

Evansville marine reservists, also consisting of mostly undertrained teenagers, were just as stunned by the activation. An Evansville reporter interviewed the company and their families at reserve headquarters in July as they struggled to deal with the situation. In an article titled "Evansville's Marines Hone Up as They Await Marching Orders," the reporter noted, "the call to arms caught the local reservists on their weekly drill night in the old Marine Hospital, 2700 W. Illinois st. They went through their regular training routine—it takes a lot to upset a Marine—but the air was charged with a feeling of : 'This is it.'"[7]

The primary instructor for the group, Capt. George C. Schmidt, told the reporter, "We're not getting hysterical. There [These] men knew this could happen when they signed up. No one's running around yelling 'Let me at the Commies.' But they have a job to do and they're ready to do it." The notions the captain conveyed, however, may not have been felt by the wives. "In the club room, the reservists' wives played bingo just like on any other drill night. They concentrated on the game, a little too hard maybe. They laughed at each other's jokes, a little too long maybe. And it might strike you as unusual to see a mother give her young son a quick hug for no reason at all in the middle of a bingo game," the reporter noted.[8]

The *Indianapolis Star* carried several front-page stories about the Indianapolis marine reserve unit with one piece noting, "An Indianapolis Marine Reserve unit of 26 officers and 500 enlisted men last night became the first Indiana outfit scheduled for mobilization under the Korean War crisis. . . . Its members last night prepared to wind up personal and business affairs and started packing. Some gathered at battalion headquarters in the Marine Reserve Armory, 2830 East Riverside Drive, to check whether official orders finally had arrived."[9]

In late August, Hoosier marine reserve companies from Indianapolis, Fort Wayne, and Evansville boarded trains for Camp Pendleton, California. All but the Evansville group would receive at least a month of combat training before going overseas. About half of the Evansville unit was flown over to help support the

Hoosier marine reservist Denning Campbell waves good-bye to his mother. In foreground is Fort Branch, Indiana's Wayne Poole.

Inchon landing after only two weeks of training. All three Indiana companies bid sad farewells to their relatives and friends. In the state's capital, the reservists received an especially supportive sendoff. "A police escort, the Indianapolis Newsboys Band and the cheers of hometowners will form the sendoff for Indianapolis' own 16th Marine Battalion as it marches off to war tomorrow night," reported the *Star*. "Mayor Al Feeney urged all citizens to assemble along the line of march to cheer the Marines as they ride in 12 buses from the Naval Armory east on 30th Street to Capitol Avenue, south on Capitol to South Street, east on South Street to Illinois Street and north on Illinois Street to Union Station. 'We've been more than a little lax in seeing men off and we're going to make it up as far as possible. I hope all who can will be there for the sendoff,' the mayor said."[10]

Andy Jacobs, Jr., recalled the send-off for two reasons. One had to do with the teenager's misunderstanding of military language. "[My] orders were to report to the Marine Reserve unit . . . on 10 August at 0800 hours, but [I] didn't yet understand military time. [I] reported at 4:00 PM, thinking [I] was four hours early, but, in reality, [I] was eight hours late and the MP's had been looking for [me]." Jacobs's superior officers accepted his explanation as "an honest, but stupid, mistake."[11] The other memorable event was the parading of the reserve company through the streets of Indianapolis and a brief speech by Gov. Henry F. Schricker. (Jacobs could not have known that fifteen years later he would, at this same place, make the same type of speech to another generation of Hoosier reservists on the occasion of that group's departure for Vietnam.)

A *Star* reporter caught the sadness of the Indianapolis departure: "The Armory thronged with relatives and friends, most of them standing silent and dry-eyed as they watched the grim preparations for the war. Occasionally a young wife or sweetheart wiped her eyes. Tears welled frequently in the eyes of a mother. Fathers shook hands with their warrior sons in husky silence. Then the men climbed aboard busses and set out for the Union Station. Emotions flowed over in the crowded depot where thousands jammed for a last salute to the Indianapolis leathernecks, responding vigorously to the beckoning of destiny. . . . They rounded up the steps to the train shed and swarmed aboard their Pullman cars. It was a scene of orderly confusion, each man knowing where he was going and getting there on the double." Scenes of great sadness now unfolded. "Frequently a man would pause for a last kiss with a woman whose tears ran hot and unheeded," the *Star* reported. "One youth gave a smiling wave to a middle aged couple who fell sobbing in each other's arms when he had passed. . . . There were young boys still in high school and mature men with families. Some worked in factories, others in offices and on farms. There was Andrew Jacobs Jr., son of the congressman, a youth of 19 recently graduated form Shortridge High School."[12]

The *Star* also carried a heartfelt editorial about the event. "Tonight Indianapolis' own 16th Infantry Battalion, United States Marine Corps Reserves, will board troop trains at Union Station and head for Camp Pendleton, Cal., to begin active duty training," said the newspaper. "The pride, gratitude and best wishes of all Indianapolis will go with the members of the 16th Marine Battalion as they depart tonight for active duty. To paraphrase Riley's great Civil War poem, 'Good-by, men, take keer of yourselves.'"[13]

The Evansville departure was just as heartrending. A reporter noted, "A war half-way across the world came to Evansville yesterday. . . . But, for hundreds of people who stood on a rain-swept platform at the Union station here yesterday afternoon, Korea was all too close. A company of Evansville marine reserves was boarding a train. The company was headed for a period of training at Camp Pendleton, Calif. From there, anybody could tell where the company was going. Mothers and wives, some of whom a few months ago may never have heard of Korea, thronged the station platform. Now they all knew all they wanted to about Korea." Just before the train pulled away from the station, the reporter noted, "you noticed how quiet it was, how in all that shuffling crowd you could still hear the steady drip-drip of the rains as it ran down the sides of the Pullman cars and onto the track bed. And it came as a surprise when you saw how many of the women were holding handkerchiefs to their eyes."[14]

An editorial in the *Evansville Courier* lamented the men's departure by noting the difference between the Korean War and World War II: "And this going away—perhaps to a little war, perhaps to a big war—is the toughest going away of any soldiers who ever wore the American uniform. It is different from past leavetakings. It is different in more than the absence of the drum beating and farewell parades which marked some periods of our past. It is different from the going away of soldiers in World War I and World War II. It is different in its uncertainty. In those two great wars we at least knew what we were up against, what the job was."[15] The newspaper also reported, "Not a man will be in action for at least six months."[16] For several of the Evansville reservists, this statement proved to be dead wrong.

Once they arrived at Camp Pendleton, Hoosier marine reservists were divided into three groups. Those who were supposed to have had enough training received two weeks of intense conditioning and quickly were sent to Korea to support the Inchon landing. Several in this group came from the Evansville company. Despite the intensity of the conditioning, most of these men remained concerned about the short duration of training they had received. For example, William J. Ellis, an Evansville marine, complained to his wife that the two weeks of training "isn't enough. It just gives us blisters and makes our muscles sore."[17] Worry about the lack of training also came from those in charge of preparing the reservists to fight. As he began to train his charges at Pendleton, one lieutenant noted, "I was . . . discouraged. They seemed like kids, uncomfortable in their steel helmets, ill-fitting dungarees, some with leggings on backwards, and all milling about to find their places in the ranks. I was expected to have them combat-ready and on their way to a shooting war within only a few weeks."[18]

Those reservists with less prior training received four weeks of instruction and conditioning before being shipped to Korea. In a letter from Gordon Greene to his mother, the Hoosier teenager described his preparation: "We don't have time to waste. We really work hard having hikes and marches over these mountains every day." In a letter written in his second week of training, the young man complained, "I'll sure be glad to get this four weeks over with. Then maybe it won't be quite as tough." Greene described the base as "surrounded by mountains" where the reservists "are doing just about everything there is to do for combat training." The letter ended on a pessimistic note: "I don't know what to think about the world situation, but it looks like a long, drawn out affair."[19]

In a more colorful description of training at the camp, Greene also wrote a childhood friend, telling him, "We'll fall in by our sacks and fall out again, then fall in. We take off our clothes and put them on,—fall out again until the gunnery sergeant is satisfied." The rugged conditioning especially shocked the nineteen year old: "We get up at 4:30 in the morning to take a long tactical march over the mountains, our captain's favorite for early morning exercise. Today we fired on the range. I got up at 4:30, and it was still dark when we got to the range." Greene's comments were also a clear indication of how little training reservists typically possessed. "I had never fired an M-1 before and my darn cheek is swollen bad from the recoil," he wrote.[20]

Donald Burton recalled, "I was still in high school when I joined the marine reserves in Evansville, Indiana, in 1948. I remember going to a summer training camp at Little Creek, Virginia, in 1949. Of course, none of us saw the war coming. It seemed like once the war started we were activated right away and on our way on a train from Evansville to California. When we boarded the train, my whole family was there—everyone was crying—most of us were just teenagers. There were a lot of fights on the train ride, mostly with the World War II vets who were trying to show us teenagers what marines were supposed to be like. Out at Camp Pendleton [my] group got four-weeks combat training before they sent us out. One time I was crawling along on my face and a rattlesnake came by me. When I told the lieutenant he jumped up and started running the other way. While at Pendleton, I had the chance to become a baker since that's what I'd done back at Evansville. I didn't take it though, thinking, at the time, the war would be over when I got to Korea. I was young also and wanted to see the world."[21]

Andy Jacobs, Jr., was placed in the third category of reservists; those who lacked almost any training at all. This group received the eight-week boot camp experience before being sent overseas. Jacobs recalled, "The boot camp ordeal did much for [my] physical condition and very little for [my] ego. Advanced combat training was somewhat less unpleasant, but still a long way from a lark. Showers at Camp Pendleton were ordeals; the hot water was cold and the cold water was frosty. The facility was either shunned by those who preferred a gamy smell to chattering teeth, or dashed into and out of in seconds, but [I] had an idea that worked; [I] gritted [my] teeth, stood for seventy-five seconds in the ice-cold water, then switched to 'hot' which, by contrast, seemed warm, all of this to the amazement of [my] buddies."[22]

Robert "Bud" Fitch told of his training experiences in letters to his family in Oakland City. About halfway through his training, Fitch wrote, "I must be getting in shape because we had a 16 mile hike and it didn't even bother me. . . . Today we went out to combat town, which is a mock-up of a town with building, stores, houses, streets, etc. They had all kind of signs in Korean. We fought th[r]ough the town on past the 38th parallel and onto the Manchurian border (simulated of course)."[23] (Fitch died in combat just north of the thirty-eighth parallel a few months after writing this letter.)

Called up later than some Hoosier marine reservists, Ralph Steele of Elkhart wrote home just after arriving for boot camp at Parris Island, South Carolina. "I haven't had much time to get homesick yet, but of course I'd much rather be home. I didn't think I liked Elkhart and home so much," he said. "They say we get leave for ten days after eight or nine weeks of training. I believe we're going to fly home. . . . All the guys are about my age so we all have a lot in common to tell when we can talk. One kid even bought a Bel Air too, before he left." Steele was particularly proud of the boot-camp graduation ceremonies he watched and looked forward to his own graduation. "We've got our packs and drill rifles now. We've learned the primary marching steps and commands, so now we have the rifle to lug around. It's really pretty to see a well trained outfit marching," said Steele. "When they have graduation down here they have a military ceremony, bands and such. They play the same Sousa marches we are to have. The marine band, you know, is the national band. They sure have a lot of savvy. You get a lump in your throat to watch marines marching with flags and in perfect formation, with the band playing."

In a later note Steele told of the train ride from boot camp at Parris Island to Camp Pendleton, where his group of reservists received combat training before sailing to Korea. "We arrived here safe and sound yesterday

A group of nervous Hoosier reservists arriving at Camp Pendleton, California, August 1950.

afternoon, taking only four days to get out to the base. The trip was fairly uneventful as far as a troop train would be, but of course it was a lot of fun and a bit different from regular rail travel. There always was something happening to make it interesting. We left one guy in Augusta, Georgia, when he went in after sandwiches for the troops in our car. He hasn't got here yet but he'll be in anytime. When we were going through a small town in Texas, we hit a civilian jeep, but the driver jumped before we hit the car and pushed it under a box car on the siding. We had Pullmans and ate on the diner like on a joy ride. Our group consisted of 250 men, so it took a couple hours to feed everybody. We stood two hour guard every twelve hours, two guards to a car. That gave a chance to get out in the air when we stopped." At Camp Pendleton, Steele soon discovered, the preparation for Korea was set a notch higher than boot camp:

> We're on training schedule now, and they're really putting it to us fast and thick. We had a couple five and ten mile hikes to start things off. Up and down these hills is some tough going. We're a pretty good company as there has only been a couple that couldn't make it. One thing that makes me stay on the march is that our officers go right with us, pack and all. I figure if those 30 or 35 year old broken down vets can go, there's no excuse for me. The toughest part of it is that you're on "water discipline." No drinks until you get back to the company area. We carry full canteens though, so you can hear the water splash around but can't drink it. We went from 8:00 in the morning until 11:30 on the march without anything to drink. Guess it's the best for us as there probably will be times when we won't be able to get purified water. Two of our officers are just back from Korea, and they say this terrain here is as close to Korea as you can get. There are some places identical he said. In fact it's rumored the army is going to send a few outfits here to get used to the mountains. There's room enough for everybody out here as this is the world's biggest military reservation, save Korea.

Now that our training is started we get lectures and training problems. We've got unique "classrooms," out under any shady tree. They lecture us on Korean history, people, kinds of roads as well as weapons, mapping and tactics. The fun will begin when we start running these problems in field exercises. The night before last, it sounded like a company got ambushed on the other side of the hill as all of a sudden four or five machine guns began to clatter, and you could hear the rifles crack back at them. When you're on an all night problem, you never know when the "aggressors" will strike. The artillery was firing too, so there was quite a bit of racket going on.

I don't think there is such a thing as a "shell shocked" marine. All day long you constantly hear rifle, machine gun and artillery fire, so you just get accustomed to it. Like the train whistles in the yards, you don't even notice them. The only time we do here is when they get so noisy the instructor has to stop his lecture. We're living in tents now so it's really roughing it. The only bad part is that it has rained only once since I've been here, so there is a cloud of dust with the slightest movement of air. Things get dusty in no time it seems like.[24]

While concerned about their lack of training, many Hoosier reservists who did not undergo the more advanced instructions still felt strongly in favor of serving in Korea at this point. "While we are there," wrote one young Indiana reservist, "we should show these communists where they belong."[25] Many, however, believed the war would be over before they arrived. *Time* said of the week the Evansville reservists left for California that the period "was the best week for the UN forces since the war began and perhaps the turning point."[26] *U.S. News and World Report* struck an even more positive tone, suggesting that "the Korean campaign may be cleaned up by February."[27] Greene wrote home hopefully in October saying, "By the latest news I have heard, this Korean situation is almost over." He told his mother that he believed he and other reservists would now serve on "occupation duty."[28] Meanwhile, as many Hoosier marine reservists trained for Korea, MacArthur's planned landing behind North Korean lines at Inchon took place on 15 September 1950.

William Chappell of Huntingburg found himself a part of Task Force Ninety-Five on board the USS *Toledo* at the Inchon landing. His ship's firepower softened the enemy positions. Indeed, the navy performed a multitude of valuable services in the war. All four of the navy's mammoth battlewagons, along with twelve carriers and hundreds of other ships, worked in the waters along Korea. Besides assistance in landings at Inchon and later at Wonsan, the ships hit "enemy troop concentrations, supply caches, supply lines" and helped clear dangerous minefields.[29] By 1952 ships such as the *Toledo* had thrown as much ammunition against the hills of Korea as American ships had against Japan in World War II.[30] Chappell recalled the days leading up to the Inchon landing: "We had just gotten back to the West Coast from a Pacific tour when the war started. By that time I had been in the navy six years and the *Toledo* was like home." As Chappell was cruising to Korea, he received a letter from his older brother, Tom, telling him he was already in Korea fighting with the First Cavalry.

Handsome sailor William Chappell of Huntingburg was assigned to the USS *Toledo*.

The younger Chappell's first action involved the shelling of Wonsan. Then in September, the *Toledo* and several other ships were sent to support the Inchon invasion. "Right before Inchon, the entire fleet was sent to another area to carry out a false landing and throw off the enemy. We shelled the hell out of that place, then hurried over to Inchon," said Chappell. "When we shelled there, we really blasted those positions. There was an island out in the harbor and our destroyer blew away every scrap of vegetation. I wondered at the time how any human being could survive a bombardment like that." When the *Toledo* fired its eight-inch guns, Chappell and the others on board stayed down below in general quarters: "When those eight-inch guns fired, the vibrations shook the whole ship."[31]

Chappell witnessed the dramatic attack on Wolmi Island, an event described by John Toland in his book *In Mortal Combat: Korea, 1950–1953*: "At 5:45, shells from six- and eight-inch guns began landing in Inchon from four British and American cruisers. Then six U.S. destroyers moved in on Wolmi and began pulverizing the little island with their five-inch guns. As Wolmi lay silent in a pall of smoke, Marine Corsairs flashed through the overcast sky to unleash rockets and bombs."[32] Chappell also remembered, "We were drawing some fire from the shore, from a tank there, going back and forth. We returned fire, but we were never able to hit the damn thing." The action at Inchon was not without its humorous moments. Sometime during the bombardment, a friend of Chappell's "got a fishing pole and was fishing off the fantail when a shell exploded nearby. He sure got the hell out of there when that happened."[33]

Chappell's naval group, Task Force Ninety-Five, received a prestigious presidential unit citation from Syngman Rhee, the South Korean leader. Specifically, the citation noted: "Task Force Ninety-Five has distinguished itself in support of United Nations Forces in Korea by continued devastating attacks against the enemy from 12 September 1950 through August 1951. It has conducted naval operations in support of the Republic of Korea by destroying enemy military forces, railroads, bridges and other military installations in coastal areas and by furnishing naval close air, gunfire and other support for friendly ground and amphibious forces."[34]

Samuel Muncy of Anderson proudly displays his Purple Heart awarded for wounds received in the desperate struggle east of the Chosin Reservoir.

The effectiveness of the navy's shelling and the element of the surprise made the Inchon invasion one of the U.S. military's most stunning successes. Marines and elements of the army's Seventh Division suffered few casualties and moved quickly inland toward Seoul. Hoosier Samuel Muncy came ashore at Inchon with the Seventh Division. As his unit moved toward the South Korean capital, Muncy discovered its special treatment and training in Japan placed the unit on the point. "Because of our training in reconnaissance, we were sent out on the toughest missions, night patrols and so forth. In one situation we were struggling up a hill and taking fire. Men were going down, and we couldn't tell where the fire was coming from. Then one of our guys stepped on an enemy spider hole, a foxhole that was covered with a camouflage lid. We knew then what they were doing," he said.[35] Muncy soon noticed that the North Korean troops were mostly cutting and running away. This experience gave the Seventh Division a false sense of superiority that came back to haunt the division when it ran into the Chinese at Chosin Reservoir. Donald Hamilton of Greene County reported optimistically in a letter home two days after the landing, "I think that it won't be too long before I will be home because the way everything is going it will all be over before long."[36]

A key to taking Seoul was the capture of Kimpo Airfield. Shortly after Kimpo fell to American forces, about three hundred marine reservists, a third from Indiana, landed at the field. Among them was Hoosier Charles "Barney" Barnard. Barnard captured the flavor of the fighting at this particular place and time in a letter he wrote home to his father in Oakland City: "Here we are right in the middle of the whole works. The plane landed around 5 last night. We slept out on a hill last night, right by 1st Div. G.H.Q. [general headquarters]. Over in the distance we could see Seoul burning, and the shells busting in the town. Everyone is loaded for bear around here. I am carrying an M-1 rifle and 10 clips of ammo. Some of the boys have automatic pistols and carbines with 100 rounds of ammunition—that is too much weight for me. We stayed in a graveyard last night. They are just mounds of earth, no markers or anything. It was very cool and I don't think it helped my cold very much."

As the days passed, Barnard wrote of further hardships: "There hasn't been any mail yet, but we should really get a pile of it when they get all of it up to us. We have been on the go so much that I haven't missed the mail so much as I would if we had been stationed in one place all the time. This evening I had the first good meal that has been passed out for a week. Hot dogs, potatoes, peas and pineapple. Also hot chocolate. I have on the same clothes that I had in Japan. My socks really are something to see, blackened. The dust here is very bad so there isn't much use of changing or shaving or anything else for that matter." In a letter written to his mother a week later, Barnard gave more insight into the savagery of the fighting: "You have read about the things the North Koreans did to our army people, well they buried three Marines alive. So our division didn't take any prisoners for three weeks. . . . It isn't very nice, but nobody is going to [do] that to our men the way they did." Barnard went on to observe, "The South Koreans were even worse to the ones they captured, but that's all in war I guess."[37] Another Evansville reservist, Jess Thurman, was told by a veteran World War II officer, "'not to remember anything we saw, just block it out of our minds and forget it.' This, we were told, was the best way of dealing with the scenes we would encounter."[38]

It was during this offensive that the Evansville reserve company lost its first man. John Elliott was killed near Kimpo Airfield a month after leaving the train station at Evansville for Korea. Hoosier Donald Hamilton, an army medic, reported in a letter home written on 30 September 1950 how savage the Inchon/Seoul campaign had been for the Seventh Division.

> Well, I am rested up now because we had stayed here in Seoul for the last three or four days, but I think we are moving back across the river this afternoon or tomorrow morning. We have really been hard hit since we landed in Inchon. You said in one of your letters that you thought I wouldn't hit the front, well you were wrong about that because I have been there everyday that we have been in battle. I am with a weapons platoon and stay back about 200 to 300 yds. from the main line. I have only had 4 men hit in my platoon, but I have patched up several from different outfits. There is really some bloody messes around here, you should see some of them.
>
> You were talking about the circles around my eyes in the pictures, well I believe you would have had the same if you had just walked 16 miles like I had that day. I will never say anything about training again because I wish I had more of it now. I have only had about 3 close calls so far since I have been here. I went out to get a kid and they opened up with a Tommy gun. The second time [I was] going up a hill and a machine gun slug kicked dirt up all around me. The third was a sniper here in Seoul. I think however these dangers are about over. I hope so anyway. . . . I am about half afraid to make plans for the future because everyone who had it planned what he was going to do when he got out either got killed or bad hit. I had a good friend who never talked about anything but his future and now he is rolled up in a blanket in the army grave yard on a hill just outside of Inchon. He never had a good time like other boys because he saved his money, and what good did it do him? He was cut almost in half by a 30 cal. machine gun.[39]

Despite the American casualties, MacArthur's plan worked to perfection. After Seoul fell to UN forces, the marines and the Seventh Division proceeded east and south to trap the North Korean Army that surrounded Pusan. Most of the North Korean troops, however, realizing their predicament, panicked and fled north across the thirty-eighth parallel. On 27 September troops who had landed at Inchon linked up with elements of the Eighth Army pushing up from Pusan. The war seemed all but won. In early October UN leaders wrestled with the problem of whether or not to pursue North Korean troops north of the parallel and, in effect, reunite the countries. China, at North Korea's northern border, had warned it would not tolerate such an action, but MacArthur believed the Chinese would not come into the war for fear of the powerful U.S. Air Force.

In late October American troops started northward. Because of a high ridge of mountains that split the length of North Korea, MacArthur divided UN forces into two groups. The Eighth Army was charged with rushing up the west side of North Korea and taking the capital of Pyongyang on its trek to the Yalu River on the

Chappell and the USS *Toledo* participated in the invasions at Inchon and Wonsan in 1950.

border of Manchuria. In the east, the Tenth Corps, consisting of the First Marine Division and elements of the Eighth's Seventh Division, moved into northeast Korea, landing at the ports of Wonsan and Iwo and marched toward the Chosin Reservoir. As the Eighth moved up the west coast, Bill Chappell, on board the *Toledo*, took great pride in his ship's work of shelling the fleeing North Koreans. "I knew my brother Tom was somewhere in that action, and I thought our firing would be helping him out. Then I got a letter from him. Apparently several of the rounds from naval vessels were falling short. He wrote me saying, 'quit shooting over here, you're killing us.'"[40]

Stanley Nelson of Winslow, now serving with the First Cavalry Division, attached to the Eighth, recalled the jubilation of the troops as they drove across the thirty-eighth parallel and headed toward the North Korean capital of Pyongyang, "What a wonderful feeling. We were elated. Soldiers were grinning, slapping each other on the back, just like when World War II ended," said Nelson.[41] During the golden days of apparent victory, Hoosier newspapers carried glowing reports of UN successes. Jasper's *Dubois County Daily Herald,* for example, reported on 14 October 1950 that American forces "tightened a death squeeze on 68,000 North Korean Communist troops." The same issue also announced that the late October draft call for thirty Dubois County men had been canceled because of the positive successes of the armed forces. Five days later the Jasper paper carried a front-page story telling how a former resident, Maj. Gen. Frank Milburn, "will have dinner tomorrow night in Pyongyang."[42]

Not everything Hoosiers witnessed at this time was upbeat. While traveling north one day, Nelson spied several loaded A-frames the Korean refugees typically carried on their backs. "I was pretty sure these belonged to some of the hundreds of Koreans we had seen fleeing south," he said. "Anyway, I was curious as to what was in the rice straw bags on these particular frames, so I walked over and peeked inside. They were all wrapped up bodies, mostly children." In another instance Nelson saw huge ten-wheeled American trucks tearing down a narrow road where haggard, escaping refugees lined the edges, waiting for the trucks to pass. "The edges of the road were so very narrow and beyond that was a deep ditch. When the trucks came hurling by they threw a solid wall of slushy water, knocking down those poor people. Most of them tumbled to the bottom of the ditch. Some of them looked so weak, I don't believe they got up again. The American drivers did not do that on purpose. It's just that we were in a hurry to get to the Yalu so we could go home. To me, Korean civilians were the greatest casualties of the war."[43]

Hoosier Carl Spencer recalled another chilling scene involving Korean dead later in the war during the winter thaw in 1951. "The snow was just starting to melt, and as it did, you were able to see all these bodies of little children from six months old to about eight or twelve," said Spencer. "The muddy water from our tires would wash over them and make them rock as we'd drive by."[44] Another Hoosier, Raleigh McGary of Boonville, in a letter to his wife described the North Korean people he saw as his marine unit moved north.

> The North Koreans are a lot like the Japanese in looks but that's about all. I haven't had a chance to observe them in town but I can tell you a little about the farmers. The country is pretty hilly and the farms are larger than in Japan. As nearly as I can tell the only crop around here is rice. The whole family works. The little kids cut firewood and thresh the grain out of the straw. The women work just the same as the men. It's against custom for a Korean girl to have anything to do with a foreigner so we haven't seen any of them (that is the young unmarried ones). If she is caught they may kill her, take away her name, or chase her away from home. The little kids cut firewood for us. In exchange we give them candy, food, or cigarettes. The cigarettes are the most valuable to them. We can't allow them to come around where we have our positions so we have a time with them.[45]

In late October the First Cavalry Division drove into the North Korean capital, and Nelson and his comrades received a special treat. "Bob Hope came and gave a show. He had Les Brown's Band and Marilyn Maxwell, along with some chorus girls. Because I was an engineer, I helped build the stage for the show at this large field at one of the Universities there in Pyongyang," said Nelson. "There must have been 50,000 people there for Hope's appearance and everyone was in such a good mood thinking the war was over." The thing that Nelson remembered most, however, was "the women in shorts. It had been a long time since we'd seen American girls."

Nelson found the enemy capital surprisingly large and "with many universities. The people were very subdued, held their heads down and so forth. For our part, we felt like conquerors." Some American troops, including Nelson, stayed in the capital while the bulk of the Eighth moved north toward the Yalu River. Around Thanksgiving, just when Nelson and his comrades were hearing talk about putting their rifles in Cosmoline and being home by Christmas, disturbing rumors began to drift in from the main line of American troops that was moving toward the Chinese border. Nelson started hearing that "the Chinese were coming across the Yalu in great numbers," and these stories quickly grew worse. "We heard how the Chinese troops were cutting right through us and how we couldn't get our equipment out," he said. "Another thing going around which didn't register much at the time was that the Chinese were giving medical aid to wounded Americans, whereas the North Koreans had been much more brutal in their treatment of captured American GIs."[46] Nelson received a firsthand experience of this former tendency just a few short months later.

The truth was even worse than the rumors that were at Pyongyang. Not only were American troops of the Eighth being threatened with entrapment by the Chinese, but they were also caught in an early bitter winter. Hoosier army reservist Thomas Chappell of the First Cavalry Division recalled those trying times: "I ended up in a Repo Depot in Pyongyang, the capital of North Korea. We were issued more clothing to cope with the oncoming cold weather. I had been wearing my regular size combat boots, 6½ D, but after talking with others I promptly traded my boots in for a pair of 7½ D and wore 3 pairs of socks to protect my feet from freezing. In the shuffle, my records were lost somehow and I was assigned to a field artillery unit. They only had 25 persons left in the Battalion after fighting in Taegu heading north. I wasn't impressed with those statistics, but I did as I was told, hoping it would all be over soon."

Near the Yalu River, Chappell received a new assignment. "I was . . . assigned to an outpost with a 50 cal. machine gun set up to guard our artillery. The outpost positions were the highest points surrounding the battery," he noted. "It was pretty tiring climbing to the top of a large hill to set up position." Chappell recalled the bitter cold: "It was around 35 degrees below zero one day." In another instance, Chappell remembered his squad leader letting some enemy troops escape. "I was surprised to see a convoy moving up the road in front of me, so I called the officer of the guard and asked if I should fire at them as I knew they were North Koreans," said Chappell. He told me not to fire and to be real quiet. Next morning the infantry helped us to get out, as we had been surrounded that night by the enemy. We just wished the war to be over soon so we could all go home. This was the time we had begun our strategic withdrawal toward Seoul, South Korea, just below the 38th parallel. We were surrounded by the enemy two more times before we got to Seoul."

It was during this time that Chappell experienced one of his most unforgettable moments in the war. "I was sitting on a hillside cleaning my gun and looking across the valley, when I saw a mountain top turn white. A blanket of snow had hit it. That's the most spectacular sight I saw in Korea," he remembered. Despite the beauty of the snow on Korean mountains, Chappell recalled that the most brutal force he faced in the war was the weather: "I slept on the ground in a mountain sleeping bag in 40 degrees below zero and both my feet were frozen to the point where they had burst open around the balls of my feet. While on guard duty, we had to start the trucks' engines every hour and let them run for 15 minutes to keep them from freezing up. There were times that I didn't think I'd make it back home, but I had a lot of people praying for me back home. The day I finally got the news I was going to be rotated, my captain called me to his tent and offered me a battlefield commission if I would stay. I said to him, 'Not on your life,' so the next day I was taken out of the outfit and sent home to my wife and two children. I'm not bitter, but I don't think it was right that men with a family should have to go over there and fight when there was no explanation as to why."[47] Chappell's strong feeling was shared by many of his reservist comrades.

At the time the Chinese entered the war in northwest Korea, the Eighth Army's Second Division was particularly hard hit. Many companies were understrength and ill prepared for the surprise Chinese onslaught. Some units had platoon leaders who had only recently joined the service and did not know their men. Worse, many officers were about to experience their first combat situations. "It's a story," noted two military historians, "of units who had no cleaning supplies for their weapons, who got into sleeping bags for the night without digging in, who gave up trying to establish communication with [other] units . . . because they ran out of field telephone wire."[48] The Second Division's progress toward the Yalu River was a primary concern to the Chinese, who now decided this group must be wiped out at all costs. The Chinese surprise attack was "as complete as any ever put upon an army."[49] Russell Spurr, in his examination of China's sudden entrance into the war, noted the sad lack of American awareness of the Chinese presence. Spurr observed, "The advancing Americans had shucked off their bayonets, blankets, spare ammunition, and emergency rations for what appeared to be the last and most leisurely effort of the war. Most of them dreamed only of a family Christmas," Spurr observed. "The top brass was equally euphoric. General Douglas MacArthur issued another sanguine communique claiming unresisted advance to the very borders of Manchuria."[50]

One of the most amazingly brutal portions of the ensuing American army's escape was the Second Division's agonizing run through what became known as "The Gauntlet." On 30 November 1950 the division's escaping column "expected to break through a shallow enemy position. Instead it was enveloped full length by a Chinese division already holding the ridges commanding its line of march."[51] The valley was a natural trap. As the first units of the Second Division began to drive through, "Machine-gun fire ripped up and down the mile-long line of thin-skinned vehicles which waited helplessly for someone to remove the obstruction. Trucks died in their tracks, creating more blockages and confusion." Soldiers of the Second Division "took shelter wherever they could find it. Soon the roadside ditches were choked with dead and wounded. The few officers still on their feet vainly tried to organize a coherent defense."

Spurr, who interviewed several Chinese troops fighting at "The Gauntlet," told of one Chinese group's first view of the devastation of American equipment and men down on the bloody road.

> Bivouac bags, tents, broken footlockers and ration boxes were ankle-deep across the road. Mixed in with the trash of battle were the bodies of men, as frozen and forgotten as their own forsaken baggage. Some of the squad quickly got down to looting, but the captain ordered them into defensive positions. They could be caught in an elaborate trap. Surrounding vehicles were cautiously checked out for signs of life. A jeep stood slewed across the road packed with American military policemen. The MPs were all dead and quite rigid, the blood on their parkas long congealed. Other men had been killed seated inside their trucks, jumping out or scrambling for safety underneath. One driver hung half out of his open cab, dangling arms gently swaying in the wind. The same wind rustled the snow-flecked hair of the boy who still manned the traverse on the half-track. He sagged awkwardly in his seat, helmetless, shot between the eyes.[52]

Among the unfortunate men of the Second Division who endured the dash through "The Gauntlet" was Lexington native Carl Spencer. Spencer's group had gotten almost to the Yalu River. "We were set up for about three or four days before the Chinese hit. I remember Thanksgiving up there," he said. "I put a turkey leg in my pocket to take with me." When Spencer first saw the Chinese, "it looked like ten armies coming, there were so many of them. We mowed them down as long as we had any ammunition. One night Fox company next to us got over 3,000 rounds of mortar shells on them. After that we got the order to pull back—there were just too many of them."

Spencer recalled there was no organization to the retreat. "Everyone was hollering, 'Go south! Go south!' Fleeing Americans hitched on any vehicle that looked like [it] could go through." The Chinese, however, had gotten around on both sides of the Second Division's escape route and bore down upon the vulnerable American vehicles with the intent of wiping out the entire group. Spencer recalled seeing one of the survivors of a Turkish outfit: "He came out from under a bridge with his hands up hollering in broken English, 'Don't shoot! Don't shoot! I'm a Turkey!'" As Spencer pulled out from where he'd been dug in, he and other Americans heard the rumor going around "that we were outnumbered twenty to one. The Chinese were also dropping leaflets telling how they wouldn't mistreat us and for us to surrender while we still could. I tell you that was a dark day in my life. I really didn't believe I'd get out of there alive."

Spencer found himself in the notorious gauntlet, participating in a harrowing escape down a dirt track surrounded by thousands of Chinese. As the party of vehicles Spencer joined started south through this killing field, the Americans "shot at anything we'd see. There were burning vehicles everywhere. I'd climbed into an ammunition trailer behind a truck full of GIs earlier. When I'd tried to get into the back of the truck, it was so packed, they told me to go back to the trailer. I remember there were soldiers of all kinds—ROKs [Republic of Korea], Turks, and mixed units of our guys—it was just that chaotic. Everyone was lost and separated from their outfits and just trying to survive."

Spencer's grueling ride was in "that little ammo trailer. It didn't have any springs, and on those dirt roads, the ride almost shook me to pieces. On the other hand, when the Chinese attacked, they always went after the trucks with all the soldiers, so I was spared getting shot at as much. I rode like this all the way through. They just kept on driving, and I just hung on." Spencer was one of the lucky ones. Most of those who entered the gauntlet did not survive. Spencer recalled, "When we went back south, I thought for sure we'd lost the war. We figured the whole world had gone crazy."[53] Surprisingly, just a few short months later Spencer and his comrades would be pushing the Chinese back across the thirty-eighth parallel in some of the most intense fighting of the war.

A less fortunate Hoosier serving with the Second Division was Monroe City native Everett Wayne Leffler. A member of the Thirty-eighth Field Artillery Battalion, Leffler quit school at the end of his junior year and joined the army. Serving in the armed forces, his younger sister Bettie Lou remembered, "was all he talked about doing. He enjoyed hearing his uncles talk about World War I and II." Leffler trained at Camp Breckenridge, Kentucky, and when the war broke out he was stationed at Fort Lewis, Washington. On 2 October 1950, when it looked as if the war was winding down, young Leffler wrote his youngest sister, who was a freshman in high school back in Indiana:

PFC Everett Wayne Leffler, Jr. Leffler was listed as missing in action on 30 November 1950 after his artillery battalion made an unsuccessful attempt to run "The Gauntlet."

Dearest Sis, Will answer your letter which I received about 5 days ago. Hope this finds you okay. I am just fine. Well, I am getting rested up—have been for three days now. I don't think we will see much more action. Since I got your letter, we have advanced 150 miles, so we have sure been on the go. We think it is about over unless we fight Red China, which we won't unless they start it. We don't know yet when we will come back to the States. I sure hope we do, for I can never like this place. Well, Sis, I guess I had better close and write a few lines to Hugh. Will write more soon. Answer soon. Lots of Love, Wayne

A week before the young Leffler disappeared forever, he wrote his "Dearest Sis" again, telling of the intense cold and the lack of winter clothing:

Dearest Sis, I guess I had better answer your letter, which I received about two days ago. Hope this finds you ok. I am just fine. Well, Sis, we are in action now way up in North Korea. We are getting ready for a big push. Maybe it will all be over with before long. I sure hope so, for I sure hate this place. It has sure been cold the last two weeks. It has been as much as 20 below, and that is sure cold, for we don't have any warm clothes to wear. Sure wish they would get us some. Well, Sis, it is late, so I guess I will close for now. Will write more soon. Answer soon. Love, Wayne

On that same date Leffler wrote a letter to his parents addressed to "Dearest Dad and Mom":

Will write you a few lines while I have a little spare time. Hope this finds everyone ok. I am just fine. Well, we had "turkey" for dinner today, and it sure was good. Wish we had it all the time, but most of the time we don't have anything fit to eat. It is sure cold over here. It has been about

20 below for the last two weeks. I sure hope it warms up soon, for we don't have any warm clothes to wear unless they get us some soon. We are up at the front and are moving up again today if nothing happens. I sure hope this thing is over before long, but it looks like it may last a good while yet. If everything goes ok we may be back in the states before long. All my Love, Your Son Wayne [54]

When the Chinese hurled themselves into the war, Leffler's group was the last unit to try to run the deadly gauntlet. The fleeing battalion lost every artillery piece and few of Leffler's group would ever be heard from again. Historian S. L. A. Marshall tells of the impossible situation confronting Leffler and his comrades when they began their escape attempt.

> Artillerymen have a love for their guns which is perhaps stronger than the feeling of any other soldier for his weapon or any part of his equipment. That guns will never be deserted simply because danger threatens is a point of honor around which the artillery has largely built the solid discipline of its corps. These batteries were not less lacking in awareness of professional obligation than were others. But as at Omaha Beachhead one battalion lost its guns because the mover was riddled, and there was no other source of power at hand. Perhaps not every man kept the trust and did his utmost; under battle's pressure, men are not found equal. But that which needs be remembered is that hundreds died or became missing in the effort to save machined metal which in the nature of the situation was beyond salvation. . . . The 38th Battalion [Leffler's group], at the far end, last to get the call in the entire division, lost every gun and vehicle. It could not even get on the track, such was the chaos extending out over seven miles. There is no record of the retreat of this unit as a unit. Some of its men got back to allied lines by traveling cross-country under the cover of dark. Many did

not. The 105s were left in enemy country. For this, it was said in parts of the American press that their action was discreditable, the consequence of bug-out fever. They could have escaped this charge had they been able to put wings on the tubes and fly with them beyond the encircling ridges.[55]

As for the teenage Leffler, he was declared missing in action as of 30 November 1950. His body was never returned to his native state. When the defeated Eighth Army began to pass through Pyongyang on its way south, Stanley Nelson saw on their gritty faces, "the expressions of a big letdown. There was also a sense of panic too. The Chinese were right behind us now, and although I had yet to see one, they sounded like fierce warriors. It was obvious they meant business and were not what we called 'rice paddy boys.'" Nelson's group of engineers were one of the last to leave Pyongyang. "We were put in charge of blowing up bridges, burning equipment, and so forth. The main thing was to make it difficult for their T-34 tanks to come through," he said.[56] When the Eighth finally got back south to safety, Spencer recalled how all the units were completely mixed up. "I saw men from every division over there wandering around searching for their outfits," he said.[57] The chaotic retreat of the Eighth from northwest Korea was the longest in U.S. military history. The rapidness of the retreat, however, saved the bulk of the Eighth's men and their equipment. This was not to be the case over on the east side of Korea, where Hoosiers such as Charles Garrigus, Jr., and Donald Faith, Jr., fought and died.

"The boys . . . will be back by Christmas."

Gen. Douglas MacArthur in *Time* magazine, 4 December 1950

"The real heroes are dead."

Audie Murphy

CHAPTER FOUR

BITTER RETREAT

The marine's First Division and elements of the Eighth Army's Seventh Division, dubbed the Tenth Corps, had landed in Wonsan, on the east side of North Korea, in late October. They marched inland from the coast toward the Chosin Reservoir and, beyond that, the Manchurian border. About this time, Gen. Douglas MacArthur related to an assistant in a brief moment of flippedness that "the boys . . . will be back by Christmas." A magazine correspondent overheard the statement and reported it to the public.[1] MacArthur had further assured President Harry S. Truman at a hastily called meeting on Wake Island in mid-October that Chinese intervention was highly unlikely, and if it occurred, it would bring "the greatest slaughter" of Red forces.

That the Chinese might hurl themselves into the war should have been of grave concern to Gen. Walton H. Walker on the west, where the Eighth found themselves extended far beyond their main supply bases. The Tenth Corps, including Charles Garrigus, Jr.'s group, which moved up the east side of the peninsula, faced a more chilling reality if the Chinese did indeed come into the struggle. Strung out along a single precarious mountain road, the Tenth Corps was particularly vulnerable to entrapment and possible annihilation. The Marine Corps component of the Tenth Corps, however, under Maj. Gen. O. P. Smith had wisely established several bases of supplies and men along the single narrow supply route with primary perimeters located at Koto-ri and Hagaru, the latter near the south end of the sprawling Chosin Reservoir. Highly organized and trained to fight under the most severe of conditions, marine units stayed in close and constant contact with one another. The Seventh Division, labeled Task Force MacLean, which would eventually come to rest northeast of marine lines at Hagaru, lacked the organization of Smith and his men. "The communication in Task Force MacLean," noted military historian Clay Blair, "was deplorable. The unit had no radio contact with the 7th Division Headquarters . . . or with Hagaru. . . . In effect . . . the elements of Task Force MacLean were not connected, physically or otherwise."[2] Because of this lack of organization, all the ingredients were present for a catastrophe.

Back in Indiana in October, Gladys Garrigus read the uplifting news of the war's sure end but still harbored great fears concerning her son's safety. She wrote Charles and pleaded with him to send any information he could regarding what he was doing in Korea. About the time of the "Home by Christmas" campaign, Garrigus sent his mother a letter in response to her request. Enclosed was a snapshot of himself standing beside two of the three-quarter-ton trucks he maintained. The trucks were mired in heavy mud. "It was typical," he explained, of the conditions he had to work with in Korea.[3]

On Thanksgiving Day 1950, marines of the Fifth Regiment enjoyed a hot meal while occupying the east side of Chosin Reservoir about midway up that body of water. The next day this group received orders to leave their positions and proceed south to Hagaru then west to Yudam-ni to wheel west and hook up with General Walker's Eighth. To protect the marines' flank, Col. Allan MacLean's group of three thousand GIs arrived on the east side of the Chosin. MacLean, who at forty-three still maintained a robust body and aggressive spirit, had seen heavy fighting in Europe in World War II. Colonel MacLean and his Thirty-first Regiment team were to link up with Garrigus's unit of the Thirty-second Regiment, commanded by thirty-two- year-old Lt. Col. Donald Faith, Jr. Faith, who had yet to experience leading men in combat, was placed under MacLean's command. From their Chosin base, these two army units would help in mopping up the enemy in northeast Korea and protect the flank of the UN forces' main thrust up the west side of the peninsula. However, tens of thousands of Chinese troops waited patiently, as the convoy of tanks, trucks, jeeps, and men slowly snaked over and around hill after hill, to spring a deadly trap on the oblivious Seventh Division.

Letters written from October through November by Solsberry's Donald Hamilton, convey his experiences with the Seventh Division as it moved north toward the Chosin Reservoir and its dismal fate. Ironically, Hamilton and many other American troops believed that they would be home for Christmas. In a letter written in early October, Hamilton told his parents, "We finally got part of the way to where we are going or at least where I hope we stay. It looks like we may have to go through Manchuria before it is all over. It is a little chilly up here, but we have rather good clothes so it doesn't bother us too much. I received some mail today, but it was back mail. I look to get some more mail this afternoon. I didn't get to take over mail clerk, but I don't care because this company is really chicken s—— anymore. I will be glad to get back to C Company as aid man. I think we go back to the company tomorrow. . . . We never hear much news over here, only the bad. I guess they just don't want to get our hopes built up. I still believe I will be back to Japan or the states before Christmas."

In another letter the homesick Hoosier asked his father, "Oval, you were talking about going fishing. Did you catch any? I am sure going to do a lot of hunting when I get back, that is if the varmints over here don't track me down first, and I don't believe they can do that." Hamilton told his mother of a growing problem that eventually spelled doom for the Seventh Division once the Chinese came into the war. "The 7th division has about 700 Koreans attached to it and they are always getting the s—— knocked out of them when there isn't an officer around. They are no good at fighting, they are so yellow that when we get in a fire fight they would lay down and refuse to go. There are several of them who refused to fight." In a particularly upbeat letter written on 1 November 1950, Hamilton related, "I can't hardly write because the boys are seeing who can tell the biggest war stories. You should hear some of them."

By the middle of November things began to change for the worse. Nobody was telling war stories. Hamilton wrote his parents about the incredible cold the Seventh was beginning to endure. "It's really cold over here, several degrees below zero. Don't look for much mail from me because it is too cold to write." About this same time Hamilton wrote, "It doesn't look like I am going to make it home for Christmas this year, but I hope to be back shortly after Christmas." Hamilton added other thoughts as his unit drew closer to its final fate. "Those Chinese won't want much of what we have to give them. I went out today and done a little target practice. My rifle messed up a little so I guess I will have to go get it repaired tomorrow," he wrote. "The 32nd is (or has been) trying to clean out the guerilla bands, but as yet we haven't found any. They can move a little faster in the mountains than we can. I have about three months pay coming now, and I don't think I will draw a penny until I leave Korea, and by then I should have a nice little pile of money coming. It doesn't look like I will get a chance to send you anything for Christmas this year unless that I can get back to Japan. I don't know whether I will make Sgt. or not but I still have a chance to make it. Oval, you were saying in your last letter that you didn't want me to re-enlist. Well, you don't have to worry about that if there is any kind of work to do in civilian life." In his last letter home, written just a few days before the Seventh Division was trapped by the Chinese forces, Hamilton wrote:

> We are sitting here in the same place, and I think we are going to stay here until the 22nd. I don't know where we are going when we leave, but they say we are going back to Iwon, the place where we landed here in North Korea. It came out in the paper yesterday that there was 5 divisions

going to Europe from here and that one would go straight to Europe and that the other 4 would go through the states before going. It also said that the U.S. troops would be relieved by other UN forces, so I have a little hope in going to Europe before too long.

Where we are staying now is a valley and the mountains on both sides of us are covered with snow. It is really beautiful, but everyone is afraid we will have to cross those mountains before too long. We hardly ever hear any news here but what is 4 or 5 days old so the war could be over and we wouldn't know it. Well, Oval, I guess hunting season is going strong now. I was planning on doing a lot of hunting this year, but since they declared open season on Koreans and Chinese, I guess I will stay here for a little while. It is a little more exciting at times. This company went on a raid of the villages around here last night, at about 0100 and got 15 prisoners that came out of the mountains to get something to eat. There is one thing I would like for you to do, that is send me about a pound or two of candy and things like that about every week or two, but send small amounts so I can carry it when we move around. We just can't get things like this over here.[4]

Had the Chinese not come into the war, it is a likely bet that members of the Tenth Corps, such as Garrigus and Hamilton, would have long remembered the terrible winter conditions of that campaign. Winter struck northeast Korea with a fury in November 1950. On 10 November the temperature dropped to minus ten degrees without warning. More extreme temperatures soon followed. One historian noted that "the cold was so intense men became dazed and incoherent, some went numb, others cried in pain."[5] By late November temperatures dropped to minus thirty-five degrees. Inactive GIs and marines often froze to death in their foxholes. A survivor, Alan Cork, recalled that the Thirty-second Regiment "had only summer sleeping bags and most had just a pair of long johns, a light field jacket and a parka shell pulled over. Most did not have gloves."[6] Truck drivers such as Garrigus struggled to carry out their jobs in the most difficult circumstances—the roads in the Chosin campaign "were among the poorest and most precarious of any used in war by American forces." No American armies, noted Roy E. Appleman, "before or since have fought in as harsh of or hostile environment."[7] The cold often paralyzed trucks and drained batteries while troops riding in the back of three-quarter-ton trucks sometimes froze solid. Letters written by Boonville native Raleigh McGary give great insight into the brutal weather conditions under which the Tenth Corps struggled and the hope American troops had at this time that the war was all but over.

November 19, 1950

We moved north 60 or 80 miles from Wonsan and are dug in in a graveyard between Hamhung and Hungnam or some such towns. This has been established as a rendezvous point for the 1st Marines. What we are going to do is a matter of much speculation but I'm not going into that. I hope we are leaving Korea. Since I wrote you last it has been pretty cold, too cold to write a letter even. The sun came up and warmed us up a little yesterday. I've been too busy most of the time to notice how cold it really was. . . . I hope you aren't having as much trouble keeping warm as we are. We have our hole lined with straw and manage to keep pretty warm in our sleeping bags (they're wonderful) but the rest of the time we get cold and huddle around a fire (not allowed at night of course).

We have been eating C-rations. They contain quite a variety of foods. 3 cans of food; three cans of cookies, sugar, coffee, jam, matches, cocoa, and others; 2 cans (small) of fruit (peaches, apricots, pears, or fruit cocktail). The foods consist of a variety of beans with pork or frankfurters or ham; spaghetti and meat; chicken and vegetables; beef stew; ham and lima beans; and a few others. We trade

BITTER RETREAT

around and manage to get something worth eating. They also contain cigarettes. We get a day's ration at a time.

It sure would be nice to take a bath and change clothes. I'm still wearing what I left Japan in and instead of changing I just add more. All I change is my socks and not very often on those. I've managed to wash 3 times and shave once. My teeth are in pretty filthy condition. . . . I hope my letters aren't as bad as they seem to me. I should get some mail from you in a day or so. Then maybe I can write better. All my love, again.

In other letters McGary's thoughts showed that he and others still held out hope the war would soon be over.

November 25

I guess this was my lucky day. I had to finish the letter by firelight (3 from you and one from mom) and I was awakened the next morning with "pack your gear we're moving," and we have been since then. I don't have any idea where we are except that it's on the side of a mountain. I spent Thanksgiving Day on a much higher mountain. I think the elevation was about 5000 feet or more. It rained all day and night and left us with 0-degree weather. We just finished our

Raleigh McGary of Boonville shortly after he and the First Marine Division escaped the trap set by the Chinese at the Chosin Reservoir.

Thanksgiving dinner. It took till today to catch up. According to the latest word we are supposed to leave Korea by the 15th day of the new offensive which was to have started this morning. We haven't started yet but probably will in a little while. . . . MacArthur is supposed to be over here now, and he seems anxious to get the M.C. [Marine Corps] home. I hope so!

I find it pretty hard to write letters. My hands are about frozen. I sure would love to jump into a nice warm bed. If we leave here in 15 days, it won't be too long. Of course we shouldn't plan on it, but it makes the separation more bearable if you keep thinking—well, it's only for another month. At least that's the way it is with me. I expected some more mail today, but it's about 4:30 and none yet so I guess tomorrow. It's getting colder by the minute so I'm going to close for now. Love forever

November 27

I'm sitting in our tent wrapped around our oil stove freezing to death. It isn't too bad, but the wind can sure find places to come in. The weather around here isn't like anyplace I've ever seen—it gets almost warm when the wind isn't blowing, but when it does it comes from the north pole. . . . I don't know if I should tell you the gossip—but I will. It seems we are supposed to stay here until we go home. That will be by the 8th of December (we leave Korea at least). Every time I have told you any such news we have moved farther north. I'm taking another chance. If it's any colder north of here, I don't want any. It's late so I'll close with oceans of love.

November 29

My pen is frozen up and doesn't write so well. I didn't have time to mail the first part of this letter as we have been pretty busy and losing sleep every night. It seems impossible to get a good night's sleep in a combat area. I'm really filthy and will just have to take a bath (<u>AM</u> <u>I KIDDING</u>) today. We have our tent fixed a little better now, so I'll heat some water in my helmet and wash my hands and face and maybe under my arms. I believe that is what is referred to as a whore's bath.

We had about an inch of snow late last night. I was standing watch so I nearly looked like a snowman when it was over. We are going to make some snowmen to fool gooks. (Well, it's an idea isn't it—O.K. forget it). For the first time, I didn't have a roof on my foxhole so it was full of snow before I realized what was happening. There I was pulling snow out of the hole and putting up a shelter in the middle of the morning—2:00 am. It's a wonder someone didn't shoot me for a gook. I'll have to get this in the mail so I'll close with barrels of love. See you Christmas—I hear MacArthur said. Love, 'til the well runs dry.[8]

The Chinese sprung their trap in late November, shattering the hopes of Hoosiers such as McGary. As already noted, the Eighth on the west side of Korea made a hasty and panicked retreat south when the Chinese attacked. The Tenth Corps experienced a different fate. The Seventh Division had engaged the Chinese earlier and found them reluctant to fight, leading the division's command to regard the new foe with contempt. All this now changed. As the temperature dropped drastically and heavy snow fell, the Tenth Corps, including approximately 3,000 members of Task Force MacLean, found themselves facing at least 120,000 battle-tested Chinese soldiers. American leadership was simply dumbfounded by the staggering change in events. "The Chinese," MacArthur wired Truman, "have come in with both feet." Truman quickly called a meeting of his staff and told them, "We've got a terrific situation on our hands."[9]

For Americans such as the Garrigus and Hamilton families, who had loved ones fighting in northeast Korea, newspaper accounts painted a grim picture. The *New York Times*, for example, spoke of "waves of Chinese Communist infantry" sweeping down upon vastly outnumbered U.S. troops.[10] The primary paper for the region in which the Garrigus family lived, the *Evansville Courier*, also offered a gloomy assessment of the situation in northeast Korea. One headline noted that "80,000 Communist Suddenly Confront 10th Corps in Northeast."[11] The next day the same paper announced that the Thirty-first and Thirty-second Regiments were surrounded, and their only supply route had been cut.[12] The marines, strung all up and down a single mountain road that led from the coast seventy-five miles up to the west side of the Chosin Reservoir, now began to leapfrog back to safety. While marine comrades held the perimeter at Hagaru, about ten thousand marines began to pull out from Yudam-ni, retreating toward the relatively safe position at Hagaru. The marines fought every inch of the way, stopping their columns just long enough to go up the steep mountains and drive off scores of Chinese ambushes and attacks. Hoosier marine reservist Paul McDaniel remembered how the convoy was stopped cold at one particular spot and marine officers asked for volunteers to try and knock the Chinese off the mountain. "We were told some of us would not come back down that mountain, but it was the only way we could escape the trap," he said. McDaniel went up with Item Company of the Third Battalion, Fifth Marine Regiment. Only about two dozen men returned in fighting condition. McDaniel was severely wounded but was rescued by an old Evansville acquaintance, Robert Egan, who found McDaniel lying by a ditch and helped place him on a truck with scores of other wounded.[13]

Donald Burton, another Hoosier marine reservist, recalled the Chosin campaign and the narrow escape he experienced:

> My group landed at Wonsan in October of 1950 and went up north toward the Chosin Reservoir. We dug in on this mountain at Chin hung-ni. It looked, at first, like the war was almost over, and then the Chinese came into it and

surrounded us up at the reservoir. On top of that it turned cold—really cold. I believe it got over 40 degrees below at times, not counting the windchill, and we were out in the field. Both my feet ended up freezing before it was over with. For awhile, it looked like we wouldn't get out at all. When the marines started the breakout back to the coast, my company, along with two others, went up to take Hill 1081 so the marines above there could all get out. On the march up the Hill 1081, we discovered it was so cold that the water froze in our canteens. We'd have to break ice in a stream to get to the running water beneath to get something to drink. Like I said, things were so bad, nobody actually thought we would get out of there. When we finally escaped, the first thing I did was call my mother and dad and told them I had made it.[14]

Indianapolis native Howard Suttmiller was among the marines who secured Hill 1081. He recalled a dramatic episode in which the American engineers had to drop a prefabricated bridge to replace a key structure that had been destroyed by the Chinese. "They leveled the bridge off with the bodies of dead frozen Chinese—stacked them like wood," said Suttmiller. On the way up to Hill 1081 Suttmiller remembered how "it was about 40 below, and we had to move very fast. A lot of our guys worked up a sweat in the process. Then they stopped so that hands and feet froze very quickly. Myself, I got in my sleeping bag, took my socks and shoes off, changed them, [and] put the others down in my sleeping bag to dry off so that the next day I had some more dry socks to change into. Overall, I believe we had about 40 percent of our group who went to Hill 1081 to turn in for frostbite injuries. The thing I most remember about the Chosin campaign was the cold. It was at least forty below with about a eighty below chill factor, and we had to try and fight in that kind of environment. As I said earlier, I changed my socks everyday. At night I'd crawl into my sleeping bag— remember we were sleeping on the ground—and I'd pull my parka

Sgt. Howard Suttmiller of Indianapolis (left). Suttmiller had just returned from a hot, dirty motor patrol in central Korea, looking for North Korean guerrillas.

over me. It wasn't fun being shot at, but for me, the cold was the worst thing."[15]

David Graham of Evansville also recalled the horrible cold and the difficulty involved in maintaining a sleeping bag—an item essential for survival. He said:

> You really have to experience such cold to understand the feeling of helplessness that comes from such incredibly difficult circumstances. We operated in cold weather with the temperature down to 40 below zero, plus the cold wind blowing. Our sleeping bags were the only thing that kept us from freezing to death. They were very important to us. But if you are ever in that kind of temperature, you will find things freeze stiff as a board. At night your bag would get moisture—rain, snow, whatever—and in the morning the bag would be frozen stiff. Then you were told to roll up your sleeping bag and move out. Now if you've ever tried to roll up a frozen, six foot long board, you'd have some idea of what it was like trying to roll up a frozen sleeping bag. Can you imagine going into a firefight dragging a six foot frozen sleeping bag behind you? You sure couldn't leave them behind and tell someone to bring them up to you at the end of the day when you are ready to dig in for the night. No, they must go with you.
>
> Now on this day, mine was frozen stiff. There was no way I could begin to roll it. The very best I could do was kind of fold it over in half to about 3 feet in length. Then I was afraid it was going to crack apart. I found a piece of com [communication] wire and tied it around my waist, folding the sleeping bag into half and carrying it behind me. During the early morning we got into a firefight. I was on the ground and crawling through the weeds, trees, and brush under fire. My sleeping bag became entangled in some weeds and com wire. I was all tangled up and pinned down and naturally scared as hell. All I could do to free myself

and get out of there was to get my knife and cut my bag loose. We moved out, and I never saw my bag again.

That night I told my Sergeant that I had no bag. Naturally, he didn't have an extra one. So I had to do without. A buddy gave me a blanket. I thought I would freeze to death that night. The next night I got one from a buddy, who had gotten shot and evacuated. Those who lost their sleeping bags and could not find another likely died. I was one of the lucky ones.[16]

The marines fought for two bloody weeks and finally escaped to the coast and were evacuated. At the cost of about seven hundred killed, the First Marine Division inflicted forty thousand Chinese casualties and took three Chinese field armies out of the war for at least a year.[17]

Elements of the Eighth Army's Seventh Division on the east side of the Chosin when the Chinese struck were not nearly as lucky. Less prepared than the marines, the Seventh had few options when the Chinese attacked. The Tenth Corps, with basically one mountain road upon which to escape, appeared to be completely surrounded and trapped. The country held its breath and waited to see what would happen in northeast Korea. Meanwhile, communications from this front virtually ceased. Garrigus and other members of Colonel MacLean's group seemed to have disappeared off the face of the earth. A telegram came about this time informing the Garrigus family that their son was listed as missing in action as of 27 November. As it turned out, that date was the start of Garrigus's cruel five-day struggle for survival.

Samuel Muncy remembered the days leading up to the Seventh Division's crisis. "We figured it would be like South Korea, just colder. We were told later our coldest night there was about forty degrees below zero, seventy-four degrees below counting the windchill. The bad thing was the army was supposed to send up our cold weather gear the next day but then the Chinese closed the door." Gen. David Barr, commander of the Seventh Division, flew in the day after the Chinese struck. "Barr told us we were in a tough situation and would have to fight our way out," Muncy remembered. "Then he got back in his helicopter and flew off. At that time we didn't know how bad things were." Muncy also recalled, "We were down in this valley surrounded by mountains. Of course if we had known what was about to happen we would have dug in on high ground. Even after the second day we were hit, we were still in the dark about how many thousands of Chinese were in the mountains—we still had orders to go north to the Yalu [River]."[18]

On 27 November the Chinese struck the Thirty-first Regiment in below-zero weather, blowing horns and bugles and shooting flares. They quickly swarmed into GI positions "firing burp guns and mortars, throwing hand grenades, and shouting shrilly."[19] Because of the lack of communication, the scattered elements of Task Force MacLean "fought separate and desperate actions."[20] Over in Faith's and the Thirty-second's perimeter, the fighting was fierce as well. Cpl. Alan Cork, an Iowa native, was one of the lucky survivors from the Faith group and vividly remembered this terrible time of struggle. Although Cork was not a native Hoosier, his account, shared here for the first time, offers an important testimonial to what Hoosiers who served east of the Chosin endured:

Iowa native Alan Cork, whose accounts of the Chosin battle give great insight into what Hoosiers endured in November/December 1950.

It seemed to me that I was the last man off of the hill that had been a company position, and there was no way that I could take the road back to D Company. The only choice was to take a very steep hill to the rear, and I began the descent and lost my footing, causing me to fall down the hill. It was fifty feet or so before I hit bottom, and the tumble knocked all the wind out of me. Even so, I had to keep going as there was shooting and it was at me. I got up and ran through the brush and small trees, and I really didn't know which way to go, until I heard Sergeant King holler, "Who's there?" and I screamed, "It's me." He yelled for me to come on in and I ran as fast as I could through the snow and trees and bushes and still was falling all the time. I wear glasses, and I remember when I took that dive off the last hill, they were knocked off my face. I was so scared, I picked them up and put them on, but didn't waste time cleaning them so that I was seeing through the dirt and snow mixture. Sergeant King and Corporal Green helped me into their position, and I remember Sergeant King asking me how far back were the Chinese. I said they were right behind me, and Sergeant King told me to follow the road to the new position, so I took off after getting my glasses cleaned a bit and catching my breath. I had just gotten around the bend in the road when I heard the machine gun let go and a loud explosion. That was the last time I saw King or Green.

I made it to where my platoon sergeant was standing next to a jeep, and he said that he had heard I had been killed. He asked how it was, and I told him I'd lost all my equipment, radio, and how the telephone was not worth a damn, and the battery for the radio would not last. I was telling him in general terms of my problems when he broke in and told me this: "You don't know shit about combat." Then he began to tell me about his combat in World War II.

As Cork's group moved to a new position, Cork was able to catch a ride. "I was still tired from running down the road and I had sat down in the passenger seat when Sergeant Madden asked me if

I wanted to ride shotgun, and I said yes. The unit began to move out, and I was thinking how lucky I was. The rest of my platoon had to walk, and I saw that they had begun to descend the hill toward the water and cut across a frozen finger of the reservoir." Cork glanced down the road and saw "lots of men lying down on the right with their guns pointed up and across the road, and since we were moving so slow I had a few conversations with the troops. I made a smart remark that they must think that they were on the front line of combat." Then all hell broke loose. "The jeep windshield had been put up, and it was shattered by gun fire and of course the driver really hit the gas. As we took off skidding and sliding across the road, I made a few attempts to return fire," Cork said.

During that first night's attack on Faith's group, Cork was told, after the first round of fighting had ended, to find a foxhole and get some sleep. Unfortunately Cork had lost his sleeping bag and dreaded trying to get any rest in the subzero weather. Then he spied a dead body in a winter sleeping bag. "The bag had lots of blood on it, but I took the body out of it and took the bag over to a foxhole so I could lay in it," he said. Before Cork could sleep, he needed food. "I went off and found a C ration can of beans and was trying to thaw it out near a fire. I had just got a few beans loose and was bringing the can closer to the fire when a machine-gun burst hit. That was the last food I saw for the next week." When Cork returned to his foxhole, he discovered someone had taken the bloody sleeping bag.[21]

Fearing air strikes, the Chinese pulled back the next morning and scattered groups of GIs from the Thirty-first and Thirty-second Regiments reformed their perimeters. The commander of the Tenth Corps, Gen. Edward Almond, did not seem greatly concerned about the initial Chinese engagement. From Hagaru, Almond helicoptered into Faith's perimeter on 28 November and talked over the situation with Faith and others, while nearby, Garrigus tended his trucks. Almond had come to confer with and encourage the leaders of the beleaguered task force. "The enemy," Almond told the shaken men, "is nothing more than the remnant Chinese divisions fleeing north. . . . Don't let a bunch of Chinese laundrymen stop you."[22] Before the commander of the Tenth Corps left, he hurriedly offered three silver stars for valor, one to Faith and two others to men that Faith was told to choose. Faith protested such arbitrary awarding of medals for valor, and when Almond left Faith tore his medal from his uniform and flung it into the snow. The next day Garrigus performed an act of extraordinary heroism, the first of several daring and courageous actions the brave Hoosier sergeant would carry out during the five bitter days of fighting east of the Chosin.

The struggle that took place on the evening of 28 November proved to be even more brutal and intense than the first night's action, and MacLean's inlet camp was almost overrun. The situation was so serious that many units did not "take time to carry rations to the front line. When the food did reach the soldiers after dark, it was frozen and the men had no way to thaw it except by holding it against their bodies."[23] Faith's group, which included Garrigus and Hamilton, fared little better than MacLean's. The next day MacLean decided it would be best for Faith's regiment to consolidate with the Thirty-first at the inlet. Before moving out, Faith ordered several trucks to be unloaded of their cargo so the rapidly mounting number of wounded could be carried out in three-quarter-ton trucks. At dawn on 29 November, about sixty vehicles began the dangerous dash through heavy enemy fire. As the column crossed a final bridge to arrive in MacLean's perimeter, Chinese fire increased in volume, and two American trucks carrying valuable ammunition and rations were hastily left behind by nervous truck drivers. Later that same day Garrigus gazed across the bridge and saw enemy soldiers cautiously approaching the abandoned supply trucks he had previously cared for. "On his own initiative," the first sergeant suddenly decided to return for the trucks. Unarmed and dashing "across . . . 300 yards of open snow covered ice," Garrigus brought the first bullet-riddled truck across the bridge to safety. Then, ignoring the yell of his comrades, Garrigus ran back to get the second truck. His second trip drew the unwanted attention of even more Chinese, who now bore down with murderous and concentrated fire in an attempt to stop the daring Hoosier. As Garrigus maneuvered the lumbering truck over the frozen ground, he could hear bullets whizzing by or smacking loudly into the truck's body with sickening thuds. Miraculously, the bullet-riddled truck made it into the safety of the American lines, stalling as it rolled into the friendly confines of the inlet perimeter. Inside the perimeter the sound of the dying engine gave way to the "hurrahs" of GIs. These soldiers had taken brutally hard hits from the Chinese and the sergeant's surprising stunt greatly lifted their morale. "Through Garrigus' quick thinking actions," a later report noted, "the supplies were taken from the very grasp of the enemy."[24]

That same morning Colonel MacLean was either killed or captured by a group of Chinese whom the commander mistakenly identified as Americans coming into the inlet perimeter. MacLean's absence put Washington native Faith in charge of the task force.[25] Ferocious evening attacks by the Chinese continued. Cork recalled

Lt. Col. Donald C. Faith, Jr., of Washington (front and middle). Faith was posthumously awarded the Medal of Honor for his actions at the Chosin Reservoir.

these nightmarish encounters: "At night was the worst time. I had no radio or telephone, so I would go over to my unit CP [command post] and ask how things were and what to do. They had run out of shells for the 81mm mortars and the platoon was being used as a blocking force wherever it was needed. The last time I went over to my company area, all the ones I knew were gone with other units, and by this time it was hard to recognize anyone. One of my friends came by, and I told him he looked terrible and his reply to me was that I should look at myself."[26]

On 30 November General Barr, commander of the Seventh Division, came by helicopter to Faith's headquarters, where he learned of MacLean's disappearance. Although their conversation was not recorded, Faith probably told Barr of his plans to break out of the trap by dashing several miles over a narrow mountain road to the more secure marine base at Hagaru.[27] Further, Faith planned to load an estimated five hundred wounded men in trucks and jeeps, bringing them out as well. Given the horrible conditions of the road, the bitterly cold and snowy weather, and the thousands of Chinese who now infested the hills, the breakout plan seemed an impossible task. Yet more shocking news came to Faith at this time. The beleaguered marines would be unable to send any men to help Faith's party move southward. Other than daytime air support from a handful of planes, Task Force Faith, as it was now officially called, would be on its own.

The night before the attempted breakout was a brutal one. Shortly after midnight the Chinese attacked with a greater intensity than all other previous attacks. "All through the night," recalled one survivor, "we heard the cries from our friendly wounded within the perimeter who were suffering from the cold."[28] Five times before dawn the Chinese "came into the American lines." Each time a breech occurred, Faith organized a handful of men to throw the Chinese out of the perimeter. So desperate was the lieutenant colonel for men "that he grabbed walking wounded from the aid station and led them to the front line to plug holes." By morning some men were so fatigued "they actually fell asleep in the middle of battle."[29] Faith's determination and actions helped save the fragile perimeter.

Medical supplies were completely exhausted by the next morning. Thus the condition of Faith's group on the morning of the attempted breakout was especially poor. A surviving officer described the hellish scene: "By dawn on December 1 members of the task force had been under attack for 80 hours in sub-zero weather. None had slept much. None had washed or shaved, none had eaten more than a bare minimum." To add to the deteriorating situation, most of the men were either wounded or crippled somehow by the bitter cold: "Everyone seemed to be wounded in one fashion or another . . . frozen feet and hands were common. The wounded who were unable to move froze to death. Trucks and jeeps and trailers were ransacked for ammunition and any kind of fabric that would serve for bandage or clothing." Just as discouraging on that bleak dawn loomed a rapidly declining weather situation. "Everyone could see that the weather was growing worse," noted the officer, "which meant the loss of air support and aerial resupply; that relief from Hagaru in army force less than regimental size could never reach us; that another night of determined attack would surely overrun the position."[30]

Garrigus was probably given authority over the trucks in the convoy, most of which were now heavily loaded with wounded. Vehicles typically carried fifteen to twenty injured men, though some had as many as fifty on board. The beginning of the breakout seemed disorganized, much of this no doubt stemming from the exhaustion of the troops. "I . . . vaguely recall," said one officer, "the confused situation of trucks being lined up under occasional mortar fire."[31] Another reason for the lack of smoothness in the operation may have been caused by very poor communication between scattered groups of GIs. Some of the men did not know a breakout attempt was occurring until they saw trucks and men leaving. Meanwhile, the enemy observing from the high ground as the American vehicles lined up on the road and loaded up the wounded could easily discern what was taking place.

Soon mortar fire rained down on the hapless trucks, causing many casualties and more wounded for the already over-loaded vehicles. Adding to the chaotic conditions was the growing number of killed or wounded officers and noncoms who normally held the enlisted men together in difficult times. Still, preparations continued. Stomping their feet in a hopeless attempt to stay warm, Garrigus and the other truck drivers in the convoy hurriedly drained precious gasoline from nearby inoperable vehicles to fill the working trucks that now held groaning men.

Just as the convoy began to leave, Chinese, swarming down from nearby hills, suddenly overran several key machine-gun defensive positions at the edge of the perimeter and turned those weapons on the American lines. The chance that the convoy would fail was more than Garrigus could stand. Rallying "a group of soldiers," the fearless Garrigus led "a daring charge, regained the machine guns" and immediately turned the weapons "on the enemy, killing 60 or so and wounding many others."[32] Because of Garrigus's bold actions, the Chinese firing died down and the perimeter was safe once more, allowing the convoy to continue.

Given the lack of communication and the loss of leadership, it is not surprising that the column soon began a disorganized fight for survival. One major noted that once started, the troops "flooded down the road like a great mob and tactical control broke down almost immediately. Officers tried frantically to re-establish control and to order men up on the high ground where they could protect the truck column."[33] "We started out in column," Muncy recalled. "So many officers were gone by this time that the sergeants were mostly in charge. Unfortunately, there was hardly any communication from one end of the column to the other. For example, I didn't know of Colonel Faith's death until after we'd escaped. If there'd been a leapfrog movement, where we'd set up safe perimeters, we might have gotten many more out. The way it was though was just chaos."

Except for the men who stayed with the wounded in the truck columns, the march soon deteriorated into an "every man for himself" situation. Muncy was leading one group "of mostly real young kids. Some were just seventeen and had never been in any combat to speak of. A few wanted to stay and fight, but I could tell we were in a bad situation. I told them the only way we were going to get out of there was to fight our way out—kill everything in our path. At every bend in the road the Chinese were waiting for us. They had machine guns set up." At first the GIs loaded up the dead but before long there were just too many bodies. "There was hardly room for the injured," Muncy remembered. "We took dog tags and had to leave the bodies." Soon Muncy and other able-bodied men were spending most of their efforts protecting the wounded in the trucks. "I noticed that there had been a lot of men behind me when we began, but as the line progressed, I'd look back and see fewer and fewer men," said Muncy.[34] Cork shared his memory of the debacle:

> I could not find anyone from my company, so I stayed with company A and was given a position as rifleman on the right flank. The convoy began to move, and I was about 100 yards off to the right of the road. This was not too bad, but as we began to move down the road, keeping up with the convoy was getting harder and harder and most of the men had begun to drift towards the road.
>
> The convoy had been moving for some time, and we crossed a railroad bridge. Some men had fallen off of it and broken through the ice, freezing their clothing. I have a vivid memory of a man getting shot just in front of me. He fell face first and didn't move, so I ran up to him and tried to help him to his feet. I asked a number of other men to help me get him onto the trucks, and most of them just kept walking. I finally had to threaten to shoot one man if he didn't help me. We carried the man over to the road and got a truck to stop, but it was already full of wounded and dead. I believe the main reason that I didn't get any help from most was because they were at the end of their rope.
>
> I was getting there fast myself. By this time there was no organization anywhere that I could see. I had lost contact

with A company and just kept moving, not able to think. The convoy had stopped for some reason, and since I was not with anyone, I moved forward to the front of the convoy.[35]

Many GIs who charged up hills to drive off a Chinese attack just kept going, trying to get to the frozen reservoir and walk to marine lines at Hagaru. The urge to survive now collided with the urge to help wounded comrades. Army medic Hamilton of Solsberry was one of scores of Americans who left the convoy and started up a hill to try and escape to Hagaru. As he began to go over a ridge, however, he heard someone scream for a medic. Hamilton paused for a minute to weigh his decision, then turned to help the wounded man. A friend shouted, as Hamilton started down the hill, "Don't do it," but the courageous Hoosier disappeared around a boulder as he scurried back down the hill to help a fallen comrade; he would never be seen or heard from again.[36]

At about 3:00 P.M. the convoy came to a blown bridge, forcing the trucks to go down into a muddy streambed in order to bypass the blockage. The Chinese brought down especially heavy fire as the vulnerable trucks struggled to churn through the muddy mess below the destroyed span. The deplorable driving conditions were beyond the capabilities of the men now operating the trucks, and the convoy was soon mired down in the worked-up ooze. This circumstance threatened to stop the column in its tracks.

A wounded survivor, Maj. Hugh W. Robbins, recalled the difficulty of the crossing: "For about 100 yards we bounced and crashed up and down . . . with the wounded screaming in anguish as they were jostled and slammed into one another on the truck bed. We came to a final jolting crash and stopped. Our front wheels were down through a crust of ice in a small creek, and no amount of effort on the part of our driver could move that truck."[37] Once more Garrigus rose to the occasion. The resourceful motor pool sergeant was able to put his long hours of driving vehicles through muddy Indiana farm fields to good use. "Under intense enemy fire," Garrigus brought "several trucks across and out of a deep mud hole in the bed of the stream."[38] Cork recalled examining the trucks after they got past the blown bridge and found that it was impossible to place his hand anywhere upon any of the vehicles without touching a bullet hole. Cork also remembered the convoy's ordeal bypassing the blown bridge. It was also during this time that Cork was wounded. He remembered:

> I saw the bridge that had been blown and was wondering what they were going to do. The first trucks of the convoy had driven over the side of the road and down to what may have been a rice paddy that had frozen over. I can remember big chunks of earth that looked to have been plowed up to prevent any vehicle from crossing. There was open water, and I know that they were pulling vehicles through the water and having a hell of a time doing this.
>
> There was mass confusion and a lot of shooting going on. I moved to the left of a vehicle that was being pulled across the frozen mud and water. Then I moved back onto the road where a number of vehicles were across and had formed up. They were getting ready to move out when a lot of shooting began to take place. Someone said to form an assault line and go up the hill to the right. I was a corporal and was put in charge of a few men. We began the assault on the hill and were about halfway up when I saw a Chinese soldier stand up and point his rifle at me. I quickly turned to shoot him, but was shot by him first. I was hit in my right elbow.
>
> At the time I felt a sensation of warmth but it didn't hurt yet. Then I fell down and was unconscious for a while. When I came to, I saw that the hill was littered with bodies and a few men like me were sitting around waiting for something. I wasn't sure what to do next. My arm was starting to hurt, but I could still move it. I wasn't sure if the line of GIs had continued over the hill or not.
>
> I returned back down the hill to where the convoy was still sitting. There was mass confusion, and no one at the time

seemed to be doing anything. I heard my name being called and found a friend in a ditch who had been shot in the groin. He was there with a large group of men who had been wounded, some of which were dead. I talked with the friend for a while, and he asked me what was going on. I had no idea and went looking for somebody to see if we could get the convoy moving again. I went to a 2½ ton truck and tried to wake the driver up, but he was dead. I had another man help me move the body over so I could get behind the wheel. However, after I got the engine started, each time I put it in gear, it would conk out.[39]

Unfortunately for the convoy, it took several precious hours to get the trucks full of wounded GIs to the other side of the destroyed bridge. Daylight was ebbing, and marine air support could no longer protect the men and trucks who struggled down the icy Korean dirt track. Marine aviators flying over their struggling comrades looked down in horror, observing thousands of white-clad Chinese soldiers moving down from the mountains. Aviators Ed Montagne and Tom Mulvihill flew over the struggling column just at dusk. Below them "burning vehicles lay in profusion." More chilling, however, was the sight of "masses of [Chinese] infantry" bearing down upon the Americans, "preparing for killing night assaults."[40]

About the time dusk fell at 5:00 P.M. only twenty-five of the original thirty-five vehicles remained in the column. Perhaps the saddest image of the struggle at this time is one remembered by seventeen-year-old Pvt. Louis Joseph Grappo of the Thirty-second Regiment. As the wounded private moved southward in a truck already dangerously overloaded with injured men, he gazed upon the remaining wounded who were left on the roadside. "They kept reaching out their hands pleading for help," Grappo remembered.[41] Garrigus, perhaps because of his actions back at the blown bridge, now drove the lead truck of the vulnerable convoy. As the vehicles inched forward in low gear, more able-bodied men continued to leave the column, but not Garrigus.

At one point the column was stopped by Chinese fire coming from a hill. "We were pinned down," Muncy remembered. "Some of us went up the hill to try and drive off the Chinese. We went up through this valley trying to find where the firing was coming from. All of a sudden I see dirt spattering around me. I turned and yelled 'machine gun.' I jumped behind a mound and, as I did, got hit in the legs." Muncy was put on the trucks with the wounded. Luckily for Muncy, the injuries were all flesh wounds. "When I took my boot off it was filled with blood, and then my foot swelled and I couldn't get my shoe back on," he said.[42]

Lieutenant Colonel Faith's end came as he was leading the column. At a Chinese roadblock, the Washington native assembled a small group of officers and men to tackle the blockade. The Americans won the engagement but not before Faith had a "gaping hole torn in his side by a exploding grenade." He was placed in one of the trucks where "battered for five days, weak from the cold, and exhausted from his heroic efforts . . . [he] slowly bled to death."[43] Faith received the Congressional Medal of Honor for his efforts. [See appendix for the official citation.]

Around midnight the convoy was about five miles from the marine lines at Hagaru. Enemy fire and mechanical breakdowns had taken its toll on the convoy during that long afternoon, leaving only fifteen bullet-riddled vehicles packed with groaning, wounded men. In the cab of one of the remaining trucks sat Faith's frozen body. At this point the column paused to regroup. Maj. Crosby Miller, who was wounded and barely able to cling to the hood of a jeep, remembers what happened next. The silence was suddenly broken "by two mortar rounds burst[ing] to the right [side] of the road opposite the truck column about 100 yards away. Very shortly, two more rounds hit the right of the road but closer in. It became apparent that soon we would be bracketed. I could visualize the wounded hit again and possibly a truck set fire making us an even better sitting target."

Before the first mortar rounds came, Garrigus had left the cab of the lead truck and "moved a 100 yards [ahead] and had not seen or

Yeddo's Charles Garrigus, Jr. Garrigus was awarded the Distinguished Service Cross in the Chosin battle, a campaign in which the young Hoosier sacrificed his life.

heard any movement." The moment presented the Hoosier soldier with a perfect opportunity to leave the convoy of wounded and escape to Hagaru. Hearing the mortar shelling, however, Garrigus, dead tired, cold, and hungry, reached down into his being and found one last gasp of courage and energy. He approached Miller and begged to lead the convoy in a last-ditch effort to get the trucks and the wounded to Hagaru. "It was a choice between the unknown [and] the known danger," remembered Miller. The major hesitated at Garrigus's request as he numbly gazed down the column of dented and shot up trucks and jeeps. Then he instructed Garrigus "to move out."[44] Word was passed back to prepare for a final run. The motor pool sergeant waited a few moments for the other vehicles to be advised of the plan. While he waited, Garrigus gently revved the engine of his three-quarter-ton truck, listening to the machine's increased pitch as he pressed down on the accelerator. Trucks had fascinated Garrigus since his childhood in Indiana, and now he hoped the few remaining vehicles would help take him and the others to safety. Unfortunately Garrigus did not go far. Two hundred yards down the road "a terrific blast of . . . machine gun fire hit" the lead truck, causing it to crash into a ditch and block the escape for the rest of the convoy.[45] Garrigus perished at the wheel of his vehicle.

Muncy lay in one of the stalled trucks, unaware of Garrigus's last heroic act. Muncy noted: "It was so cold that my watch had stopped. It was about two in the morning. Most of us were out of ammunition. I had only two bullets left myself. Of course most of us who were left were also wounded. Suddenly, someone came along and said the column had stopped, and we had to break up into groups of three or four. We were told to head west where the marine lines were. I had four that came with me, and we went down through this culvert when we heard the Chinese coming. We hid there in the culvert and watched the Chinese strip the bodies. The first thing they went for was GIs shoes. Then they poured gas on the trucks and set them afire. There were still wounded Americans in those trucks."[46] Cork also had an extraordinary escape.

> I got word that the front of the convoy was getting ready to make an attempt to break through the roadblock. I was still able to use my right arm, and I moved forward to where a number of men had gathered. They formed us up and asked everyone how much ammunition we had. I had just a clip for the carbine I was carrying and my 45-caliber pistol.
> I had no idea what time it was, but it had been dark for some while. We began the march, which continued on for what seemed like hours. I remember passing through a small village that had a sawmill in it. Here there was a challenge by a North Korean soldier. I was told not to say anything, to make myself as short as possible and just keep moving. We kept moving until we came to a fork in the road, and the question came up as to which way we should go. We could hear mortar fire to the left and someone said that must be our guns. Since I was a F/O [forward observer] for the 81-mm guns, I said yes, they were 81-mm guns, but it could be Chinese who had captured a lot of our weapons. I think that settled it; we took the right fork and finally ended up at a marine outpost. We were brought into their positions, and from there on I only remember being in a first-aid tent. That morning I was flown out to Japan.[47]

By an odd chance of fate, Donald Mayville worked with and observed both Garrigus and Faith during the American army's doomed struggle east of the Chosin. Mayville served as a radio operator for headquarters company and consequently found himself near Faith during much of the battle. The Michigan native especially recalled the lack of medical aid available to the wounded and the rapid deterioration of the American troops once the Chinese attacked.

> Since our radios were knocked out the first night of attack, and the one radio we had left, a voice radio, could not get out over the surrounding hills on a whip antenna, I was used as a switchboard operator and stringed telephone lines to the line companies. While at the Inlet, where we were first attacked, I went to see Captain Adams and found him gravely wounded in the chest. He started begging me for water, but I knew he couldn't have any with a chest wound. Not being able to give this man a drink made me pretty upset, especially since Captain Adams was such a well thought of officer. He used to come in the Commo area and joke with us a lot of times from Inchon until Chosin. Other officers fell in that initial attack as well. I was stringing a new telephone wire to the Command Post from the switchboard after that first attack, when I saw Lt. Col. William Reilly [Commanding officer, Third Battalion, Thirty-first Regiment] sitting up against the CP building outside, wounded, watching me, probably wondering what a baby faced boy was doing there in such a hellish place. I had my own close calls. The first night of the attack I was in the switchboard room and a bullet came through the wall and hit PFC John Hale in the back and entered his lung. We laid him on the floor and SFC Cutting took over the switchboard. My Radio Chief, Sgt. Maynard, came in and took my rifle and went back outside and was killed as was PFC Joe Harper. Next morning I picked up a rifle from one of the dead.

I recall Major [Harvey] Storms and I left the Inlet together [to join Faith's group]. I was behind the major and when we came to the first cut in the first hill, we were fired upon by some Chinese. We fired back and kept on moving, trying to stay out of sight of them. When we came upon the stalled trucks, I went over about fifty yards to the right to help a soldier lift his friend up on his back and I never saw Major Storms again. I spent the last three days in the Battalion Command Post with Faith and his remaining staff.

Just before Task Force Faith started, I remember Charles Garrigus helping us to load the wounded into the trucks. I don't know how long Garrigus lasted in the driver's seat at the head of the column, as many drivers were being picked off by the Chinese. I do remember that drivers were replaced frequently. One driver would be killed and another would climb in the seat and continue driving until he was killed too, and then another driver took over. After it grew dark, I ran out of ammo. I picked up a friend of mine in my platoon who was shot in the back and half carried and half dragged him with me to the marines at Hagaru-ri, but not until after I saw the Chinese killing the wounded in the trucks. Most of us were out of ammo and could do nothing to help. The injured that could move on their own climbed out of the trucks when they saw the Chinese killing the wounded. I was with the group that Lt. MaGill guided to the marines, where we ended up in the middle of their minefield. When I heard the guard say we had blundered into a minefield, I thought "after coming all this way I get killed in an American minefield." But they came out and guided us through it. Lieutenant Boyer told us at Hagaru that we would forget what we saw at the Chosin after awhile. How wrong he was about that. Ironically, Boyer was killed on the march from Hagaru to Hungnam.

I was in Faith's group when he was mortally wounded while wiping out the Chinese roadblock at Hill 1221. I was wounded at the same time, and when I got to Hagaru found out that I had severe frostbite on both feet and top of my ears. I was given medical treatment and left to sleep in one of the mess tents until I was evacuated the next morning by air from the home made airstrip the marines built. I remember at Hungnam, we couldn't eat a full meal because we had been eating frozen C rations and our stomachs were not ready for hot food. I spent five months in the hospital. The wound healed long before the frostbite. After Faith was mortally wounded and put in his jeep, there was no more organized resistance by American troops on a large scale. Officers and Noncoms and even PFC's took charge in small groups and guided men back to the marines. Many, many, many men made it back on their own, by themselves. I saw numerous brave acts that never got recognized for their valor that ordinarily would have been awarded Silver Stars and Distinguished Service Crosses. The heroic actions I observed from the roadblock at Hill 1221 to Marine Corps lines was something I have never seen in any combat since.[48]

For all purposes, Task Force Faith ended with the crash of Garrigus's truck. "At the end," noted Appleman, "each man had his own adventure, and some lived to tell them."[49] Garrigus and the other members of the task force would not suffer or die in vain. The task force's efforts kept a large number of Chinese tied down for five crucial days, allowing the marines at Yudam-ni to fight their way down to Hagaru where marines and surviving elements of the Seventh Division were miraculously able to retreat to the coast and evacuation.

For those who left the task force convoy and sought the safety of Marine Corps lines, one should mix any judgment with a large dose of mercy. As one survivor noted, "I too did not make that last ditch effort with the column of twenty trucks. I knew it did not stand a chance, but I thought it would make a diversion, thereby making . . . possible . . . a better chance of escape." As Garrigus, this particular survivor was a sergeant in the Thirty-second Regiment. He noted: "When many men look back, they like to think of themselves as heroes, but the truth of the matter is that when the chips are down, most try to save their hides. All I can remember is the cold, inferior clothing, worn-out equipment, the noise, the wounded, the dead."[50]

For several months Gladys and Charles Garrigus, Sr., were told that their son was missing in action, but by early April 1951 the army had pieced together enough information from the accounts of survivors to be certain that Charles Jr. had died while leading the final breakout attempt. In a letter that April, addressed to Gladys Garrigus, General MacArthur wrote that he hoped Gladys could find "some measure of comfort" knowing that her son died "in the service of his country and in the defense of a peace loving people."[51] The fragmented accounts concerning the five-day struggle east of the Chosin also shed light on Garrigus's heroic efforts, and on 7 August 1951 the fallen Indiana man posthumously received the Distinguished Service Cross, America's second-highest military honor "for his valorous conduct."[52] Garrigus's body, along with so many who died in northeast Korea that bitterly cold winter, was never returned to the United States.

While the Eighth fled south and the Tenth Corps struggled in a life-and-death drama to escape the Chinese trap, Hoosier newspapers were once again filled with gloomy reports similar to those that appeared during the dark days of the Pusan perimeter. The *Indianapolis Star* carried an article stating, "We Are Face to Face with World War III" and noted that "the situation in Korea is so desperate that we must hold there without much further retreat for it will be impossible to bring out the bulk of our men if we are pushed into attempting a series of Oriental Dunkirks."[53] The *Terre Haute Tribune* declared, a "big war is started. . . . It's war, big war of unknown duration and unknown, uncertain outcome. . . . War with China, at some point, will merge into world war."[54] The *Evansville Courier*, in an editorial on 8 December 1950, also agreed with the rest of the nation that a war with China was at hand:

How can we go on maintaining the fiction that we are fighting merely North Koreans? We can recognize the fact that we are at war with Red China without committing ourselves to hopeless land battles. We can blockade the Chinese coast. If there is as much discontent inside China as the Formosa nationalists say there is, perhaps a stiff blockade might encourage some revolting on a major scale. Who knows?

A blockade would bring great pressure on China—the China of the "simple agrarians" who, we were told not so long ago, should be appeased and treated well. Millions are starving, as matters stand now, with the best of food being set aside for the army.

It is time we were doing the practical things which can be done in easing the situation of our beleaguered troops in Korea.[55]

The *Indiana Daily Student* carried similar grim headlines: "Trapped 1st Cavalry Troops Must Escape Without Help," noted one banner headline in early November. In early December the same paper declared, "G.I.'s Await Million-Man Chinese Red Horde."[56] *Daily Student* editorials often seemed as if they were speaking about a sporting event between two old rivals rather than a war. "Get tough," argued one piece. "If the Chinese continue to fight, the American and other U.N. forces should 'shoot the works'—bomb Chinese supply lines, and take any other action to let Russia know we are not fooling in Korea or anyplace else."[57] In another issue, the editor encouraged the United States to "keep up the fight."[58] By early December, however, things seemed so grim that the paper lamented:

We are jittery for fear of another major war. The world of peace which we fought for just nine years ago has turned into a sphere of struggle and bloodshed between two political beliefs.

We seem to live in an armed camp, waiting for our former allies to co-operate, or make a false move that might send us into another total war.

While we live and fight for democracy, Communism in the world seems to think force means peace. No war has proved one country wrong and the other right. War merely shows that one country is either larger, has more men and resources, or is more skillful at war.

The world peace organization, the United Nations, has not been effective. While men are dying on battlefields, this group argues about eligibility of nations and stalls on political moves obviously started in the Kremlin to gain its end—world domination. What is the answer? We might pause on this day to consider. There seems to be no real solution to all our problems, except that we must do everything in our power to stop aggression and slavery from enveloping our nation as it has so many others in the last nine years.[59]

In January Jasper's *Dubois County Daily Herald* suggested the answer to the crisis was to "restore the world to its creator," adding, "amid the confusion and turmoil of a world conflict between two diametrically opposed ideologies which threaten to precipitate us into a third world war, there is one hopeful note to brighten the sombre picture of the infant new year of 1951. That note is the rediscovery and general recognition of the Supreme Being, at least on this side of the Iron Curtain. Whatever may be said of 1950, it started the trend, a definite movement that before the end of the year had grown into a crusade—almost a migration of nations, back to the camp of the Lord of Hosts." Even the sports page got a word in on the matter. In one column a syndicated sportswriter declared, "I'm mad. I'm burned up. It seems to me that in this country of yours and mine, we're acting like a lot of jittery old maids. . . . World War III, or no—and probably no—Americans don't belong under a bed wringing their hands."[60]

Regarding the Tenth Corps's perilous situation in early December 1950, the *Indianapolis Star* declared in a glaring headline, "Allies Face Tragic Trap."[61] The *Evansville Courier,* whose community had scores of its sons at the Chosin Reservoir with the First Marine Division, carried a more optimistic headline, telling how the American forces had launched a drive "TO BREAK [the] TRAP."[62] Three days later the *Evansville Sunday Courier and Press* lamented that the war "Appears Militarily Decided; First UN Army Decisively Defeated." A map in the same issue features a map of the "Scene of Dramatic Escape Try."[63]

Editorials in Indiana newspapers screamed for the use of the atomic bomb just as they had in July 1950 when it looked as if the North Koreans were going to push UN forces out of Korea. The *Star* argued, "American troops retreating before the massed divisions of Communist China cannot match the manpower thrown against them. If they could match the firepower of the enemy, however, there might be some hope for victory or at least a successful evacuation from Korea. If atomic bombs can provide the firepower necessary to equalize the strength of our armies and save the six precious divisions we have in Korea, they should be used."[64] Hoosier citizens also warmed up to the idea of using the bomb. One Indianapolis minister, in a letter to the *Star,* argued, "We have the atomic bomb! That is not an accident. It is, in my judgement, God's doing. His plan for mankind runs constant down through the ages. He had a definite end in view. He will not allow all His 'good seed corn' to be destroyed. He has sent his bands of driven saints to this new land for a purpose. His plans punctuate human history. Britain would most certainly have been overrun by an inferior race had not God destroyed the Spanish Armada by letting loose the most terrible gale that ever swept the face of His great deep. That is a comparatively modern instance. God has long been doing things like that all along. The Old Testament history cites repeated instances where a whole people was swept off the earth to make way for his ongoing plan. . . . Yes, we have the atomic bomb thank God."[65]

Another Indianapolis citizen, in a letter to the same newspaper, called for a move to total wartime production. "What is it going to take to get the President to immediately put our manufacturing facilities into war production—manufacturing war planes, guns, tanks, ships to transport our men and war equipment, military clothing, etc. etc. etc.? We should turn to all-out war production at once, back up our soldiers, sailors and marines with the maximum of war equipment and supplies. The men of the armed services will do the job if we at home forget the civilian $ sign and instead produce military tools of war for their use in preserving a free country," said the letter.[66]

Yet another Hoosier called on President Truman to resign: "If Mr. Truman ever had the confidence of the masses of people in this country, he has now lost it. It is time for Mr. Truman to resign. He has been tested and found wanting. With his departure we would then expect the removal of his entire administration. They all have been proven wrong, futile and badly scared. We cannot expect our men in the armed services willingly to follow this type of leadership. We have suffered the worst disgrace in the history of this country. We seemingly are allowing our men in Korea to shift for themselves and evidently we are willing to allow them to be sacrificed without making every effort, including the use of the atomic bomb to back them up."[67]

Gerald H. Hammerstein of Evansville wrote the *Evansville Press,* deploring, "Can't you hear them cry? Can't you perceive their desperation? I'm talking about fellows who are human, God-loving sons of tender mothers, who, but a few short years ago were snuggled and protected with American parental love. And, who at this very hour are quite likely to be praying to God that He takes their parents into His domain so that they shall not suffer to hear of their children's ominous rodent-like death, thanks to us and our foreign policy of appeasement and political ethics toward a horde of infidel Communists." Hammerstein suggested the following answer to this suffering: "If you feel compassion for our hunted, haunted, hungry, harassed, and homesick sons of a beleaguered democracy say it where it will count. Your congressman is Winfield K. Denton, and your senators are Homer E. Capehart and William E. Jenner. Their addresses are House of Representatives, and Senate Office Building, respectively, Washington, D.C. Last reports had Harry S. Truman in Washington, D.C., too."[68]

When news of the Tenth Corps's escape came, the *Courier* in bold headlines declared, "25,000 AMERICANS BREAK OUT OF TRAP." A day later an editorial spoke thankfully of the Tenth Corps's narrow escape.[69] Charles "Barney" Barnard of Oakland City had been one of the fortunate marines to escape the Chinese trap at the Chosin. On 22 December 1950 Barnard wrote a letter to his father sharing his feelings about the dramatic episode, feelings likely shared by many of his comrades. "The fighting is all over for us, at least for the present. I think that people in the United States are beginning to realize there's a war over here," wrote Barnard. "Before, no one payed much attention to it, unless they had someone over here. The Marine Corps had taken quite a few losses, although not as bad as we first thought. I think around seven thousand killed, wounded, and missing. Frost bite is one thing which took a heavy toll. We were all hoping that the government will make some kind of peace treaty." Barnard closed his letter by summing up his feelings on the Korean matter: "We don't want this country, it isn't worth keeping."[70]

In January 1951 the parents of Donald Hamilton received a letter from a Japanese friend of their son's. Her name was Sadako, and she and the Greene County native had talked of marriage. The young woman shared her grave concern for Hamilton's safety, "I received from him, last time he written me 4 of November. I haven't received any letters since. Perhaps I worry too much. What do you think about him? Do you think he got wounded. . . . I don't think so, also I hope not so."[71] The Hamilton family suffered many years of agonizing doubt because their son was listed as missing in action. As for Sadako, she never saw her lover again.

"I'D GIVE ANYTHING TO GET OUT OF THIS LINE COMPANY."

Letter from a Hoosier marine in Korea, September 1951

"YOU WILL HAVE MY UTMOST; I SHALL EXPECT YOURS."

Gen. Matthew Ridgway upon taking command in Korea

CHAPTER FIVE

THE IMPERFECT WAR

At the time of the Eighth Army's hasty retreat and the Tenth Corps's narrow escape, the war began transforming into its final form. Ironically, it was the Chinese who were now confronted with the temptation to cross the thirty-eighth parallel and unite the two Koreas. Just before Christmas 1950, however, both sides—the UN forces and the Chinese—paused to regenerate. Part of this downtime was because the fleeing UN troops moved south quickly by modern transportation and the Chinese were on foot and unable to keep up. Fate, however, wrought an important change to the war. The Eighth's commander, Gen. Walton H. Walker, lost his life in a traffic accident on an icy Korean road in late December and was replaced by square-jawed Gen. Matthew Ridgway. Ridgway faced what appeared to be an insurmountable task. Since the Chinese drive, the Eighth had fallen back almost three hundred miles while the Tenth Corps recouped near Pusan, leaving the American troops holding a line roughly at the same point as where they had started in July 1950. The new commander was shocked at the lack of morale among his new charges and quickly made plans to put the UN forces back on the offensive as soon as possible. Touring among his men, the rugged Ridgway declared, "You will have my utmost; I shall expect yours."[1] Ridgway's confident manner and practical fighting strategies soon helped turn the tide for the UN effort.

The aggressive Ridgway wanted to launch an immediate attack on the Chinese, but his broken army was not ready for an offensive. Instead, as fighting slacked around Christmas, the Americans rebuilt and rested. One Indiana marine, recuperating with the First Division near Pusan, wrote his mother on 24 December, telling her, "Well, tomorrow is Christmas, and we . . . have a huge tree in the mess tent with decorations." Having gone several days without substantial food at the Chosin, the young Hoosier wrote again two days later, emphasizing the wonderful meal he had received for the holidays: "We had turkey, dressing, shrimp cocktail, corn, peas, mashed potatoes, sweet potatoes, olives, pickles, celery, mince pie, fruit cake, fruits, and nuts."[2] Rest and good, hot food, however, did not last long.

On 1 January 1951 the Chinese began another drive south, the first since the November/December debacle. UN forces again gave ground, but this time, as Ridgway noted, "as a fighting army, not as a running mob."[3] Now the situation of late 1950 was reversed, with the Chinese troops finding themselves greatly overextended. By the middle of the month the Chinese drive had bogged down. During the offensive the UN forces had given up real estate in order to buy time, and Ridgway realized that his forces could not move beyond the thirty-eighth parallel unless the United States was willing to commit to a much larger war. Knowing this was not likely to happen, he devised a plan emphasizing firepower over manpower. Ridgway believed that the Chinese eventually would tire of their great losses and agree to recognize the thirty-eighth parallel as the boundary of the two Koreas. Although a wise strategy, it exacted a great number of American lives.

Around February 1951 the marines were moving north into the guerrilla-infested tract around Andong. The marines had yet to be placed near the firing line, as they were still recuperating from their Chosin ordeal. Hoosier marine reservist Robert Whitehouse recalled one particular episode following an incident in which a marine radioman was killed by a guerrilla sniper. Whitehouse said:

The fire came from a village, and the old man [commanding officer] was so enraged by our guy's death that he ordered us into the town to seek out and destroy the enemy. We started burning down some huts, not knowing the North Koreans had stored ammunition in the thatch roofs. Soon ammo was going off all over the place. On top of that, we were told to expect booby traps as well. I was walking down a street, very cautiously, watching for any guerrillas who might pop out of a building. I finally came to this fairly large structure and inside I could hear a whining noise. It sounded like a little crying kid. I went in pretty fast, not taking as much time as I should have because I thought a kid was hurt somewhere inside. A gunnery sergeant snapped at me, warning me to slow down and check things out, but I was in too big a hurry.

Inside I found a lot of these big ceramic pots, large enough for a man to hide in. Meanwhile, the whining I had heard to begin with turned out to be coming from in back. As I moved in that direction, I saw that a huge sliding door had been knocked down and set afire. It was still smoldering when I came up to it. The whining sound was coming from beneath. Without thinking I picked the door up and found a shivering wet dog. I picked the poor thing up and tried to settle it down. While the poor pooch was licking my face, the gunnery sergeant came up to

Evansville's Robert Whitehouse takes a break during the static portion of the war.

me and said, "Well, Bob, that was real smart. Not only could you have been killed, but you've saved a dog so someone can eat it later." I felt kind of bad about the whole deal and was worried about what would happen to this poor dog. The sergeant had been right about the dog getting served up for dinner. The Koreans often ate dog.

As we walked out of the building, our colonel drove up and saw me with the dog. He said, "What do you have there, marine?" and I showed him the animal. Then I heard him say "I use to have a dog just like that." So I said, "Well, sir, would you like to have this one?" Turned out he took the dog so I didn't have to worry about it anymore. I understand he kept it for some time.[4]

As the marines wrestled with clearing out bands of guerrillas, the army began to put Ridgway's plan of attrition into practice. The UN forces drew the Chinese into battle, then used their superior firepower to kill as many of the enemy as possible. Giving up ground no longer mattered as long as the enemy sacrificed great numbers. Scottsburg's Carl Spencer vividly recalled the tough fight back to the thirty-eighth parallel. "It seemed like it was just one hill after another. One time we went for thirty-seven straight days, taking hill after hill. This was in the winter, and it had snowed more than usual and was very cold. We'd take the hills in the daylight, and the Chinese would attack in the evening, usually after midnight. I suppose the Chinese knew we were not accustomed to thirty-inch snows. They were dressed in these thinly padded coats and wore tennis shoes. I don't know how they did it."

Spencer recalled that most of the battles the Second Division fought with North Koreans "were in our favor. We didn't back down. I can't remember losing a hill to them. With the Chinese, however, there were just so many of them that they'd back us up. They just kept on coming at you. Fortunately, our artillery and planes really made a difference and helped equalize the number problem."

About the time of the Eighth's resurgence, Spencer recalled resting in a foxhole when his group came into contact with an enemy patrol. "They were about fifty feet in front of us. I heard some mumbling then saw a light from a small flashlight. It was 37 degrees below zero that night. I suspected they were huddled together looking at a map," he recalled. "When I saw that light pop on, I got a grenade and threw it on the other side of them for illumination. Then I began firing. Of course I drew all their fire, but then one of our machine guns opened up too. The next morning we found four wounded and three dead." Another time, while Spencer lay in a foxhole at night, a Chinese soldier crawled over close to where the Hoosier lay and requested to trade some pot for some American cigarettes. "I told him 'yeah, here are some cigarettes' and I popped over a grenade. I missed him, and he started cursing me, told me I didn't have any principles." In another instance about this time, Spencer watched a GI who had just lost both his feet jump off a stretcher and start walking on the stumps of the bones after being given too much morphine.[5]

During the transitional period of the war, the UN air force contributed essential efforts to the war cause. Indeed, the air force had been a fundamental part of the UN endeavors since the war erupted. During the period of the Pusan defense, for example, the UN control of the skies had been of primary importance. Like the navy, the air force attacked enemy supply lines, ranging "over the whole peninsula, hitting truck convoys, rail lines, marshaling yards, bridges," and any concentration of troops that could be found. As the war on the ground moved to its static stage in late 1951, the tempo of the air war greatly increased. By early 1952 the UN applied the "leverage of air power to try and achieve a settlement."[6]

Perhaps those who were most appreciative of the air force's efforts were those Americans such as Spencer, who occasionally found themselves surrounded and trapped by the Chinese and North Koreans. Spencer, who fought in the desperate battle of Chipyong-ni, recalled, "Luckily for us our planes dropped in plenty of supplies. I saw a lot of them shot down getting stuff to us.

The pilots were real unsung heroes."[7] Another Hoosier, William Cunningham, who loaded planes with supplies dropped to the surrounded marines at the Chosin, saw the great holes that had been cut into the planes' metal bodies by enemy fire. "You could see a lot of daylight through the holes," Cunningham recalled.[8] Many Hoosiers, such as Dexter Crane of Loogootee and Marvin Boeglin of Huntingburg, served in the air force.

Boeglin had been ready to start his senior year in high school when South Korea was invaded. After his senior year, Boeglin "went to the recruiter's office at Washington, Indiana. The marine quota was full for that month, so I turned around and went to the air force recruiter's office across the hall. . . . When I was accepted into the U.S. Air Force, I was very interested in getting into an 'outfit' that involved flying. After basic training, I had a choice to go to gunnery school or air refueling training. I chose gunnery school; therefore, I was on my way to combat-crew training, where I would become a member of a flight crew as an aerial gunner."

Boeglin was assigned as a combat-crew member (gunner) on a B-26 Invader (light bomber). The young Huntingburg man was twenty years old when he arrived in Korea. Within two weeks he was flying missions from Kunson air base. "We had three squadrons of B-26s and two squadrons of F-84 jet fighters, so it was a very busy place. The B-26s were twin engine planes and very sturdy. We flew a lot of night missions, dropping bombs on trains and truck convoys. We'd look for their lights, in the distance. Once we marked the lights, we'd have

Marvin Boeglin of Huntingburg. An air force gunner, Boeglin flew on the last bombing mission of the war.

them even if they turned their lights off when they finally heard our engines. We'd drop flares then fly out of the light. I was able to watch through the plexiglass, and often I saw the enemy trying to put out the fires our bombs had started. We flew all the way to the Yalu [River], and sometimes did daytime bombings. They worked the B-26s almost 'round the clock some times. When a plane landed, they'd just bring on a new crew."

The missions that Boeglin and others carried out could be deadly. "One of my best friends, George Cherrington of Galesburg, Illinois, was shot down. He was a very religious man and very responsible," said Boeglin. "George and I had trained together. He even came home one time on furlough to Huntingburg to meet my family. On his last mission, George had volunteered to replace a young gunner, who George believed wasn't ready to fly on this particularly dangerous assignment. George's plane was shot down, and only two were able to escape the spiraling plane. George was not one of them."[9]

Letters written home by Boeglin at this time give some indication of how dependent the war efforts were on the air force and how little time crews had to rest. In one he noted to his wife, "I didn't get a letter written last night because of my missions. I got #35 in last night, #36 this morning, and I'm going for #37 tonight. . . . I've had about 5 hours sleep in the last three days. Maybe we'll get back early tonight and I can get to bed for a change. Hon, I'm sorry for the short letter. I hope I get one from you tomorrow. I'm so tired I can hardly hold this pen." In another note Boeglin reported to his wife, "I went to the 3:30 combat briefing and then ate a little chow. I went to Mass and Communion at 5 o'clock and then came back to the hut. The engineers and I then went out and checked over the plane. I armed the turret and then came back to the hut. I laid down and slept a while and just woke up about a half hour ago. I feel a lot better now. I have to shave and shower in a few minutes again. I love this good old water over here."[10]

Dexter Crane joined the air force in January 1951 with sixteen other young men from the Loogootee area. "At that time the war was getting hot, and I had always wanted to go into the air force and fly. On the other hand, my father didn't want me to go into the service, but when I turned twenty-one I joined anyway. Things looked very bad over there at the time," said Crane. He took advance instruction at Lackland Air Force Base, San Antonio, Texas, to become an airplane engine mechanic. The Loogootee man then began working on C-119 cargo planes. "In September of 1952, I volunteered for Korean duty. We flew out of Japan. There I was a mechanic, then crew chief. Later I became a flight engineer. I recalled that sometimes I flew thirty-six hours without sleep. There was very little rest."

Not only was air force duty difficult in terms of a lack of rest, but it could also be dangerous. Crane remembered, "We often flew in without escorts and between the mountains to drop supplies. I remember one of the planes which flew in a sister squadron had a monkey they kept and sometimes took along for luck. The plane went down on a mission and all aboard perished, including the monkey." Crane's group called themselves the Pack Rats. "We dropped supplies all over South Korea. We also hauled the dead back to Japan. The smell was almost unbearable, but we put up with it because they were our boys," said Crane.[11]

By February 1951 the fighting began to intensify. Harold "Sonny" Bender of Boonville served with the army's Twenty-third Regiment, Second Division. He had been in Korea for less than a week when he first faced combat. In a letter written to his mother on 12 February, just three days before one of the pivotal battles of the war, Bender tells of the discomforts and dangers he faced. He wrote:

Dear Mom,

    I am writing in my foxhole, and my hands are awfully cold. This is the first time I've had a chance to write. I am about 20 miles south of Seoul. It might help you to know that I was assigned to a mortar squad and I am behind the front lines. It is awfully hard work, but there is a better chance of coming home.

I don't know whether we will stop at the 38th or not. We are not very far from the parallel. My foxhole is up on the side of a mountain looking south over a railroad trestle that has been bombed out. The big guns are going off all the time shooting over our heads. The chow here is not too bad, but there is no PX here, so if you get a chance please mail me a box of candy bars, etc. It snowed all night last night and it is about 5 below 0 at night around here. It becomes fairly moderate during the day.

I am in the 2nd division, and there is a lot of talk that maybe we will be pulled out and sent to Europe. I sure hope so! As for me, I sure would like to know what we are fighting for. It certainly couldn't be for this land nor the people in it. The land isn't worth anything, being all mountains, and the people don't care one way or another. There are plenty of Chinese around here, but we are pretty safe. They outnumber us almost 20 to 1, but we have better guns and equipment. They have no air force nor artillery; that is what makes it somewhat safe. There is nothing to fear except guerilla bands that are in the mountains around us. I will write as much as I can this time because it is difficult to say when I will have another chance. From here on, if I fail to write often don't worry because I will be back someday.

This war over here is the worst fighting our troops have ever undergone according to the men that were in the last war too. You have to fight the cold as well as the enemy. But as cold as it is, I hate to see summer come, because when it does, the rain starts and a foul odor arises from the ground because these people use human excretion for fertilizer. All streams are polluted and drinking water is hard to get. We were issued large cold weather sleeping bags about two inches thick that zip up all around you, but there is one catch. You can't use them, because if you did you would never get out in time, in case there was a raid.

I sure wish I could go back to Japan. It is such a much nicer country and the people in it are much nicer. These South Koreans bow to you every time you get near one. It is hard to get used to. Well, I'd better sign off as it is getting dark, and we can't have lights after dark.

Lots of love and don't worry!

Sonny

One of the most crucial battles of the Korean War took place in early February 1951, and many Hoosiers participated. A tremendous Chinese onslaught caused the Eighth to fall back. As the Americans retreated, the Chinese were able to surround the Twenty-third Regiment at a little hamlet called Chipyong-ni. The village stood at a key position for protecting the withdrawing UN troops. The Chinese were determined to wipe out the American regiment and relentlessly pressed their attack. For three long bitter days and nights, American troops along with a French battalion fought a desperate fight for survival at Chipyong-ni. In a letter dated 19 February 1951, Bender recalled the battle while downplaying his part in it. He wrote:

Dear Mom,

Well, I get a chance to write now; up until last night we were completely surrounded and mail couldn't go out. You might have read about the battle in the papers. It lasted almost 3 days and 2 nights and the 2nd Division together with the French killed 36,000 Chinese. Every day when the sun would rise up and the battle sort of died down, we could look across the rice paddies and see the dead Chinese, like flies on flypaper. . . . The battle started at 9 p.m. February 13th and lasted 3 days. The first night I kept peeking out of my foxhole with a ringside seat to the battle. I tried to see something to shoot at, but didn't have much luck so I finally went to sleep and slept through the thickest part of the fight.

It looked about like the 4th of July; all you could see were tracer bullets, rockets, and flares.[12]

Spencer, also with the Twenty-third, recalled how American and French troops found themselves in a bowl-like area surrounded by thousands of Chinese. "Our intelligence had goofed up because there was a railroad tunnel into our area and about eight hundred Chinese had been able to sneak into our lines. This was going on while we were attacked from the outside, too. It was a mess. Luckily for us, our planes dropped in plenty of supplies. I saw a lot of them shot down getting stuff to us. Those pilots were real heroes," he said. Because the Americans were not only surrounded, but also had Chinese who had infiltrated the perimeter, UN troops were unable to take prisoners during the struggle. "We couldn't let another night come and they be in there with us," Spencer recalled sadly. "We just didn't have enough men to guard them."

The fighting at Chipyong-ni was some of the most ferocious of the war. Spencer vividly remembered how "the Chinese and us were almost on top of each other, and they had us surrounded." The Hoosier native suffered two wounds while fighting. "I saw a Chinese throw a grenade at me and dived into some brush just as it went off. It got me with some shrapnel," he said. "Then I made the mistake of taking my eyes off the one who'd thrown the grenade; there were just so many Chinese to shoot at. While I was distracted elsewhere, the fellow that had hurled the grenade shot at me, and the shells hit my rifle. A part of my rifle was then pushed into my hand. That hurt worse than the grenade explosion."[13]

While Spencer, Bender, and their comrades fought and suffered in Chipyong-ni's life-and-death drama, a unit of the First Cavalry Division was sent to help break the siege. Winslow native Stanley Nelson, who served as a combat engineer, recalled being approached about the mission. "An officer came along asking for volunteers to ride on the front of a lead tank to look for mines. We'd done this many times before, and when the sergeant volunteered, I told him 'No way, it's about my turn!' I just thought it was going to be a kind of [a] routine run." The night before the mission, however, Nelson had a disturbing dream that he couldn't shake. "I dreamed I walked into Williams Café back home in Winslow, Indiana, on crutches. It seemed so real I had trouble putting it out of my mind." Nelson soon had plenty to occupy him to get his mind off his dream. The Hoosier native was about to experience one of the most incredible adventures of any American GI in the war who lived to tell about it.

"The day started out much like any other day. At that time I did not realize that in the next few hours my life would be changed forever, both mentally and physically." Oddly enough Nelson and his comrades were not told the exact nature of their mission, that they were going to attempt to break through to Chipyong-ni. Nelson, however, thought it odd that so many tanks were being assembled for the task. "I was beginning to notice this was going to be a larger operation than usual," he said. "Several tanks, about twenty-three as I learned later, and a company of infantry were assembling. Ahead, about two and a half miles, was a mountain range. The road we were on led straight to the mountains, and the air force had begun bombing and strafing the mountainsides that were ahead of us. It appeared that no one could survive such an assault; however, I knew better. It was a clear day, and the ground was well covered with heavy snow. The temperature was about zero." At this time a request came for five volunteers to sit on the lead tanks and watch for mines. Since Nelson had often performed this task before, he volunteered. He recalled:

> My job was to clear mines that might be in the road and to protect the blind side of the tank. There was a 50-caliber on the turret of the tank which I would man. We also had several charges of TNT prepared to blow mines or other obstacles that might be in the road. The first few tanks in front had no one on them except another combat engineer and myself. The tanks to the rear were loaded with infantry. Finally, the column started to move a few hundred yards

into a no-man's-land. We received a few rounds of heavy mortar fire, and I was knocked from the tank. Someone in the tank noticed this and stopped and let me get back on. Then we continued toward the foot of the mountain.

As the column proceeded up the mountain, enemy small-arms fire intensified. Nelson, firing his tank's 50-caliber machine gun, soon ran out of ammunition, leaving him only his rifle for defense.

Nelson said that nearly halfway "up the mountain the column stopped for a few minutes. Suddenly we were in the middle of several hundred Chinese." The fanatical Chinese troops, carrying satchel and pole charges, fell on the column in waves. "As my tank was stopped, I leaped from the tank to a small ditch for cover. In doing so I had jumped over the head of a Chinese soldier. As I hit the snow and rolled, he was on top of me instantly. He began trying to beat me to death with a wooden pole he was carrying. He struck down on my head hard twice, but I was able to knock him off his feet. Now we were fighting hand to hand and somehow my left forefinger and thumb got in his mouth, and he was biting very hard. If I was going to escape, I had no choice but to gouge out his eyes." When the enemy stood up, screaming in pain, an American on one of the tanks shot and killed the Chinese soldier, enabling Nelson to scramble back on to the tank. The bite marks would be permanently embedded on the remaining parts of Nelson's fingers.

The movement of the column continued as did the ferocious Chinese attacks, and Nelson climbed back on one of the tanks. He began reloading magazines for another soldier. "I was on that tank for only a few minutes when I received a bullet through the center of my left foot. I knew this was very bad because the foot was totally blown apart. About nine or ten others that were on the tank were also wounded as badly or worse than I was. I beat on the turret of the tank and asked the tank commander to let the wounded be put inside the tank. He replied there was no room in the tank for the wounded. Then he announced he was going to stop the column and that the wounded were to unload to the side of the road in the snow-covered rice paddy. He said if we did not and fell in front of the tanks he would be forced to run over us," said Nelson. Most of the wounded soldiers dropped off the tanks and crawled to the rice paddy.

The column moved ahead as the wounded Americans, including Nelson, were left behind. As soon as the last tank had passed by, the Chinese began to shoot into the pile of wounded GIs lying on the frozen ground. Nelson recalled "being shot through my right shoulder, side of the neck, and right ankle. Everyone else that was near me was being shot also. I could feel or hear the bullets ripping through flesh." A few minutes after the firing ceased, the Chinese started to mill around very cautiously. "They checked our hands for watches and rings and our mouths for gold filling in our teeth," said Nelson. "They knew that most carried wallets, so they checked pockets. Then they began to take our heavy winter clothing, field jackets, and parka overcoats. For some reason they must have thought I was too much alive because a Chinese soldier took his bayonet on his rifle and pushed it into my ribs. I dared not move."

Then for some unknown reason one of the Chinese soldiers became enraged at Nelson and "jumped astraddle of me and began beating me in the head with a GI entrenching tool, using the sharp side. After two licks I think I could hear someone screaming for him to stop. The beating stopped and I slumped back into my helmet, which was filled with blood. The blood had started to run back into my nose. I was afraid to move, however, so I tilted my head to the side and let the blood run out of my helmet all the while trying not to be noticed. After searching and kicking us again a few more times, this group of Chinese moved out into the mountains."

Nelson now lay in the freezing cold, half dressed, listening to the sounds of dying men all around him. "I remember most called for their mothers or talked to their mothers telling them how sorry they were that their death would bring such grief to the family. It had now become dark, and I kept thinking I could crawl back to our lines; however, I was not able to move more than two or three feet," he said. "Again I could hear people talking and their feet crunching in the snow. I lay really still hoping to gain no attention. When the group stopped near me I could make out that they were American POWs." This group was a band of captured American infantry who had been assigned to guard the tank column but had at some point been left behind by the tanks. "Most were wounded and were trying to carry or help one another. There was an officer in the group who recognized that I was not part of the infantry that had been with the tanks," said Nelson. "He asked me what I was doing here, and I stated that I was with the combat engineers who had led the column. He said, 'You had it pretty tough, didn't you?' As we were talking, two Chinese soldiers tried to pick me up, but after carrying me a few feet, they threw me down and stated that I was too big."

About this time a Chinese officer put his pistol to Nelson's head. "I was so scared that I literally could not speak. All he had to do was pull the trigger a little tighter," Nelson said. "The American officer who had just come along began to plead for my life through an interpreter and admonished the Chinese officer of the Geneva Convention. He also told me I was a POW and that I should act like one. This moment has never left my mind. I believe my heart was beating so loudly that it could be heard. My only thought at that moment was that I would bring unbearable grief to my mother if I died." Fortunately for Nelson, the American officer's pleas were successful and the Winslow man's life was spared. "The officer also talked with two or three other Americans that were in the rice paddy with me but was unable to help any of them because there was no one able to carry out any more wounded. None of us looked like we could survive the night anyway. However, before they left, the American officer told me that he would try and get me out of there," Nelson remembered.

The Chinese pulled out, leaving the wounded Hoosier in the bitter cold to fend for himself. However, more Chinese soon came by. "The POWs and the Chinese moved out, and it was quite awhile before another group of Chinese soldiers walked past. This group again kicked and searched a few of us, but they did not shoot anyone. I was beginning to wonder if I would make it back to Winslow, Indiana, and if I didn't, how this would affect my mother," said Nelson. "I began to feel colder and colder as the Chinese had taken my winter clothing. After some time there seemed to be a faint warmth come over my body. I was unaware that I was freezing and getting frostbite." As if things were not bad enough already, Nelson now experienced the terror of a heavy artillery bombardment by his own troops. "It was not long before a barrage of artillery came in on me, and the ground started to explode all around me. I did not hear this barrage come in. One round hit near my feet and I was hit again in the foot and leg," he said. "A piece of shrapnel tore the remainder of my left foot off. Another piece took the entire calf off my leg and a seven-inch piece of bone out of my fibula. Again I thought this might be the end. Luckily, that was the last shelling we would receive that night. I was still alive and still had a glimmer of hope." By this time Nelson was literally freezing to death. Salvation, however, came to him in an unexpected form. Nelson said:

> I again heard footsteps crunching in the frozen snow. I lay very still. This person turned out to be the Good Samaritan who probably saved my life. It was a Chinese corpsman or aid person. I expected very little. I spoke some Chinese and told him that I was very cold and I was thirsty. I had been eating the blood-soaked snow that was around my head. The soldier took out a canteen of water and poured me a small drink in a gourd cup and then he bandaged my foot and head. After that he lit a cigarette and put it in my mouth. He did me no harm, just left and went back down the mountain. To my amazement, he returned

Stanley Nelson convalescing after losing a leg in the battle of Chipyong-ni. Nelson received a Silver Star and a croix de guerre in that battle.

later with a large straw mat which he wrapped around me very carefully. He also took one of his winter mittens and put it on my left hand, which had been bitten by a previous soldier. Nothing was said except "thanks friend." I believe at this time all the other wounded had died that were there with me in the rice paddy.

Nelson's rescue occurred the next morning. "I had not heard anyone for some time with the exception of some small-arms fire and some artillery," he said. "That was all I heard for the remainder of the night. There was a light dusting of snow, and the moon was very bright at times. When morning came, I was still alive. I had hope." Nelson's first sign of rescue took the form of an American helicopter flying up and down the mountainside. "I could tell by the tubes on the side they were flying out the wounded from Chipyong-ni," Nelson said. "After a few passes the helicopter stopped and hovered over me and the dead. I could feel the turbulence from the rotors as they came close." Nelson was able to move his right arm a little but thought they failed to see him, or they thought it was a trap and were afraid to land. "As they left, my heart seemed to go with them. It must have been in early afternoon that I began to hear motors in the distance. They seemed to be coming closer and closer. I was not sure if it was our troops. After some time it was quite apparent that there was a convoy of trucks and jeeps coming up the mountain toward me. As they came closer and started to pass, I moved my arm trying to wave. I heard one of the soldiers on the truck say 'hey, there is one still alive.' The truck moved on and a jeep pulled to the side and picked me up. I was loaded into the jeep and driven to Chipyong-ni. I remembered hearing the officer that picked me up tell the medics in the aid tent that this soldier had been out on the mountain all night and to see that he got attention soon. I was given shots and a water soaked gauze bandage to chew on. I was eventually evacuated through channels to the fourth field hospital."[14] For his efforts, Nelson was awarded a Silver Star and croix de guerre. The citation for the Silver Star read in part:

During the engagement of Task Force Crombex, Private Nelson courageously engaged the enemy to prevent attempts to destroy the armor and covered his tank's blind side with his own weapon. Although hostile rocket launcher crews made all-out attempts to stop the advancing column, and fanatical troops carrying satchel and pole charges attacked the column in waves, Private Nelson, though wounded, constantly displayed outstanding fighting qualities and an eagerness to close with the Chinese. Aided by his courage and selfless devotion to duty, Task Force Crombex smashed through the 4½ mile defensive position, killing over 500 enemy, and arriving at the objective in time to repulse a strong assault by the Chinese against the encircled 23rd Infantry Regimental Combat Team. Private Nelson's gallantry reflects great credit on himself and the military service.[15]

The French commander at Chipyong-ni, Lieutenant Colonel Monclar, was so moved by the efforts of Americans such as Nelson and Spencer that he recommended several men, including these two Hoosiers, for the rare French military honor, the croix de guerre. Interestingly, a month after the Chipyong-ni siege, Oakland City's Gordon Greene accidentally met Monclar. He told of this chance encounter in a letter to his mother. "Back at Wonji, I walked up to this French battalion, and I was giving them cigarettes, sharing gear, etc. when up walked this commander whose picture was in *Life*. All the French snapped to attention, and I was dumbfounded, I just stood there. I told him that I was a U.S. marine and he invited me to have a cup of coffee. I really like the French; they're alright."[16]

The eventual success of Chipyong-ni's defense in February 1951 was an important turning point in the war. By blunting this major Chinese drive, UN forces halted the enemy's advance and disrupted their overall plan. Historian Clay Blair considered the episode one of the more pivotal aspects of the war. The Twenty-third's stand, "which had shattered major elements of four Chinese . . . divisions, was . . . one important tile in the mosaic of victory at this time." All in all, the Eighth's work in February 1951 came to be "one of the greatest victories in the history of the United States Army."[17] The Chinese, however, made two more pushes before the war became static along the thirty-eighth parallel.

On 22 April 1951 tens of thousands of Chinese and regrouped North Koreans attacked all along UN lines. Much like the late-1950 Chinese entrance into the war, the enemy's spring offense came as a cruel and unexpected shock. The degree of surprise of the Chinese attack was evident in two letters written in February by a Hoosier marine. In one he notes, "It looks to me as if we're waiting for spring, and then we'll get into high gear and finish this up." Toward the beginning of March the Indiana marine was even more optimistic: "I think that when we reach the parallel the chinks will be ready to talk peace terms. We're sure giving them a working over."[18] A series of letters written by Robert "Bud" Fitch to his parents back in Indiana also conveyed a strong flavor of what life was like on the line in the days leading up to the 22 April battle. In a 17 February 1950 letter, Fitch described life in a combat zone and complained about the cold:

> Well the picnic is over. We are here at a base close to Pohong or Pohong-Dong (they are both the same place). The whole 7th Regiment is here, but I don't know where any of the rest of the 1st is. The Reg. just got back after 10 days rest so we should be here at least a week. There are a lot of us in this tent. We sleep on the ground and have our gear piled all around, over, and under us. We have a small stove and some oil lamps. I can hardly see to write though. After all my training in telephone and then rifle man, I got put in a mortar section, since I was in the mortars back in the reserves. This camp is set up in a sea of mud but is frozen most of the time anyway. It is quite cold and a really sharp wind blows all the time.

A week later a letter from Fitch described the first time he saw the raw horrors of war. "It took us three days to move up from Pohong, and we rode on open trucks all the way. The roads were bad, and we had to wait sometimes for 4-6 hours while we forded where bridges were blown out. It sure got cold and my rear end is flat. There are some gooks lying around here, but they are froze so they don't smell." In March, on the first month anniversary of his being in Korea, Fitch's letter conveyed a sense of his growing confidence as a marine. "We are waiting for an air strike on a hill we have to take. The 5th Marines (who have been in reserve) were supposed to take this objective, but they didn't get here in time, so the 7th is going ahead. We are now taking the city of Hongchon (see map) which will put us about 8 miles from the 38th. The first battalion is taking the mountains, overlooking it." Fitch also noted the difficulties and discomforts endured by he and his comrades: "A lot of time up here they can't get chow to us and there is hardly any water. I thought maybe we would get a chance to wash up when we got down by some water, but we didn't even stop. We found a spring though and had some water to drink. Also we got some candy bars and a half loaf of bread to go with our rations." The letter, similar to most written by Hoosiers in Korea, speaks of the harsh weather. "We walk over here all the time with our gear, and it sure is a time. With all those clothes on, I sweat when I am moving, and then I get cold when I stop. It's hard to write with mittens on. Well that's about all the news for now, so I'll sign off. I am fine and hope you are all okay," Fitch said. Two months after coming to Korea, Fitch found himself in the middle of an important marine operation. On 17 March 1951 he wrote his parents telling them in some detail what his life was like:

> I just wrote yesterday, but I am behind and I have a chance, so I will rattle off a few lines. We took our hill this morning and have set up a roadblock. We are supposed to be relieved by the 5th marines tonight or in the morning. They are three days late now. We will probably be off the

lines a few miles and have a chance to clean up. I broke down and washed up today. Also brushed my teeth. First time in 17 days.... It is warming up some, and we will soon be able to get rid of our Parkas and shoe pacs. Still gets plenty cold at night, though. We got an egg, a loaf of bread for every four men, and a can of beer today: what surprises! We are fighting the gooks the only way it can be done—by assaulting every mountain and ridge by foot.

By late March, Fitch and many of his comrades were desperately hoping that the war might end once UN forces reached the thirty-eighth parallel. In a letter written on 24 March, the young man shared his hope with his father and gave him some specific information about the enemy's technology:

I guess you read the letters I wrote mom and have got most of the details. I sure enjoy your letters and the clippings you send. We have reached the 38th almost all along the line now. If they decide not to cross, the fighting might come to a close. It's out of our hands now for sure. Contrary to most reports the "chinks" we have run into are well equipped and have clean uniforms and are quite husky and well fed. You are right; we have a tremendous advantage of firepower. When we attack a position, we call in air strikes, pound them with artillery and mortars, and then rake them with machine

A photo of Hoosier Robert "Bud" Fitch taken shortly before his death. A number of letters written to his parents in Oakland City chronicle Fitch's difficult journey and ultimate fate.

gun fire. When you see how well dug in they are, you see how they were able to stay. They have some artillery and mortars and are very effective at the use of it.

In early April Fitch's group began to hit heavy Chinese resistance after the Americans crossed the thirty-eighth parallel. Details from a letter conveyed Fitch's growing awareness of the powerful Chinese presence:

> Well, we crossed the 38th yesterday, and we sure hit the chinks. April 4, we were set up on the highest mountain (naturally) overlooking the 38th, and the 4th we took the hill we are on now. We are supposed to be the first unit of the 8th Army to assault a position across the 38th. We are set up in a former chink position so we didn't have to dig any holes. They are sure dug in around here. You can tell they have been here quite a while. We have been moving ahead at top speed for about five days, and we are losing a lot of men because their legs are going out. Our section's chief left us the day before yesterday. His legs just couldn't take it any longer. We did quite a bit of firing with our mortars yesterday, and I did O.K. as gunner. We are just north of Chunchon, and our objective is a big reservoir across the 38th about 5 miles. We were relieved for about 2 weeks to rest up, but I don't remember the date. I just had to go change the range on my gun. We are staying here today. Good news! They say we may get a counter attack today.

In his last letter to his mother, written before Fitch was killed in the 22 April offensive, the young Hoosier told of the circumstances leading up to the Chinese attack, and of his own growing sense of his coming fate:

> Well, we've been in one place for 2 days now. The gooks opened some gates on a big dam up the way, and the

river is so high they can't get supplies across. They are afraid they will blow the dam and flood the whole valley. That wouldn't bother us; we are so far up in the hills the water would run off into the ocean before it would get near us. It has been raining all day today. I'm set up in a trench dug by the gooks and have a shelter over me so I am pretty dry. There are some nice bunkers (pill boxes) not far from here, but I have to sleep near the gun.

I cut my thumb on a ration can this morning and can't write too well. Maybe it will get infected, and I can go back and have it fixed. I had a Corpsman fix it up though. You know, you are supposed to regret that you played around and didn't study hard in high school, but I don't feel that way at all. We got 3 new men in the section. They came over with the 7th draft. The next one is supposed to replace all the men who came over with the division last fall. Then they can start on the replacement drafts. That's about all for now so I'll sign off.[19]

Ronald Burton of Evansville vividly recalled the beginning of the nightmarish Chinese attack on 22 April: "The closest I came to death was probably during the big Chinese offense that spring. The marines [First Division] had fought back up to the thirty-eighth parallel and a little beyond. I was running along a ridge trying to get into my position when the Chinese attack came. A fellow marine tackled me at the same moment a shell cut a tree in half where I'd been standing. The marine saved my life. Just prior to that same action, me and my foxhole buddy had dug out this big bunker area and covered it with brush where you couldn't tell it was a foxhole. The night of the attack the marines in the foxhole next to ours were killed by some Chinese who came into our lines. In the morning you could see where the same Chinese had walked over our bunker but had somehow missed us. The night the big Chinese attack came was the most scared I was in Korea. It was at this time I realized I was really in a war."[20]

Indianapolis's Andy Jacobs, Jr., described the ferociousness of combat during the April battle in his book *The 1600 Killers: A Wake-up Call for Congress*:

> At about 1700 hours, 23 April 1951, George Company, which for three weeks had been climbing over and digging into the mud of what seemed like most of the mountains in central Korea, was suddenly ordered to "saddle up" and move out. This was strange. In all the maneuvering of those past weeks, the outfit had never moved so late in the day nor with such little notice, but on this day we marched north along rice paddies as the sun descended to [our] left.
>
> After an hour of easy walking, not counting about thirty pounds on each back, [we] began to ascend onto a mountain which was destined to be recorded in Marine Corps annals as Hill Nine-O-Two. Darkness and real war were approaching. As George company neared the summit, it was absolute hand-in-front-of-the-face darkness. The people of George Company were already cotton-in-the-mouth thirsty with nothing left in their canteens.
>
> For a couple of hours, the Marines took turns sleeping. Then at about midnight, not with a bang, but with thousands of them and tracer fire to match, the replacements of George Company became combat veterans. Flares soared and parachuted above the chaos of battle. The Chinese could be seen with armbands fashioned from white rags obviously for the purpose of mutual identification among their ranks.
>
> As if the massive gunfire did not shatter spirits enough, the Chinese chose to serenade the god of war with bugles. There were the horrible human shrieks from those cut down by the blizzard of tracer fire. The Bible speaks of "the quick and the dead." The battle speaks of the quickly dead. At daybreak, as a Marine aircraft swooped down in close ground support, [I] was struck violently in the head and began to bleed profusely. The pain was sharp as [I] fell back

onto the rocks which were the roof of the mountain. "Oh my God." Those were the frightened words that faintly echoed [my] thoughts.

Jacobs quickly realized he had been hit by a spent shell from an American plane and was not seriously injured. He now turned his mind back to the battle. "The evil pandemonium of Hill Nine-O-Two had raged on through the night. In overwhelming numbers, the enemy eventually overran the entire Third Marine Battalion," said Jacobs. "In later reckoning, G Company would be credited with blunting the Chinese Spring offensive of 1951. It was rather like being celebrated for blocking a kick with your face. War propaganda can be sardonically amusing. When the other side stands its ground, it's *fanatical suicide tactics*; when your side does the same, it's *heroic rear guard action*." Jacobs's experiences during the hectic battle moved him to write some verse in which he endeavored to capture some sense of what had happened to him:

> In life and death and youth and age
> Some problems do arise
> But often woes that seem the worst
> Are blessings in disguise.
> A nation's call to take up arms
> Could breed a cynic's eyes
> Or mold a boy into a man
> A blessing in disguise.
> The laborer who sweats and toils
> Has no jewels that wealth buys
> But his are gems of healthy limbs
> A gift not so disguised.[21]

Fitch's Able Company was almost overrun the first night of the Chinese spring offense. Through grim and ferocious determination, they barely hung on. Able Company experienced many casualties including Fitch, who died a day before his nineteenth birthday.

Fitch's and the other marines' sacrifices enabled an essential part of the UN line to hold.

In March 1951, as UN forces were struggling to stabilize the front lines, Harold "Sonny" Bender of Boonville received a stroke of good fortune in an unusual form. He reported it in a letter to his mother on 15 March:

> Dear Mom,
>
> Well Mom, I'm back in Japan again in the hospital, but don't jump at conclusions. I wasn't wounded, shot, or even scratched. I was evacuated [to Japan] with hemorrhoids. . . . We were attacking a mountain somewhere when I left my outfit. We had been under heavy enemy fire for about 3 days, so I couldn't very well write when I was there. These piles are sort of uncomfortable, but they are the luckiest thing that ever happened to me. . . . My hemorrhoids started with a bad case of the GI's (diarrhea). I think carrying all that weight might have helped some. I'm going to chow right now, I'll write some more later.

In early May Bender reported to his mother of his concern about having to go back to Korea where heavy fighting continued. "From the looks of the news we are going to cross the 38th; if they do I hope I don't have to go back to Korea. I hope that anyway. I wouldn't even want to be in that filthy hole in peace time." The dutiful son also told his mother not to worry when he did receive his orders to return to combat. "I see by your letter that worry is causing you to lose sleep; don't let it. When you go to bed, think pleasant thoughts. I sleep my best during trouble," he said. "It sounds funny but when the Chinese were attacking [at Chipyong-ni], I would go to sleep like a baby. During the day they started shelling our positions, and we had to get down in our holes, and I went to sleep and slept through four hours of mortar barrage. It's lots easier that way."

In his last two letters home before his death, Bender told of a chilling new order that indicated the increased intensity of the fighting. "They passed out an order today that we are to shoot all refugees on sight in case they might be Communist sympathizers. It'll be rough on the innocent ones. Boy!" Ironically, Bender's very last letter was on Red Cross stationary—typically used when a soldier was in the hospital with an injury:

Dear Mom,

I bummed this sheet of paper and envelope, because I left mine at the bottom of the mountain. We are out of reserve and back up on the front lines. Everything is very quiet up here. I'm going to write this fast as it is getting dark. We are sitting way up on the peak of a high mountain. From my foxhole, I can see the valley with a river far, far below. We are not exactly on the front lines. There are ROKS in front of us (that's South Koreans), but they will run as soon as anything happens. We are back here more or less to shoot them if they begin to retreat. I wish I could describe it up here, but I haven't that much time, and I'm not sure when I'll get to mail this.

It's pretty rich, the 23rd was on line for 2½ months and got 10 days rest and the 38th was in reserve 2½ months and on line 10 days. It's not quite fair. Every time the Chinese start pushing they call up the 23rd and all the time the 9th and 38th were on line there was hardly a shot fired (this pen is about to give out). I forgot to tell you I got your 2nd package and a letter dated the 19th of April telling about Alan [his younger brother] wanting to get the white coat altered. Tell him that is perfectly alright, that he'd better get all the use out of it he can. Also tell him that if the draft starts squeezing him, to get into either the Air Force or the Navy. At least I have a clean bunk at night and decent chow. Tell him I congratulate him on his graduation. This may arrive early or late. This is all the paper I could bum and it is getting dark.

Loads of Love,
Sonny[22]

Harold "Sonny" Bender of Boonville. Bender was killed in action just as the war stabilized along the thirty-eighth parallel in mid-1951.

Bender perished during the last big Chinese offensive in mid-May 1951. Twenty-one Chinese and nine North Korean divisions hit the UN line with their main thrust directed at the U.S. Tenth Corps and the South Korean ROK Third Corps. "The latter was routed, as it had been on every previous occasion when attacked, and the enemy made a penetration of nearly thirty miles. The collapse of two more ROK divisions again threatened the flank of the US Second Infantry Division. The men of the 'Indianhead' division held fast, suffering over nine hundred casualties while inflicting an estimated thirty-five thousand on the Chinese," noted a historian of the conflict.[23] As the Second Division retreated, two companies, including Bender's, were ordered to hold back the Chinese while other Americans escaped. South Korean troops quickly fled the initial Chinese onslaught, leaving the American lines vulnerable to attack. Bender sacrificed his life holding the thin line while his comrades retreated. His body was not returned to his native Boonville until 1954.

By June 1951 the war had grown static, with fighting now taking place along the thirty-eighth parallel in most instances. One of the issues confronted during the Korean War concerned treatment of African Americans. After World War II the armed services continued to practice segregation. By the time of the Korean conflict, however, some progress toward integration had been made. In 1948 President Harry S. Truman issued an executive order for the armed forces to begin moving toward desegregation. The Korean War accelerated this process. "Heavy combat forced the military to use all its manpower efficiently," noted one historian. Still, in the beginning, there were all-black units fighting in Korea. The Twenty-fourth Infantry Regiment, a famous all-black unit, unfairly earned the reputation as a "bug out" unit. Thirty-nine of its members were convicted of "misconduct before the enemy" and sentenced to prison terms. Later, closer examination of the trials clearly demonstrated that "the 24th Infantry . . . fought as well as other American regiments." Gen. Douglas MacArthur later said, "I am willing to concede that these court martials may have been excessive."[24]

Hoosier African Americans Ira Neal and Herbert Crowe experienced the complex situations faced by black Americans who served in Korea. Neal recalled, "I got three hundred and sixty-five dollars for reenlisting after the war started. I wasn't thinking about Korea, and anyway three hundred and sixty-five dollars was a lot of money back then. They also told me I could go back to Japan and rejoin my unit, which was an antiaircraft group. This would mean I would likely miss combat. It did not turn out that way at all. I went to Seattle where they found I hadn't had much infantry training, so I was sent to Fort Lewis for this training. At the time, I still thought I'd go back to my antiaircraft group in Japan. Instead, they sent me to the Twenty-fourth Infantry Regiment—the all-black unit."

Neal was assigned to a weapons company and arrived in Korea in March 1951. In Korea he joined a mortar platoon and soon became a forward observer. What really puzzled Neal was that he had been aware of Truman's push to desegregate the army in 1948, but even by early 1951 Neal saw little or no results from the president's efforts. "In October of 1951, something happened. We were pulled off the line, and in three days my unit didn't exist. We were reassigned and mixed into white units," Neal said.

In Japan, Neal walked guard at graves registration buildings. "These structures were just filled from top to bottom with our dead. It was almost beyond comprehension to see that many dead in one place and then to think they were our own people—and my age at that," said Neal. "At night it was incredibly depressing. Then in

Korea I saw more gruesome results of combat. You'd walk up on guys with their arms shot off, their bodies ripped apart. One day I was getting water from a creek and there lay a dead guy with the water running through a big hole in his chest."

There were humorous moments as well. Neal remembered one time when Korean workers brought up some food to his unit "and the enemy started shelling just at that moment. You could hear it coming in, and we scattered into foxholes. But in spite of the shelling, there would always be one or two guys dumb enough or hungry enough to run over to the food, grab some, then run back to a hole with a couple peaches or whatever."[25]

Herbert Crowe of Boonville also remembered his training for Korea as being totally segregated. "There were hardly any whites at all. We experienced a lot of prejudice too while we trained, which struck me as kind of odd since we were now in uniform and getting ready to serve our country and all," said Crowe. "Things were moving so fast though, that most of the time you just went on and didn't think about it."

Crowe began his service in Korea on Kodijo Island, guarding prisoners and digging latrines. "From there I went to bringing up supplies to the front line. Sometimes we would stay up there while those on the line went back to get shots or whatever. It was so cold on the line, and we wore these shoe pacs. They'd make your feet sweat; then they'd freeze," he noted. "We were later told to change socks all the time, but for me I heard that too late. Got my feet frozen up there. When I went to the hospital for my feet I saw some of our guys with what they called 'rat fever.' It was an awful thing to see."

Crowe never came across an integrated unit while serving in Korea. Still, when Crowe returned home, he found his Korean experiences worthwhile. "Because of the things I saw over there, I had a whole new sense of how great this country was in spite of its weaknesses," he said. "I was also proud of my combat infantry badge because I know it meant I had done something." When Crowe returned home, he reunited with two other brothers who also served in the armed forces during the war. "It was so great to be back home, especially after Korea. Korea made me learn to stand on my own," Crowe said.[26]

Despite positive assessments of their war experiences by some African Americans, the Chinese and North Koreans were quick to try and take advantage of the unjust treatment often given to black soldiers in Korea. The *Indianapolis Recorder* reported in August 1953:

> As war-weary American prisoners of war are being returned to freedom once more, they—especially the Negro soldiers who have constituted nearly 90 percent of the men freed since the truce—revealed to reporters an existence of steady lessons in Communism . . . . Here is the story of why and how the Reds promoted their doctrine among colored American soldiers:
>
> The Reds rated racial bias in the United States as the weak spot in the American armor of democracy. They felt that it would be easier to turn Negroes into Communists than other Americans because of the indignities of segregation and bias suffered by them. To promote the indoctrination program, the GI's said, the Communists separated the Negro GI's from the white captives. Basically, the more a PW accepted his "lessons" the better treatment he received in the concentration camps.[27]

Most efforts to brainwash African-American prisoners, however, did not prove successful.

By late summer of 1951 the conflict evolved into a grinding stalemate as UN and Communist forces fought along a front that hardly moved for the remainder of the war. As battle-line movement slowed, the Chinese and North Koreans were able to bring up artillery, causing the conflict to become a war of attrition. A letter written by Hoosier Gordon Greene to a childhood friend gave testimony to this new situation: "Things are getting a little too rough.

Joe Chink isn't playing fair; he's using artillery and mortars and we've spotted some tanks. Our company is shot; we've got a corporal for a platoon sergeant, and so many replacements at one time can foul up an outfit when thrown into combat for the first time. The guys they're sending over must be scrubs, for the outfit isn't the fighting unit it was last winter."[28]

Ralph Steele of Elkhart arrived in Korea in August 1951, joining the front lines and the static war in September. "My first view of the country was from the ship's deck. As the purple-colored land began to appear on the horizon I thought this would be the beginning of a test of manhood," Steele recalled. "At that moment I knew I did not want to fail." In September, Steele experienced his first of many close encounters with death. "A call came over the radio that a marine patrol had been clobbered and needed assistance to bring back the wounded. I and a few others volunteered to go help. We got to this stream where they were bringing the wounded across. As I waded out to meet the marines carrying the wounded, I saw these splashes of water and heard these snaps. Then I remembered how I had heard these same snapping sounds on the rifle range at Parris Island. That's when I realized I was being shot at. Oddly, no one else was paying any attention, so I also went about my business."

This was also the first place in Korea Steele witnessed the brutal consequences of war. "A dead marine on one of the litters had been hit in the forehead. Everything was normal about his face but behind it the face was just mush," Steele said. "As they carried him, the face would move around like there was Jello behind it. That's an image I'll never forget."

By fall 1951 the war had transformed in most instances into sharp bitter engagements often involving patrols. Steele remembered, "By the time I got over there, the thing had become more static along a battle line like World War I, and there were a lot of patrol actions. I know this sounds like it would be less dangerous than a full-scale battle, but it wasn't. You'd go out and seek out the enemy until you brought fire to bear, count his weapons, note the calibers, and note his positions so you'd know where the strong points were. We'd ambush too and sometimes they'd be ambushed back. Even during the time of the armistice talk, we had thirty-four killed in our area alone. Day in, day out, this kind of thing would just wear on you." Small actions could sometimes extend into major engagements as Steele found out. He said:

> The night before we were to assault Hill 749 [Bunker Hill], we were attacked in several waves during that entire evening. I remember I sure didn't want to be there. The enemy would blow their whistles before they attacked. They'd also call to us. "Hey marines go back home to Alabama!" I still wonder to this day why they picked Alabama. We were on top of this ridge, and I was in a foxhole with the platoon sergeant just before the attacks came. I thought to myself I'd just love to take off running south. I knew I could run all the way to Pusan, I was that scared. What made it even more scary was you couldn't see what you were shooting at there in the dark. But you could hear the sound of attacking troops crashing through the overgrowth down below where we were firing. All night you'd hear the firing all up and down our ridgeline as the enemy probed for a weak spot. Machine guns are suppose to fire in short bursts to preserve the barrels, but that night ours just fired constantly. After awhile you'd see tracers from the machine guns going off in different directions because the constant firing had ruined the barrels.
>
> In September of '51, we went up Hill 749 [Bunker Hill]. I was laying on the ground firing up the hill with a BAR [Browning Automatic Rifle]. The fellow lying right beside me had his boots next to my face. I had just run out of ammo and had turned the BAR over to put in a new clip when an explosion knocked me down the slope fifteen yards or so. Next thing I knew my BAR was gone, and I was having trouble getting my breath. I saw my jacket was ripped to shreds. The only place there weren't holes was right around

my upper chest and face where they had been protected by my friend's boots. If he hadn't been lying there to take part of the blast, I'd been dead for sure.

After being wounded I crawled up toward a gook trench line where a bunch of other marines were taking cover from the mortar attack that had knocked me down in the first place. As I crawled along, I noticed big streaks of fresh blood, and I kept praying it wasn't coming from me. Then I saw my friend who'd been lying beside me before the mortar blast dragging himself toward the trench too. His foot was just shredded and that's what had been leaving the blood trail.

When I got to the trench, a bunch of us who'd been hit huddled down in this bunker. A corpsman came running up the slope under heavy fire to get to us. He later received a bronze star for coming to us under such heavy fire. A marine asked me if I was okay; I guess I was pretty pale by then. I told him that I thought I'd been hit. He took off my jacket and said "Jesus Christ, you're bleeding like a struck hog." Then I passed out from shock.

When I came to, the corpsman gently told me he didn't think I would make it off the hill since he thought he saw bubbles in my blood. I was given a morphine shot, but now the hard thing was getting us wounded to the other side of the trench and off the hill. When I started over the lip of the trench, marine fire whizzed right past my face, so I fell back into the trench. One bullet came so close, it knocked my helmet off. Well, that ended that possible escape route. I wasn't gonna let myself get shot by a fellow marine. Then the corpsman said to go down to the end of the trench where we wouldn't be in danger of our own fire, and there'd be litter bearers waiting for us there. When I got there, right before I went over the top, I saw what I thought was a step. I put my hand there for support and found out it was an enemy crapper. I went in one arm up to my shoulder in pure shit. I thought then "Gee whiz Ralph, this just isn't your day."

After I was hit by the mortar blast, I went to battalion aid, then to a MASH [Mobile Army Surgical Hospital] unit where I had surgery. They brought me into a squad tent in the late afternoon. The operating table was two wooden rocket cases standing on the end of a plank. There were Coleman lanterns hanging over it. I remembered them pumping the lanterns up and how the pieces of shrapnel they took out of me made a noise when being dropped into a pan. I was then flown in a C47 to Kimpo and a hospital. At the time they didn't know the extent of my injury at the MASH unit. When I got to the main hospital, they saw I wasn't hurt too bad, so they sewed me up leaving some shrapnel in me. The doctor told me—"This will add some weight to your name." Two weeks later I was back on the line.

Elkhart's Ralph Steele, January 1952.

Steele survived the seesaw part of the war and vividly recalled the day he left the line. "Leaving combat was a strange experience. I got in the back of this truck, and as I left my unit, the guys I had been with just stared at me the whole time until we disappeared from each other's sight," he said. "There was all this guilt because I was leaving those guys."[29]

Robert Whitehouse was another Hoosier who discovered how dangerous a patrol could be. Whitehouse, a marine, had been in Korea for almost a year and had survived the Chosin campaign and the horrendous April Chinese offensive of 1951. He had a reputation for fearlessness but one day before patrol, Whitehouse felt an overwhelming feeling of dread. He said:

> I started giving my things away and making arrangements for my family to be told where my stuff was and so forth. When I told one squad sergeant who I didn't get along with that I wanted him to have this navy foul weather jacket I had stored away, he got spooked too. Finally, an officer called me over and made me tell the other sergeant I was okay about the patrol. He didn't want the others spooked, you see.
>
> Before we went out, I talked everything over with my squad—drew a diagram on the ground of how we were going to carry out the patrol. Then I told them if they saw anything move—anything— just cut loose with everything you have—don't hesitate—just shoot. So we started the patrol going out down through this minefield. We disarmed some mines and moved forward. Eventually we came to the face of a mountain and checked out what we hoped would be abandoned bunkers. Then we did an about-face and headed back. It was at this point we started receiving fire and had to take cover. To make matters worse, there was nothing but open ground between where we were pinned down and the ridge where we had to go. We never did figure out where the fire was coming from.
>
> The lieutenant decided we'd go back the way we'd come out, which is a real no-no. We were taught not to do this from the beginning, and here he was ordering us to do so. So we're pinned down in the gully, sending a couple of people at a time across this open space. Each couple had to haul ass up this ridge, zigzagging while taking fire, then they had to go back through the minefield. I was the last one out. As I was running up to the ridge to safety, I saw the last two guys before me had stopped to hide in some reeds. I thought "Oh no, I don't have time for this shit." I turned

around to them and told the guys not to stop, to go on up the ridge. So one says, "Sarge, they're going to kill us." I told them, "They're going to kill you if you don't get up to that ridge." I chased them out and made them go up the hill. I followed right after them and got within twenty feet of the crest of the hill. I was almost there when I got hit in the neck.

I'm carrying my rifle in both hands running up the hill when I felt this burning pain like someone had put a hot cigar to my neck. Then I begin to lose sensation in my body. First my arms dropped. I started to yell but couldn't talk. I dropped my rifle and went down to my knees. As I started to fall, I realized I was going face first into a puddle of water. With my last ounce of strength, I turned my head so I wouldn't drown. That was the last movement I made for a long time.[30]

Paralyzed from the neck down, Whitehouse would miraculously recover the use of almost his entire body but only after two years of painful convalescence.

Kenneth Dougan of Spurgeon especially remembered the terrain in which he fought during the last stage of the war. "Everyone lived in trenches and bunkers upon the line, and when you came out in the morning you could see clouds floating down below—we were that high up in the mountains," he said. One of the great frustrations of this type of warfare was the taking of a hill one day only to be ordered or pushed off the next day. Dougan remembered his unit's unique solution to this seesaw aspect of the war. "There was this one hill—Hill 55—we must have won and lost it half a dozen times. The last time we took the hill, we went and set up all kinds of explosives in it—every tunnel—every bunker—just hundreds of pounds of stuff. Then we just left it without a fight. The next day the enemy of course retook the hill. After they settled in we blew the thing completely up—the whole hill—when we went back, there wasn't anything left."[31]

David Graham relaxes in a foxhole.

Occasionally the war had a humorous side. David Graham, a southwest Indiana native, remembered his quasi-comical experiences with Korean honey pots. He said:

> In case you don't know what a honeypot is, man, you are in for a treat. You just cannot believe the smell. Koreans put all of their human waste from the little villages in holes in the ground to later use to fertilize all their crops. Many times we sat up in the hills and watched while the farmers of the village spread the "honey" over their rice paddies.
> On one occasion we sat up in the hills for 3 or 4 days and watched while they covered their rice paddies. After about 4 days, we got orders to move up, we had to go straight through these rice paddies in front of us. The question everyone asked was, "If all hell breaks loose, are you going to hit the deck?" Like everyone else I said, "I'm not going to get down in that shit." Well you know what happened? As we

were moving through, we were raked with machine gun fire. Flat on my belly, down I went. You cannot imagine how quick you can hit deck (with out even thinking about it) when they are firing machine guns at you. This, however, wasn't my first episode with Korean "honey." The first came a few weeks before I had to lay down in that rice paddy.

We had been receiving fire from this little village when we got orders to go in and secure it. We had to go house to house and clear everything. We were going through this village firing and being fired upon. In a fire fight a lot of things happen real fast. You really do not have time to think when being fired upon. A whole lot of your actions and movements are pure instinct. As we were going house to house, I ran around one of the huts while being shot at, and one foot went into a honeypot clear up to almost my waist. After we cleared the village, man did I stink. No one would get close to me. No one wanted to get close to me; no one wanted to talk to me; no one would get in a fox hole with me. In combat, there is no way to shower and clean up and in combat you do not have a change of clothes.

I approached my Sergeant and he said to me, "Get away from me. You smell like shit." No one who hasn't experienced something like this can understand. Here I am, twenty years old, in a strange country halfway around the world, away from home for the first time in my life (except one week at Boy Scout camp), and no one would even talk to me. You talk about a lonely feeling. I just went and sat down by a tree and cried like a baby. Like I said before, at this time in my life this was very serious.[32]

By the end of 1952 both sides seemed ready to work out a truce agreement. Still, several sticking points caused the war to continue for several months longer. The UN increased bombing missions to bring the enemy to a final peace accord. The last full month of fighting in Korea, in June 1953, witnessed some of the highest number of air engagements and air bombing of the conflict. Finally, a truce came on 27 July 1953. Huntingburg's Marvin Boeglin flew on the last bombing mission of the war. "Liberty Squadron (Eighth bomb squadron) had been chosen to fly the last bombing mission, because the squadron had flown the first bombing mission of the war," said Boeglin. "Our plane was in the air at this time over North Korea where we dropped our load of bombs. It was quite an unforgettable experience. The night was illuminated, as everyone expended all of their armament and explosives to keep from having to pack it home. I will never forget what the ground looked like when all that started going up in the air."[33]

Loogootee's Dexter Crane proudly wears his air force uniform. Crane was one of a select group of Americans secretly flown to Indochina to help the French just after the Korean War ended.

During the thirty days following the truce, the war often looked as if it would reignite. Dexter Crane served at an air base near where the front line had been and recalled how American fighters were often scrambled because "it looked like the fighting was getting ready to start again." After the war ended, many servicemen went home. "This left the air force short handed," Crane recalled, "but we still had to bring in supplies to Korea from Japan. We got little rest during that time." In 1954 Crane was stationed in Japan when he received an unusual assignment two months after being sent overseas. He noted:

I had been given an intense examination, and they took my life history. From this, I received a special clearance status. In 1954 they picked fifty-two of us from the air force and secretly sent us to Hanoi, Indochina. We had a French interpreter in our outfit, and American markings were taken off the planes. Our job was to teach the French how to fly our planes as they were fighting the Communists in Indochina. America wasn't suppose to have troops there helping the French, so we were told to dress in civilian clothes in public and carry cameras like we were tourists. We had two 6' 6" French Africans who guarded our huts at night, armed with submachine guns. Still I slept with my 45 under my pillow. Toward the last it was difficult to rest at night. You could hear firing in the distance almost the entire night.[34]

Crane's group were the first Americans to go into Vietnam. They would not be the last. Andy Jacobs, Jr.'s father's words as a Hoosier congressman in 1950 would prove prophetic: "If we send the money [aid], our boys will follow." Many Americans who came to serve in Vietnam would also be loyal, hardworking Hoosiers.

"EVERYBODY WILL SOON FEEL THE
PINCH OF THE KOREAN WAR."

Oakland City Journal, 27 July 1950

"THIS WAR IS NOT LIKE THE LAST.
WE LACK A UNITED SPIRIT TO WIN."

Letter from a Hoosier marine serving in Korea, December 1950

"THE SECRETARY OF THE ARMY
HAS ASKED ME TO EXPRESS
HIS DEEP REGRETS."

Opening line of the telegram from the Department of the Army to
Mr. and Mrs. Paul Bowling of Washington, Indiana, 9 June 1951

CHAPTER SIX

THE HOOSIER HOME FRONT

World War II brought the American nation together as no other force in the country's history. On the home front, war-supporting activities such as drives for scrap metal, paper, and rubber demanded high levels of community cooperation. Adolescents took especially active roles in these collecting efforts, forming "Junior Commandos" and "Tin-Can Colonels" groups to help win the war.[1] Indiana was no exception to this home front zeal. Gordon Greene wrote of his boyhood in Oakland City during the war in his novel, *A Star for Buster.* In one episode he described the frequent scrap-metal drives at his school: "The halls of the school were lined with cardboard boxes of all sorts of scrap-metal and with the name of the homeroom written on the outside of the box." In competition between homerooms, Greene's class almost took first place. A last minute surprise, however, changed the outcome of the contest. "The homeroom with the most scrap had done so because some student's father had donated an iron anvil from a blacksmith's shop," he said.

When the war ended in Europe in May 1945, Greene remembered how Oakland City's main street "was closed to vehicular traffic as people gathered in clusters to celebrate right in the middle of the street." Greene and three of his friends, including Robert "Bud" Fitch, climbed to the roof of one of the main street buildings and, using trash can lids and washtubs as noisemakers, celebrated with the adults down below. "We were beating on the washtubs with hammers and banging the trash can lids together and screaming as loudly as possible," said Greene. "No one heard us above the screams and shouts of the others . . . but it really didn't matter to us. We knew that we were sharing in a moment of history."[2]

At its onset the Korean War seemed to promise that America would once more be united in endeavors requiring great self-denial. Indeed, to most Americans the crisis in Korea heralded the beginning of a global conflict with the Soviet Union. *U.S. News and World Report* suggested, for example, that World War III could come "in 8 weeks or less."[3] The magazine further predicted new price-and-wage controls along with possible rationing.[4] Consequently, at the beginning of the war Americans at home approached the conflict in Korea just as they had World War II, pledging themselves to great sacrifices.

Hoosiers, in those early difficult days of the Korean struggle, also got behind the war effort. One leading state newspaper quickly challenged Hoosier citizens at home "to be worthy of their [fighting men's] sacrifices."[5] A few days after the war came, most Hoosier newspapers carried a somber story about the state's first casualty. The *Terre Haute Tribune* reported, "The bad news came in an Army telegram, delivered to the young soldier's mother, Mrs. Fred Pope, New Castle." The sobbing mother told reporters, "I knew something was going to happen to him . . . ever since this thing started."[6] News stories such as this caused the state to move rapidly to a wartime mentality. Teachers in the Indianapolis school system, for example, while attending their first teachers' assembly, were told, "As teachers we are in the front lines. In this war we are as important to the safety of the world and future generations as the Army in the field. There is a great need for a more simple, clearer concept of democracy."[7]

Other Indiana communities quickly got behind the war effort too. Evansville, home of several mammoth war-production plants during World War II, eagerly announced its industry once again "ready for war." This southwest Indiana city, one local paper declared, was "'ready, willing and able' to convert its facilities to war production—if and when the government gives the word."[8] Wolf and Dessauer, a Fort Wayne business, quickly pledged to assist any employees who entered the service for Korea. Those workers were to "be paid the difference between the compensation they receive from the Government and their salaries at the time of induction, for a period of one year."[9] Some early war efforts carried a more negative tone. Draft boards in the state, as they had done during War World II, quickly set "get tough" policies, and Indiana's state selective service head, Adj. Gen. Robinson Hitchcock, declared, "Every court in the state will be asked to impose on [draft] delinquents the maximum penalty of $1,000 fine and a year's imprisonment."[10]

There was even talk in early September of closing down the state fair, as had been done during World War II. One Hoosier paper reported, "Because of the seriousness of the international situation, there is some talk of the State Fairgrounds being taken over again for defense or war—as the case may be. . . . The Fair is ready. So are Hoosiers. No one wants to see the Fair disbanded again. It's the pride of thousands of Indianians. But, if it is necessary in the national fight for peace, Hoosiers are ready to sacrifice their nine-day classic. Yes, this may be the last State Fair for awhile. The State Fair may once again have to go to war."[11]

Several articles in Bloomington's *Indiana Daily Student* in the summer of 1950, not surprisingly, concerned the draft. "The local draft board is busier than Santa Claus on Christmas Eve. By the way, college graduates are not being accepted for Officers' Candidate School with open arms as many persons seem to believe," the paper noted.[12] Another piece informed male students about options regarding the draft and about "the advantages of enlisting."[13]

Another article in the *Daily Student* called for a new GI Bill for Korean fighting men. "There are quite a few veterans on campus this Summer. Their books are paid for by the provisions of the G.I. Bill of Rights," the newspaper noted. "So are their tuition and some of their living expenses. But what about this group of young men just like us? They're fighting in Korea, but when they get back to the U.S., if they get back, they have no G.I. Bill that guarantees them an education. . . . It's time for Congress to give the matter some serious consideration, as Representative Dwight L. Rogers, Democrat, of Florida, recommends."[14] Male students were also encouraged, by the *Daily Student,* not to give up on their school work just because they might soon be drafted:

> With the situation in Asia growing steadily worse and the draft quotas growing accordingly, many male students have quit studying.
> True, we are facing the possibility of an all-out war, and many students have already taken their physical examinations. But these students must remember that when they leave IU, they leave a permanent record here.
> At some future date these students may want to continue their education or take a position that will require that they present their college records.
> In either case low grades would be a handicap. It would be hard for the student to return to campus and have to work hard to bring his grades up while he is becoming accustomed to his studies again.
> Then too, a prospective employer is not going to be too pleased to see that a student's grades dropped, because he was subject to being drafted. He would rather see that the student maintained a high quality of work despite outside adverse conditions.
> Many veterans of the last war regretted their attitude before they went into service, because their grades counted against them when they came back.
> Your record is important. Why not keep it a good one, even if you do face an interruption in your education?[15]

In early September the *Daily Student* reported the university's first casualty and noted, "Word was received yesterday that Indiana University has lost her first son to the Korean War. He was Lt. Ralph C. Gustin, '49, of South Bend. To a long list of gold stars will be added one for Ralph Gustin. I.U.'s sacrifice to her country has been one of strong men and women. They have fought for their country in many wars and in many places. They have died so that other men might remain free. Their place in the hearts of the members of the I.U. 'family' is very dear. They shall not be forgotten."[16]

Many Hoosier newspapers carried articles that hinted at the economic impact of the war on the state's home front. Three days after the war started, the *Evansville Press* reported: "American intervention in the Korean war became more than the main topic of conversation in Evansville today. Noticeable business spurts appeared in lines that became extinct during World War II. . . . Stock brokers offices were crowded. Hoarding talk was heard again. War rumors bred so fast in several factories that plant officials asked The Press for reports from the Korean front to circulate to foremen. . . . New car dealers reported increased interest ranging from 'a lot of lookers' to 'more sales.'"[17]

One of the state's leading newspapers, the *Indianapolis Star*, carried an editorial three weeks after the war broke titled "All Out for Victory." In the piece the editor declared "the President . . . has called upon the American people to make new sacrifices in the cause of peace and liberty. We believe that Americans throughout the nation will respond to his challenge with enthusiasm and patriotism." In the same article the *Star* noted some of the home front hardships that might soon be required. These included "higher taxes, for increased production" and "controls on credit and essential materials."[18] A day later the *Star* carried an aggressive editorial on the front page asking the state's citizens, "Where Do You Stand?" The editorial strongly condemned Hoosiers who took economic advantage of the war situation at home, while "gallant Americans are giving their lives . . . [in] faraway Korea." The Indianapolis paper especially criticized "hoarders—greedy panic buyers and money-mad speculators." Of the three, however, the paper saved its strongest criticism for hoarders, who were "even more useful to Russia than our slimy native Communists."[19] In another editorial the *Star* declared, "This much is to be said for the wartime hoarder. . . . He deserves a handsome medal from the enemy."[20]

Attacking the practice of hoarding became a popular theme in many Indiana newspapers. Jasper's *Dubois County Daily Herald* carried an editorial on its front page strongly denouncing the practice. "Perhaps no one understands the hazards of war, even on the home front, better than the men who were in the armed forces of our country in prior wars." These veterans, the *Herald* related, were now sounding a warning against statewide hoarding "by well-meaning but misguided housewives" along with motorists "who were anxious not to get 'caught short' on tires." The article further noted that the state's VFW commander, Jasper native William M. Cox, pledged all Hoosier VFW posts to "an anti-hoarding policy" in which members would seek out hoarders and reveal them to the public.[21] The *Indianapolis Star* quickly picked up on commander Cox's declaration by announcing its full support for the VFW's "stop hoarding drive."[22]

The *Terre Haute Tribune* also admonished Hoosier housewives, "The urge to lay in a stock at the moment when trouble threatens is a little selfish: it's action on the thought, 'Come what may, I'll have sugar,' or coffee, or whatever it may be. If there is not then shortage, the sudden surge of buying is very likely to create one," the newspaper said. "It upsets the normal routine of supply and sends prices upward. And it is unlikely that the ordinary householder, following this quick urge to buy in an emergency, can lay in enough of a stock to carry through real trouble."[23]

In one sarcastic cartoon on the front page of an Evansville newspaper, a housewife is shown holding an extraordinarily long shopping list. She is telling her grocer to put the items "in my car in the alley—I don't want the delivery boy to be seen unloading at my home."[24] Indianapolis merchants blamed local "panic buying" by housewives for causing an upward price spiral. "Panic buying here, touched off by the Korean crisis, is creating artificial shortages . . . and will result in unnecessary government controls if not curbed," one group of Hoosier merchants warned.[25]

Hoosier housewives were often resentful of being labeled the most likely group to hoard and blamed the merchants for taking advantage of the Korean crisis by raising prices. One angry Shelbyville woman wrote the editor of the *Star* complaining, "We read quite a number of articles in the papers putting the blame on the housewife for prices going up. Why not put the blame where it belongs? Everyone knows there is no shortage of sugar, coffee or rubber. The man or men that put prices up took advantage of the situation and hiked up prices. Which is the more to blame, the housewife who tries to provide certain foods for her household, or the man who puts the prices up just because he can? What kind of patriotism does he have? If we had the right kind of government women wouldn't need to worry about whether or not they could buy enough food." The woman went on to point out that prices for many less wanted items such as peanut butter had also gone up recently and asked, "Are the women hoarding peanut butter too?"[26]

Another woman wrote from Bicknell, near Vincennes, pointing out, "Hoarding against scarcities has never been my practice but an item in The Star makes us housewives wonder whether we should begin hoarding against higher prices. The item stated a well-known manufacturer has raised the price of his products because of increasing prices of raw materials. Recently in The Star we read of a military secret being 'spilled' in Washington by a high ranking officer who later elaborated on the secret to the questioner. Seems to me the FBI is busy enough with non-Americans, without our military giving out information. If anything needs to be rationed how about rationing parties in Washington as well as alcoholic intake?"[27]

Another concern on the Hoosier home front during the early portion of the Korean War involved a fear that government price controls and rationing would soon be mandated as it had during

World War II. The *Lafayette Journal and Courier* voiced its opinion about the matter, declaring, "All civilian and non-war expenditures must be drastically curtailed so that the armed forces may have everything they need to stop the Reds."[28] Many Hoosier leaders believed the economic dynamics of the war were already causing rising prices. On the other hand, the *Evansville Press* argued that prices were already "soaring" even before the war started, indicating the Korean crisis was not necessarily causing the sudden inflation.[29] Whatever the cause, rising prices were a reality for Hoosiers. One mother wrote her marine son during the early portion of the war, complaining, "You were talking about hamburgers being high—everything is high. Coffee is 95 cents a pound and I used to drink quite a bit. I guess I'll have to drink plain water."[30] The *Daily Student* reported an increased cost to citizens but argued it was a necessity of a just war. The paper noted:

> Your taxes are going up.
> True, they're high now. But they're going to be higher. They are going to have to pay for a war. It's not too big a war in size, but it's the most important we've ever fought.
> It's going to cost. It's going to cost an awful lot to run this war. It's going to cost much more than that to prepare this country for a bigger war that may come.
> If that war comes, taxes may mean the difference between freedom and. . . . Make no mistake. Your potential enemy—with or without the A-bomb—is strong. With 17–1 odds in his favor, he's not to[o] apt to take seriously the "God given rights of man."
> You won a war with superior might a few years ago. In 1944 you paid the highest taxes in the history of America. After the war you wanted them cut. They were.
> Now they're going up again. You're going to be asked to throw billions into the cause. It isn't a bad cause. Look at your children playing in the yard. Look at a baseball game. Look at your educational system. It's a good cause. It belongs to you.

Dig, brother. Your pocket is just as deep as the Grand Canyon, the street-chasms seen from the top of a New York skyscraper, or the colors in the flag over your head.[31]

The small-town *Oakland City Journal* declared its opinion in an editorial in July 1950: "Everybody will soon feel the pinch of the Korean War one way or another. People right here in Oakland City are daily realizing the increased seriousness of the situation . . . soon your pocketbook will feel the pinch of extra taxes." The *Journal*'s editor, however, believed "rationing and price control will not be necessary if the American people 'play ball with the government.'"[32] One Hoosier sage, a funeral home owner named Lem Crockett from Evansville, fretted over possible government controls. Crockett told a reporter for *Time* magazine, "with the war, we just can't have the range [of casket sizes]. They make you stabilize. . . . It's too bad, but that's how it goes."[33]

Not every Hoosier accepted the argument for the need of strong government regimentation at the Korean War's onset. One Indianapolis native wrote the *Star* warning, "If this country can be subjected to the regimentation of a war dictatorship under less than an all-out war to defend the country itself from Russia, the one power capable of waging such a war, then the still continuing threat of a war with Russia may saddle such a war dictatorship on the American people for another 10 years—or even permanently."[34] Other Hoosiers agreed. Indiana had a reputation for not welcoming the federal government's interference in state and local affairs, and people in the state had a general distrust of leaders in Washington. One Indiana woman declared in a letter to the *Star*, "I don't believe in hoarding nylon. We can live without nylon. But how long can one live without something to eat? We are told there is plenty. Of course there is plenty, we know that. But that is beside the point. There was plenty of sugar during [World] War II and some other things, but the government wouldn't let us have it, and we haven't forgotten."[35] An Indianapolis resident also chimed in on the subject regarding Hoosier distrust of national leaders during the Korean crisis: "Are we already dead—or just asleep? And what does it take to wake us? Contact with other folks proves that everyone is just as afraid of the future under the present government as I. But they can't see what they can do. They know there is much more we need to do, but no one trusts the present 'ins' to do it."[36]

Another Hoosier critic of the war suggested the government draft wealth, noting, "I am sure the majority of the American people do not value financial investments more highly than they do human ones. In view of this fact I would like to suggest that one of the provisions of the companion draft law be the conscription of wealth; as a starter I move that all wealth in excess of $25,000 be handed over to the government to run the war. This might make the 'all-out' effort become more real. . . . If we are really in earnest about this war: let's go all out in the draft and include men, labor and wealth. Let's try to be honest and expect sacrifices from ALL or NONE of our people."[37]

One Indianapolis man offered a more balanced view on the subject: "On the home front we are now passing through the first phases of public over-buying and hoarding that characterized the early days of World War II. We hope that this manifestation of hysteria will not reach an extreme that necessitates government rationing and controls. There will be a shortage of material required by the government for the battle front in Korea. . . . If our intelligent businessmen will use their heads we will be able to avoid many of the pitfalls of profiteering and black marketing." The writer added, "Cut out stupid 'scare-buying' or we will have scarcities and will have the attendant government regulations such as price controls and rationing—that we all hated."[38]

Hoosiers were also apprehensive about potential sabotage and civil defense during the early months of the war. Indiana's manufacturers, for example, were warned by Gov. Henry F. Schricker on 17 July 1950 "to be on the alert for possible sabotage as the state began gearing for war armament production." The governor said at a press conference, "The State Civil Defense Organization already has done 'considerable work' toward establishing air raid warning and disaster relief forces, but that individual factories must set up their own internal security crews."[39] Also at this time Arthur M. Thurston, superintendent of the Indiana State Police, sent a telegram to all civil defense units in the state asking them to establish contact with the American Red Cross "for maintenance of communication and water supply systems."[40]

Thurston's message was driven by the fear many Americans and Hoosiers had about a possible Soviet nuclear attack. The nation had been spooked by 1950s civil defense publications, such as *You Can Survive,* which proclaimed, "Know the bomb's true dangers, know the steps you can take to escape them!" Such simplistic booklets warned that contamination could be avoided by "simply taking refuge inside a house," or if inside a car, "by rolling up the windows."[41] Other government booklets on the subject were not nearly as optimistic, and Indiana newspapers quickly picked up this more negative emphasis. The *Evansville Sunday Courier and Press,* for example, carried a headline declaring "U.S. Tells Nation How to Prepare for Atom Bomb Blast."[42] Meanwhile, the *Evansville Press* tried to calm nervous Hoosiers in that city about a recent construction explosion, which the paper explained was "not an Atom Bomb."[43]

One Indiana citizen suggested the development of a locally trained group to counter any surprise atomic attack on the state: "Let's look at what may happen. Over Evansville, or simultaneously over a number of towns, out of a blue sky or down from the stars, without warning, will come the most horrifying package of doom in human history—an atomic bomb—or a cluster of them. There will be a fiery flash brighter than dozens of suns that in a split second will blind all who are unfortunate enough to be outdoors in its immediate radius of scorching fury. . . . This is where trained civilians of the national defense plan training program will render essential service. It will be their job to take over the evacuation of the remaining civilians, to restore and maintain order, to care for the injured, to take sanitary measures, to arrange for feeding, clothing, and housing refugees and to start decontamination of the devastated areas."⁴⁴ In west-central Indiana, Vigo County's civil defense unit quickly took action to prepare for any acceleration in the war. The *Terre Haute Tribune* reported that county's civil defense director had publicly emphasized, "Our people must be educated on defense against atomic attacks."⁴⁵ In Bloomington, the *Indiana Daily Student* reported how the city had established a "city defense program, similar to World War II Civilian Defense Organization . . . to work with the county defense program. The set-up includes an atomic defense plan."⁴⁶

The state's capital also readied for a possible atomic onslaught. The *Indianapolis Star* carried a front-page article titled "Doctors Prepare for A-Bomb Attack," which explained what the city would do in case "all Indianapolis hospitals would be destroyed and most of the doctors killed."⁴⁷ A leading doctor in Indianapolis called for the state to "provide enough funds to create huge stockpiles of essential drugs to be used in event of atomic bombing." One doctor, who cochaired the physicians' committee in Indianapolis, estimated an atomic bomb dropped on the Hoosier capital would cause 150,000 casualties.⁴⁸

Hoosiers, however, did not lose their sense of humor about the situation. Maurice Early, who wrote "The Day in Indiana" column for the *Star,* queried the public half in jest. "Are you thinking about getting a house in the suburbs or in the country to be safe from A-Bombs?"⁴⁹ More seriously, in another column, Early related how the Korean War was psychologically affecting Hoosiers on the home front. "Defeats in Korea and the impending devastation of World War III is having a lot to do with changing mental attitudes and anxieties, a member of the staff of Norways Sanatorium believes," Early wrote. "He illustrates by citing persons worrying about a supposed ailment, such as heart trouble. Now he is likely to forget that and focus his anxiety on the threatening international situation. It is merely trading worries." Early went on to point out that "some persons are likely to be benefited mentally by the increased activities in preparation for defense. Among such persons are the retired, who will get the jobs, and elderly women, who can be useful in some war-time activity. It is the belief of the mental doctors that the emphasis being directed to defense against possible atomic bombing in almost every community is more likely to lift the blues rather than cause gloom. All this preparation for a disaster is activity. The psychiatrists explain that activity is the best antidote for anxiety. Defense preparations offset fear."[50]

Perhaps the most troublesome worry on the Hoosier home front, during the first few months of the war, was fear of the state's Communist party membership. Overnight FBI agents and the Counter Intelligence Corps increased "their vigilance over known communists in Indiana."[51] One Indianapolis citizen vividly described his view of this danger in a letter to the *Star*: "It is reported that the FBI knows of some 1,200 to 1,500 card-carrying 'Commies' in Indiana, together with several thousand 'Pinks' and 'Fellow Travelers.' While these aggravators may live mostly in Mishawaka and Lake County, there are enough members in Indianapolis to cause trouble." The article proceeded to relate the kind of damage Hoosier communists might ultimately inflict. "Let us imagine a fall day in 1952. The State Fair is at its best and thousands of visitors line the streets or loiter in our taverns. The roar of bombing planes is heard. Great explosions occur at the Western Electric, Naval Ordnance, the Harvester, Kingan's, the Flour Mill, Bridgeport Brass and the Allison plant. Anti-aircraft guns speak, but the gunners seem to have taken poor aim. The planes disappear. Police and firemen and rescue organizations rush to the scene. Flames are rolling high. At the same time several small fires start throughout the city. The heart of the city is deserted. Then, as if by magic, the loitering crowds are armed with machine guns. They walk quietly in and take over the Statehouse, the Courthouse, the Federal Building and the City Hall." The writer went on to argue that a citizen army could stop Communists in Indianapolis from doing such damage "if citizens were organized and allowed to buy proper ammunition . . . . A 12-gauge shotgun loaded with an ounce ball makes for a fair smooth-bore rifle. They were used exclusively in shooting buffaloes in the West and a Commie's hide is no thicker than a buffalo's hide!"[52] Another Indianapolis resident advised hunting down all known Hoosier communists and locking them away: "If a skunk were devouring all the chickens on the farm it would do no good to go out and kill a million rabbits, innocent, docile souls, to right the wrong. To kill our innocent boys and those of other nations will do no good, so why not pen up in isolation wards all those who are the real menace."[53]

Worried Evansville citizens also fretted over a possible Communist threat. Two months before the war began an Evansville paper reported, "Four million [Communist] adherents in America are getting regular instruction on how to blast our country's productive heart and war potential out of existence."[54] One of the city's newspapers also reported that the FBI knew where local Communists were "and how to find them." The article added, "periodically, local FBI men visited an Evansville business office checking upon a former woman employee either known or suspected of being a Communist."[55] The state's VFW declared "a home-front war on Communism" shortly after the Korean War began and directed all state posts to ferret "out Communists within the state" and "familiarize themselves with the membership of listed Communist groups."[56]

Despite the early fears of another world war, perhaps no other conflict in American history faded so quickly from the public eye as the one in Korea. By mid-summer 1951, a year after the war broke out, the conflict entered a static stage, remaining so for the remainder of the war. Total mobilization on the home front never came to pass. *Time* magazine reported that "the Korean war was being fought by a small segment of the U.S. people . . . and only a minority of Americans—servicemen outside the battle zone, families of the men in action and civilians subjected to military duty—were directly concerned even in a secondary way."[57] Slackening of war concerns on the Hoosier home front was also evident. Fear of the possibility of hoarding, for example, quickly faded. The *Star* noted in this regard, "The Korean crisis so far has caused no hoarding sprees here. This reflects not only the patriotism but the common sense of the average Indianapolis citizen."⁵⁸ A survey completed in the central part of the state by officials of a large grocery store chain bore out the *Star*'s observation, "There is no unusual buying which would indicate hysteria and fear of World War III," the report noted.⁵⁹ Already sensing the lessening interest in the war, frustrated Hoosier marine trainees instructed their wives: "Go back home and tell everybody there's a war on."⁶⁰ However, the spirit of that particular phrase, so common on the Indiana home front during World War II, did not reappear during the Korean War. Neither did "the pinch of the war" predicted by the editor of the *Oakland City Journal*. Indeed one Oakland City man fighting in Korea correctly sensed the Korean struggle would never garner the support on the home front that World War II had. "This war is not like the last," the young Hoosier observed in a letter to his father in late 1950. "We lack a united spirit to win."⁶¹

As *Time* magazine had noted, however, the war remained all too real for Indiana families that had loved ones serving in the

Photos taken by Hoosiers of typical scenes in Korea.

Courtesy of Arthur Hart

struggle. One problem was the financial difficulties that families endured when the primary breadwinner traveled overseas to fight. One Hoosier woman whose husband had just departed with the marine reserves attempted to figure out how she could "feed and clothe herself and her 4-year-old on $110.00 a year." A Marine Corps spokesman noted, regarding the problem, "We've never had a situation like this." In desperation, the Indiana woman sent a copy of her living expenses to her congressman, Winfield K. Denton, and to Sen. Homer Capehart with a letter explaining how she and other reservist families "are being pinched by the recall order."[62]

Gordon Greene sent more than 120 letters to his elderly mother, and in almost every letter the Oakland City teenager lamented the economic hardships caused by his service and particularly the bureaucratic breakdown that kept his mother from receiving government payments while he was away from home. A month after leaving Indiana, Greene wrote, "I checked on the allotments last night and you will get $75 per month. Just when it will start I don't know." The next month Greene wrote his mother, "I hope you are doing the best you can because your allotment won't come through until the first of November. . . . We are due to be paid tomorrow, so I'll be sending some money. I don't see how you can make it." Amazingly, it would be eight months before Greene's mother finally received the payments. Her son responded to the news by writing, "Glad to hear that you finally got your full allotment. I know you are in bad need of it. If only you could have gotten it sooner."[63]

Older Hoosiers serving in Korea had to worry about the financial woes of wives and children. Paul McDaniel of Evansville departed so quickly that he had to leave his wife and young daughter in the care of his parents. McDaniel's mother was especially vocal about the lack of government support for the two dependents. In one letter she fretted, "I guess the allotment don't amount to a thing. It's awful to take you away and not even take care of your baby." In another letter, Mrs. McDaniel complained, "We sure are sore because they are not paying [your wife] for all that time you've been in that Hell over there." A week later McDaniel's mother told her son, "I know you are going to really think of dirty deals when you hear the back pay isn't to be paid. I sure was mad. Still am. . . . I thought that would almost clear up the loan." Because of governmental red tape, allotment payments were painfully slow in arriving. Frustrated by this problem, Mrs. McDaniel wrote to her son in late November, "What do you think of the allotment checks not starting like we expected them? Guess Truman gave it to some other country."

The mother also missed her son's presence, writing, "I do wish you were home. I just can't seem to hold out on things. I have so much pain in my chest, and I'm afraid its my heart." When marines were trapped at the Chosin Reservoir, Mrs. McDaniel wrote, "We have the little radio on and the Korean news don't sound so good. We hope it's not where you're at." Unknown to her, her son was fighting in the worst part of that action. In her most heart-rendering letter, the Evansville mother wrote her son, "I guess we won't have much of a Christmas without you. The baby is too young to know much about it, and we don't have money to do with either. . . . I know we will be having our Christmas when we can have that sweet face of yours to look at."[64] Another Hoosier, a teacher and mother of a teenager called to service during the war, wrote her son telling him, "I took your picture to school with me. It sure is nice Billy, and I can at least smile when I look at it because you are there smiling right at me."[65]

Younger Hoosier siblings missed big brothers who were away from home. One older sibling fighting in Korea wrote his high school-age brother telling him, "Sorry you got into it up at Jasper [Indiana]. Just remember what he looks like, and it will be taken care of when 'the boys come back from over there.'"[66] Another Hoosier big brother wrote home to his mother saying, "I was glad to hear the kids did so well on their report cards."[67] Older siblings also offered younger brothers advice about the draft. "You will be getting out of school about now," wrote one. "I hope the draft isn't getting too close to you. Sometime I will tell you how it really is over here. Only a fool would want to get into the service."[68]

In general, letters home to worried families were chatty and reassuring. William Marshall, a seventeen-year-old Hoosier, wrote home from boot camp, "I wish you wouldn't worry about me. I am O.K. and not homesick very much. When I think of home I look at the sun and the sky and know I'll be home before too long. The sun and sky I look at is the same one you look at."[69] Stanley Nelson of Winslow addressed his letters to "mom and kids," telling them in one letter, "Just a few lines to let you know I am fine and hope you are the same. I got the pictures of ma and the other boys the other day. . . . I have a mustache now and have put on a little weight. I don't know if you will know who I am when I do come home."[70] Ralph Steele of Elkhart often mentioned news of his relatives in his letters home. "Sounds like Arlene [a sister] is having it pretty tough as I can well imagine. Don't see how she can hold out working that way. I want to drop her a line this week if I can. I imagine Susan [a niece] is getting cuter and brighter all the time. I'm anxious to see how the kids have grown."[71]

One difficulty was the feeling of helplessness on the part of Hoosier servicemen when they received news of a family tragedy. Marvin Boeglin of Huntingburg, upon hearing of the death of his mother-in-law, wrote his wife, Jeanette, "Hi Hon, Well I really don't know how to start this letter. I received a letter from Carol this afternoon and she told me about your mother's death. I should really say our mother's, because she always treated me like a son since I had been going with you. I'll miss her very much, but am happy to know she is in heaven. I prayed real hard for her at Mass this evening and know God will hear my prayers. I know this has really been a strain on you, so please hon, take real good care of yourself and get a lot of rest. I don't want you to get sick by worrying. Hon, please take real good care of yourself. I love you very much hon and miss you more than ever. You are in all my daily thoughts. I love you darling."

Boeglin sorely missed his wife, who had been his high school sweetheart. "Before you know it," he wrote her, "I'll be home holding you in my arms, giving you a real big kiss and hug. . . . Goodnight and God bless you. I'll remember you in my prayers always. Tell your Dad hello and to keep the beer cold. P.S. Take good care of yourself. All my love." In his next letter Boeglin continued to convey how much he missed his beloved wife: "If I come home by plane I should have you in my arms in about 28 days. I love you darling. . . . Babe, I am running out of words so I'll say goodnight to the sweetest and most wonderful wife in the world. I love you hon! Goodnight and God bless you. I'll remember you in my prayers always."[72]

Harold "Sonny" Bender wrote his older sister June Ettensohn back in Boonville, giving her some details of his life in Korea:

> Dear June, Bud and the Kids,
>
> You'll have to excuse the penmanship. You can't very well write with these thick gloves on and when you take them off your hands get cold. Please thank Bud again for taking me to "E-town," and I'm glad Tina got to see a "choo-choo." We get very little news over here so I guess you're more up to date on the war than I am. The last I heard was we were about 5 miles from the 38th parallel. Our CO [commanding officer] estimated another 2 weeks to close completely up to the 38th. I was initiated into combat pretty soon after I arrived here; as I wrote mother. Our regiment was put in for a presidential citation. There were 6 divisions of Chinese or about 60,000 and 3 regiments of us or about 6,000 men. The battle lasted 3 days and 2 nights. I would like to tell you folks at home where I am, but just don't know. We won't have to use our little code system, as they do not censor the mail. If you ever read in the paper where we are, please write and tell me. Well, I guess that's about all I have to say except lots of love to all of you.
>
> As Ever Yours,
> Sonny[73]

Overall, Indiana's sons fighting in Korea sorely missed their families as reflected in one letter home from a teenage Hoosier who wrote, "Don't worry writing about trivial things because that

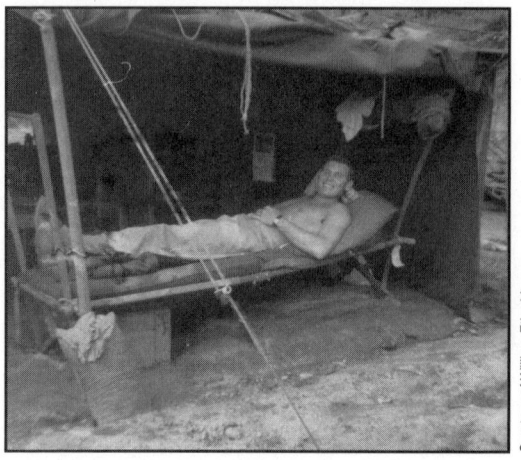

Walter Etheridge reclines in typical fashion between combat missions in Korea.

is what I want to hear. I don't wade through them. I save them and read them over many times. Just news about the family etc, is what I want to hear about."[74] This young marine perished in battle a month after writing these words.

Fighting men from Indiana developed interesting ways of informing family members of injuries and wounds sustained in combat. Most were dramatically understated. Walter Etheridge wrote his younger brother William, who was already a Korean War combat veteran, about the real circumstances of his injury. "Remember me telling you about the gook with his little mortar? Well, the asshole got lucky and dropped one in on me," wrote Etheridge. He then proceeded to relate how he wanted this information hidden from his mother and wife. "I mailed Margie my Purple Heart today. . . . I'm kind of proud of it, Bill, because it does prove I've seen a little action, but I hate to have mom and Margie worry about me. . . . I worry more about them worrying than I worry about myself." The older brother went on to confide, "Bill, you know how a guy can feel over here at times, but I always try to write Margie and everybody a cheerful letter."[75]

Oakland City's Charles "Barney" Barnard wrote his parents telling of "my little accident." Barnard was part of a marine convoy fleeing the Chinese at the Chosin and reported, "I was riding on the fender of one of our trucks, and another truck met us at a narrow place in the road." A sharp piece of metal sticking out from the passing vehicle caught Barnard "just where I sit down. For a minute I thought something had been broken." At the sick bay, however, Barnard was given good news. He was "only bruised and would go back to duty soon."⁷⁶ Greene, also of Oakland City, sent his mother a letter, hoping to beat the government telegram telling of his injury. "I'm in good shape, nothing to worry about. I'm in a hospital (Army Hospital) near Seoul. Sorry I couldn't have written sooner, but I've been moving up until now," Greene wrote. "I was brought by ambulance to an airstrip behind the lines and flown by plane to here. I don't know how long I'll be here or where I'll be going. But I'll write every day to let you know how I'm coming along. Tell everyone I said hello. Hope to see you soon. As Always, Gordon."⁷⁷

Steele went into some detail about his severe injury: "Guess I better drop you a line before the telegram gets there. Seems I attracted some shrapnel yesterday, my unlucky day, the 13th. They have me fixed up now O.K. so don't worry. I was hit at 8 in the morning and back at the aid station about noon. From there we went by ambulance to the hospital; at division they operated but were going to leave a piece in. The wound is on my right side below the ribs. . . . From there I was flown to Seoul, where I am now for observation." Steele sounded oddly cheery as he described his particular condition. "They x-rayed and the piece is in my liver. I'm fed through the veins and have a hose up my nose and into my stomach draining it. I feel O.K. so don't worry, you can't stop a marine that easy. I'll write more later, but wanted this to beat the telegram. Love, Ralph."⁷⁸

Another Hoosier fighting man prefaced his war injury by first telling about his friends' woundings: "Bob O'Keefe, my buddy from Toledo, got hit in the arm pretty bad. . . . Another buddy from Fort Wayne got evacuated on account of trenchfoot." His own injuries, the Indiana youth then reported, "are not worth turning in for . . . they are about healed now."⁷⁹ Mrs. Paul Nelson of Winslow received the dreaded telegram telling about her son's injury. It gave no details other than that Nelson "was seriously wounded in action." Nelson, who had, among other injuries, lost a left leg from the knee down, tried to soften the news. "Just a note to let you know I am fine. I guess the war department has done wrote you and told you that I got wounded," said Nelson. "I got wounded but in a pretty good place. The one in the left foot is the only one that is very bad and that is not bad enough to worry about."[80]

By far the most devastating experience for Hoosiers was the reception of a telegram relating the death of a family member. Martin Craig Brizius grew up in a large, close-knit family in Evansville. His father had been the yardmaster at a railroad yard during World War II, and this critical job had kept the elder Brizius out of the service. Older son, Robert Brizius, however, served in both Europe and the Pacific and after the war ended stayed in the army. Younger brother Craig, on the other hand, was a carefree teenager in the late 1940s who possessed a daring side. A young sister, Jackie, recalled, "Once I was riding in the family car with my mother and she had to swerve to miss some crazy kid weaving his bicycle through the traffic. When we got up to the bike we saw it was Craig."

A high school dropout, Craig Brizius worried about his future as he entered his later teens. Since his older brother had made a career out of the army, Brizius considered the armed forces, especially the Marine Corps. After completing his GED, Brizius joined the marines. The marines enabled the young Hoosier to grow up quickly, both physically and emotionally. A sister remembered, "He left for basic training 5'11" and came back 6'2"."

Brizius was sent to a base in the Philippines after basic training, and the family was relieved that he would be serving there instead of Korea. During the last part of January 1951, the family received a letter from its son telling them he would soon be coming home on leave. In February, as Brizius's ship sailed eastward, it met another ship headed for Korea. Marine troops on Brizius's boat were asked to volunteer to go to Korea where fellow marines were desperately trying to hold back the Chinese. Brizius impulsively joined the group sailing for combat.

Back in Evansville, the Brizius family excitedly waited for Craig's return. "Mother had gone to Henderson [Kentucky] with a friend to show up a fortune teller as a fake," one sister recalled. The fortune teller told Mrs. Brizius she had many children but that one had passed on. "Mother just laughed when she heard that and announced the fortune teller was a phoney. As it turned out, Craig had been killed the day before, but we didn't know it. We believed at the time he was on his way home." When the telegram came, Mrs. Brizius was out shopping. Her children assumed the message was about when their brother Craig would be arriving home. "We thought it was a telegram saying he was in California and coming home." Jackie remembered, "When mom pulled into the driveway she just sat in the car for the longest time. Of course, we were so excited about showing her the telegram, but when she came to the house she told us 'your brother's dead.' This was before we even opened it."[81] As with all such telegrams to Hoosier families, the dispatch was brief and to the point:

> We deeply regret to inform you that your son Private First Class Martin Craig Brizius USMC died 9 March 1951 aboard a US Naval hospital ship of wounds received in action in the Korean area in the performance of his duty and service of his country. Return of remains to the United States for burial probable. Please telegraph headquarters US Marine Corps Washington DC collect whether you desire remains interred in government cemetery at government expense or shipped to you for private burial. If shipped to you preparation encasement and transportation of body prepaid by government and certain designated funeral expenses as per detailed information being mailed you not exceeding seventy five dollars will be reimbursed by Marine Corps. If sent home for burial advise name and address of your funeral director and whether you desire escort to accompany body. Please accept my heartfelt sympathy.[82]

Ironically, the family received Craig Brizius's last letters home shortly after the telegram came informing the family of his death. In those letters the young man explained about his decision to volunteer for Korea. Later, the family found out Brizius had been severely wounded after volunteering to go pick up medical supplies that had been parachuted down to a group of marines and drifted into no-man's-land.

The funeral was a difficult and trying experience for the Brizius family. Craig was the first Hoosier casualty to be sent home from Korea and was sealed under glass. "The family feared his body would be too mangled up from his injuries to be shown," older sister Margaret recalled. "We were also hoping when we saw the body in the casket that it wouldn't be him—that some kind of mistake had been made. Dad went up to the casket first. He turned and said, 'It's Craig.' I was afraid I couldn't go up there and look at him. Then I remembered the scripture given to me at my confirmation 'for now we see through a glass, darkly; but then face to face.' Saying those words over and over in my mind gave me the courage to walk up to the casket where my brother lay. I didn't know his body would be sealed under darkened glass which became transparent as you approached it. Saying that verse in my head and then having that very experience was startling. On top of that, the minister used that same verse as the text for the funeral." Mrs. Brizius asked a son-in-law to accompany her to the funeral home early on the morning of the funeral. He stopped at the back of the room while the Hoosier mother went up to the casket alone to say a private good-bye to her beloved son.[83]

Mr. and Mrs. Joseph Bowling of Washington had received a telegram in early December 1950 from their son telling them he had escaped the Chinese trap at the Chosin Reservoir. The telegram read, "Love to all at home. All well and safe. Keep smiling." The telegram was signed "Fuzz."[84] His unit, the Seventeenth Infantry Regiment, had been the only American unit to reach the Manchurian border. By May 1951, nineteen-year-old Karl Bowling was due to rotate back home, and his family looked forward with much excitement to seeing his shy and mischievous smile once more. Then on 9 June 1951 came a short and brutal telegram. "THE SECRETARY OF THE ARMY HAS ASKED ME TO EXPRESS

HIS DEEP REGRET THAT YOUR SON PFC BOWLING, KARL F. WAS KILLED IN ACTION IN KOREA 29 MAY 51."[85] Despite the distressing telegram, the Bowling family held out a desperate hope there had been a mistake and quickly wrote a letter to the army asking for more specific information. The first reply offered a slight glimmer of hope. "I have your recent letter concerning your son, Private First Class Karl F. Bowling. Casualty reports received in this office to date do not contain his name. However, in view of the information furnished, an inquiry has been directed overseas to determine his present status. Upon receipt of a reply, you may be assured that you will be promptly notified."[86]

Washington's Karl Bowling. Bowling was killed in action a week before he was to return home.

Then came the final devastating report: "It is with regret that I am writing to confirm the recent telegram informing you of the death of your son, Private First Class Karl F. Bowling, who was killed in action on 29 May 1951 in Korea. I wish that I could give you more information but casualty reports of this nature are necessarily brief and contain only essential facts. However, provisions have been made for the overseas commander or Chaplain to send a letter, containing details of the operations which led to his death, to the emergency addresses designated by each person who dies overseas in the service of our country. Since these letters may be written under combat conditions, it is not known just when the letter can be expected, but it is hoped that it will not be long delayed. . . . I know the sorrow this message has brought you, and it is my hope that in time the knowledge of his sacrifice for his country may be of sustaining comfort to you. My heartfelt sympathy is with you in your sorrow."[87]

In addition to family members, Bowling left behind his best friend Joe Haag. The Haags and the Bowlings were a part of a large Irish-Catholic community that lived in the area, and Joe and Karl had been friends since their days in grade school in Washington. Haag recalled how Karl spent much of his time from junior high through high school at the Haag house. "We were like brothers," said Haag. "Karl was a girl magnet, so he was a great fellow to be buddies with." Haag remembered one episode in which the two teenage friends drove to the Indianapolis area and ran out of gas after dark. Unknown to them at the time, the small community in which they were stranded had just experienced a dramatic robbery of the local bank. Haag remembered, "Karl went up to the door of this farmhouse to ask for some gas while I stayed in the car. When Karl came back, he had a sheepish grin on his face and told me 'That old man back there came to the door and the only thing he was wearing was a shotgun.'" The two friends looked elsewhere for gas.

In May 1951 Bowling's mother called Haag to come read the letter telling of her son's forthcoming return. Ironically, Haag recalled how Bowling had written his family that until recently "he never thought he'd get home alive." But later came the telegram. At Bowling's funeral a sergeant, who had been with the Washington teenager when he died, told Haag how his friend had been killed. "Karl's unit had come under attack about four o'clock in the morning. Karl took several machine-gun bullets across his chest. The sergeant then told me Karl's last words were 'Joe I've been hit.' I've often wondered if in that last minute of his life his mind didn't jump back to all our times together in Washington."[88]

Families such as the Bowlings who lost loved ones in Korea received a number of letters conveying the condolences of the army. The regimental chaplain wrote the Bowlings telling them, "Your son gave all that he had and has joined the glorious company of those who have laid down their lives for their brethren. He has not ceased fighting and working with us. Our Great Commander has promoted him to an advanced position among the hosts of God. It is only by such sacrifice and complete devotion to duty that we are defeating the enemy. We shall all give until victory is won. He has given everything."[89] Haag was left to ponder what his friend's life would have been like had he lived. "I often think about Karl, visit his grave and think how I've gone on and raised a family, worked, and so on. Sometimes it really bothers me to think how those who gave their lives in war are so forgotten, especially those who died in Korea."[90]

Bob Doane was another Hoosier teenager who lost a best friend. Doane was in class in Solsberry at the beginning of his senior year when the news of his best friend Kenneth Ray Cox's death was delivered to the school. Doane spent that evening at home "looking out the window, facing down toward Ray's house." In the early morning hours Doane, unable to sleep, sat down and composed a poem that later appeared

Kenneth Ray Cox of near Solsberry was killed in action in September 1950 while defending the Pusan perimeter.

in his high school's yearbook. "Brave Hero" relates the memories of the adventures Doane, his brothers, and Cox shared in their youth in the rolling hills of Greene County. The poem's last lines are:

> But memory there will always be,
> When we were kids—you and we three.
> Things will never be the same,
> Because when I think of your name,
> Back rush memories, and I say,
> There never was a pal like Ray.[91]

William Barnard of Oakland City also lost a dear friend in April 1951. Robert "Bud" Fitch died in the early morning hours of the biggest battle of the war. "Bud was my best pal. We must have been friends even before I can remember, because my Mom and Bud's Mom were friends even before they were married," Barnard remembered. "So, Bud and I probably shared playtime in diapers, even though Bud was a year older than I." The families lived only two blocks from each other. "One block as the crow flies, but we never cut through a patch of woods by the Cockrum's house because it was supposed to be haunted. When we were old enough to walk off on our own, we just went right up to one another's door and knocked. If no one came to the door right away, I just walked on in. Bud did the same, except he would come in the side door if he heard my Mom giving a singing lesson," said Barnard.

As they grew older, Barnard and Fitch shared experiences of growing up in postwar America. "I guess we did about everything together. I remember my first full can of beer [a Burgermeister] was with Bud, a hundred yards down the Southern tracks behind The Palace," Barnard recalled. "The older guys who could buy beer, usually vets going to Oakland City College, would buy a six pack for you if you were a 'Palace Boy.' A 'Palace Boy' was someone who could keep a secret or would forget where he got the beer if he got in trouble."

The activity that maintained their bond as they grew older was football. "Bud was big and strong enough to be a three-letter man. When I went out for spring training at the end of eighth grade, I weighed ninety-eight pounds. The coach said, 'Anybody who doesn't weigh 100 pounds should not play football.' I grew enough that summer to make the squad and eventually was the starting quarterback my senior year." As they neared the end of their high school years, neither Barnard or Fitch could have imagined what lay ahead. Barnard noted: "Then came the big surprise. The Korean War and the activation of the Marine Corps Reserve. My brother Barney had been the first to join the Marine Corps Reserve unit in Evansville from our hometown of Oakland City. It was my junior year. Bud was a senior. Barney, who was four years older, was between college and working full time as best as I can remember. The marine reserve seemed like a good idea for several of the local men. There was the extra pay, lots of comradery, and of course, you were a marine and had a uniform to prove it. One by one a number of my friends joined up, the older graduates, then pals still in high school."

None of these teenagers had any idea that a savage war would soon break out. "Before school let out in the spring, the Oakland City bunch would practice drilling on their own in the high school parking lot. To be with my friends, I would be a rank filler, but they never let me call cadence or give commands," said Barnard. "It was great fun for awhile. Then school was out, and they all went to various jobs and I went off to work at my YMCA camp."

When the war came, the Marine Corps Reserve was called up, and the Oakland City boys could not escape their fate. Once the reservists were activated, they boarded a train in Evansville and headed west to Camp Pendleton, California, for training. Barnard recalled, "Bud was lucky at first. Because he was smart, he was sent to a communications school in San Diego. At graduation Bud was given two weeks leave, and he came home for Christmas. We had as much fun as we could, but the usual bravado was gone. My brother and the First Marine Division were surrounded and fighting their way south from the Chosin. Bud had a couple of dates, and there were a couple of parties, but he mostly hung around home. During Bud's last night home I stayed over as I had done so often in the past. In the morning he asked me to drive him to the train station, 'Mom does not want to go and see me get on the train.' I agreed, of course. The forty-minute drive was not filled with a lot of small talk. Bud said, 'Mom is afraid I am not coming back.' I tried to cover that with lots of positive platitudes. Then we both fell silent. After awhile Bud said, almost under his breath, 'I'm not coming back.' 'What?'—I challenged that and tried to cheer him up. We ended up arriving early, and I suggested just driving around, and Bud said 'No, let's get it over with.' We parked, he got his gear, and I took the car back."

In early May 1951 Barnard had an extraordinary and disturbing dream about his best friend. "The dream came in the spring. It was a Tuesday night," he said. "The senior class play was in a rehearsal, and I had the lead as Godfrey Crass. The dream was not unusual at first. I could see myself walking down to Bud's house. I walked to the front door, as I had many times before. I knocked. Nobody comes to the door. I walk in and see Bud sitting on the couch with his mother, who was crying. No one speaks to me. I think, 'What is wrong?' Bud does not speak; he just looks straight ahead and seems to be dressed in a suit (maybe his uniform). Then I am kneeling down by him and feel as if something is wrong with his legs. I looked at him and suddenly knew that he was dead. I woke up disturbed, but I realized it was a dream."

On Wednesday, 26 April, the telegram telling of Bud's death arrived for Bud's mother, but she did not tell the Barnards because Mrs. Barnard had a recital that evening, and she "did not want my mom to be upset and cancel the program. So, I did not learn about the telegram until after the play rehearsal when the director said, 'Wasn't it too bad about Bud?,'" Barnard said. "The next morning mother and I went to see Bud's mother. I told her about my dream. She said she knew Sunday, the actual day Bud was killed. My next letter to Gordon Greene told of Bud being killed in action. Gordon was in a different unit and did not know. When Gordon returned home after being rotated out of Korea, he told me he had visited Bud's unit during a pause in the Chinese offensive and learned that Bud had initially been wounded in the legs before the position was overrun."[92]

Greene quickly wrote a hurried reply to Barnard. "Boy, I'm so nervous I can hardly write. Your letter was the first to tell me about Bud. I had heard from one of the guys in his company, but I sure as hell wouldn't believe it. I guess it happened the night the chinks started their counterdrive on April 22nd. We were several miles from his outfit and fought our way back by the 24th. God is still with me, and I keep praying every day, never missing, that someone will wake up to the fact that one of us has given his life and still nothing has been accomplished."[93] The news also stunned the other Oakland City boys who had gone so eagerly into the reserve together. Barnard's brother Charles wrote his mother, "I suppose you have heard the news by now. It has been long enough for the official notice to go through. Bud's section was overrun, and he was the first one to go down. Four others were killed at the same place."[94]

The Fitches' younger son, Gordon, about ten years old at the time the dreaded telegram arrived, remembered playing at a friend's house in the neighborhood and being interrupted by his little sister, who told him to come home at once, "that something terrible had happened." The message in the telegram drove brutally to the point: "DEEPLY REGRET TO INFORM YOU THAT YOUR SON PFC ROBERT STUART FITCH USMC DIED APRIL 23, 1951, OF WOUNDS RECEIVED IN ACTION IN KOREA IN THE PERFORMANCE OF HIS DUTY AND SERVICE OF HIS COUNTRY." After hearing his grief-stricken mother read the telegram and not knowing what to do, Gordon went to his room.[95]

Bud's father, Henry Fitch, dealt with his loss by seeking information from anyone who was near his son at the time of his death. Sydney Greenwood, one of the marines from Able Company who was present at the 22 April battle, spent over a year in the hospital recovering from his wounds. While convalescing, he came across a desperate plea from Henry in the Marine Corps publication,

Leatherneck, asking for information regarding Able Company's struggle on the night of Fitch's death. Greenwood soon wrote to Henry, sharing his recollections of the battle with the heartbroken man and offering the only real consolation he could, that Bud Fitch's sacrifice had made a difference. "I spent the first evening of the battle [listening] to the clatter of weapons all that night," said Greenwood. "I remembered saying to a marine next to me, 'If the chinks break through, we will all be done.' He answered, 'Don't forget there are marines on that hill.' That remark will stay with me forever. By the courageous action of your son and other marines, the center of the UN line was saved."[96]

For many families the status of missing in action was just as difficult as the outright death of a loved one. One Hoosier family who endured the limbo created by that status was the Everett Leffler, Sr., family of rural Monroe City. The family received the official telegram on 19 December 1950. The youngest member of the family, a sister, recalled "getting off the school bus my freshman year and my parents meeting me and crying and trying to tell me the awful news they had received."[97] The Leffler family now experienced the agony of not knowing what had happened to its son. Official army letters to the family offered scraps of hope. One noted, "I know the added distress is caused by failure to receive more information or details. Therefore, I wish to assure you that at any time additional information is received it will be transmitted to you without delay. The term 'missing in action' is used only to indicate that the whereabouts or status of an individual is not immediately known. It is not intended to convey the impression that the case is closed. I wish to emphasize that every effort is exerted continuously to clear up the status of our personnel. Under battle conditions this is a difficult task as you must readily realize. Experience has shown that a number of persons reported missing in action are subsequently reported as returned to duty or being hospitalized for injuries."[98]

Five months later no word of Everett Wayne Leffler, Jr.'s fate was forthcoming, and the army sent a more dismal note: "It distresses me to inform you that no report of any change in his status has yet been received. If at the expiration of twelve months a missing person has not been accounted for, all available information regarding the circumstances of his disappearance is carefully considered under the provisions of Public Law 490, 77th Congress, as amended, and a determination of his status is made."[99]

Wayne Leffler was declared "officially dead" on 31 December 1953. Still, this resolution was far from satisfying for the Leffler clan. "We kept hoping and praying that we would hear something good," remembered Wayne's sister Bettie Leffler. "It would have helped tremendously if they had found some part of him or even something belonging to him but that never happened either."[100]

By the time the war ended, three years after North Korea's shocking invasion, Hoosiers, and the rest of the nation, were already putting away thoughts of the war. One Dubois County paper said of the war's odd close, "Had the armistice come when we had control of the whole country, [the] reaction on the home front might have been different." As it was the paper noted the end "was not celebrated" in Indiana "with demonstrations of joy as were all previous armistices."[101] The *Indiana Daily Student* noted the war's less than satisfactory ending. "As the shooting in Korea drew to a close, there was no spontaneous public demonstration to celebrate the armistice, as there was at the end of World War II. Perhaps it is an indication that the American people don't think the armistice is anything worth crowing about."[102] The *Indianapolis Star* called the conflict the "strangest ever fought."[103] The *Indianapolis Recorder* offered a thoughtful, if somewhat critical, assessment of the war.

> But for some 25,000 young Americans—as well as many thousands of soldiers of other nations, and of Korean men, women and children—the war and the peace alike have ended for eternity. The question which now stands on the sky above their silent graves is: "Was It Worth It?"
>
> Such an awful question cannot be lightly answered. It has been noted that a great advance in integration of the

U.S. Armed Forces came about during the Korean War. Jimcrow was a casualty, as Negro and white soldiers fought side by side in mixed units. Yet if this be advanced as a justification of the bloodshed and misery, we will reply without hesitation: "It Was Not Worth It." Such a price is too great to pay for progress that can and should be achieved in ways of peace. We need to learn not to die together, but to live together.[104]

Next to the editorial was a political cartoon showing a gigantic crow labeled "Old Jim Crow" attacking two men labeled "peace" and "democracy." The caption declares "neither will be safe, until he is destroyed."[105] Perhaps one Hoosier citizen summed up the whole Korean matter best when he noted to a newspaper reporter the lack of celebration in the state capital at the end of the war. "No excitement here tonight. . . . It's been a forgotten war. Only the fellows who served there remember."[106]

Gordon Greene, who lost his boyhood friend, Bud Fitch, in Korea, returned from the war to Oakland City on Christmas Eve, 1951. A slow train from the West Coast carried Greene home. He arrived about 10 P.M. and noticed a clean white layer of snow on the ground. Leaving the station and walking to an all-night diner to grab a bite to eat before he surprised his family, Greene suddenly realized that no "Roll of Honor" board now existed in Oakland City to honor the dead as one had in World War II. "In April, Bud had been killed in action in Korea on the night before his 19th birthday. Although, I knew there would not be a Board of Honor for us, I was disappointed in not finding one there." Sadly, Greene began to perceive that the Korean conflict would somehow be a different kind of war in the minds of the American people.[107] The war itself, although it took more than 54,000 American lives, 927 of them Hoosiers, would be labeled "the forgotten war."

———————

"Send me just one bone of my son, and I'll accept his death."

Statement to the U.S. Army by Oval Hamilton, whose son Donald Hamilton was listed as missing in action in the Korean War and whose body was never found

———————

CHAPTER SEVEN

AFTERMATH

On 27 July 1953, the day the Korean truce went into effect, the *Indianapolis Star* pointed out that at least 140,000 Hoosiers had served during the three-year conflict. More specifically, the article noted, "Many of them—the number is not known—gave their lives. Hundreds of others were wounded. Scores of Hoosiers always will carry the marks of war injuries to remind them of the battle for the little tongue of North Asia that is only twice the size of their home state." The article also noted:

> Hoosiers served in hundreds of jobs. They helped in the fighting, and toiled in the vast network of supply lines that kept ammunition, food and medical supplies flowing to the men who battled the North Koreans and Chinese Reds.
> More than half the Hoosier fighting men were volunteers. An estimated 80,000 of them offered their services to the Air Force, the Marines, the Navy and the Army.
> Another 43,000 were called to the colors through Selective Service. Most of these served in the Army.
> But the first call, when the war broke out and rapid military expansion was needed, went to more than 16,500 reservists. . . . For the second time within 10 years they were

called to leave their homes to repel an aggressor whose aim was to destroy the ideals of American and Hoosier life.[1]

On a more sour note an editorial in the *Star* on 28 July argued, "Nobody in the United States is celebrating the Korean truce as a 'glorious victory.' Only the Chinese Communists are using those words to describe the end of the fighting. The reason is obvious. The Korean truce has been a negotiated defeat for the U.N. and a surrender by the United States."[2]

Hoosiers and the rest of the nation simply wanted to forget the war. Conversely, for those Hoosiers still in Korea, a near state of war would exist for some time after the truce. William Hyde, an airman first class in the 336th Fighter Interceptor Squadron, arrived in Korea in January 1954. A native of southwest Indiana, Hyde landed at an airfield in Taegu "on a rainy, winter day." His recollections suggest a level of danger still existed for those Hoosiers who continued to serve in Korea. Hyde noted:

> In heavy rain we made three passes at the runway which seemed to extend into the ocean. The last pass got us on the runway, but the heavy spray from the landing gear sure gave us a scare. I thought we had gone into the ocean! We loaded into an Air Force six-by-six truck, and we were transported across the Han River to K-14 [Kimpo Air Force Base], arriving as night fell. We drew live ammunition twice "to defend the flight line." Kimpo was only eighteen miles south of the thirty-eighth parallel. We often scrambled a flight of four F-86s in response to MIG-15s approaching. Our pilots test fired their six .50-caliber machine guns when on patrol or escort duty.
>
> Occasionally a "gung ho" flight (four aircraft usually) or two flights (one for top cover, one for "bait" at a lower altitude) would stage off the coast of North Korea, hoping to attract a fight with the MIG-15s. Our group executive officer, a West Point graduate, was the bait one day in "my"

airplane and had a close call. All eight F-86s returned to Kimpo with noses black from firing their machine guns. The aircraft ground crews got the "opportunity" to apply aluminum polish in order to gain a few miles per hour out of the F-86s.

Hyde recalled several events "that still stand out," but remembered one as especially chilling. "One night while on duty as CQ [Charge of Quarters], I heard a noise in the row of tents next to the perimeter fence," he said. "South Korean soldiers were on guard duty outside the fence and enlisted airmen patrolled inside the fence." Seeing a tent flap ajar, Hyde drew his .45-caliber automatic assigned the CQ NCO and entered the tent. "The occupants were asleep, but one row of clothes hangers was still moving from being disturbed. Exiting the rear of the tent, I sensed a shadowy figure going over the fence," said Hyde. "No shots were fired and only one or two men in the tent awoke."[3]

Perhaps the most distressed group of Hoosiers at the end of the war were the returning veterans. Ralph Steele, for example, came back to Elkhart and discovered that "coming home was a disappointment. I went back to my old job and found people didn't share the values I had developed in Korea. One day we were all talking about the war and I said 'Boy they really got to do something to get that war finished.' The lady next to me said. 'Are you crazy? We'd all lose our jobs if the war ended.'" Steele was soon "down about my job and about my lack of future goals. I even considered going back into the corps. About this time my father suggested I go to school and study art, which had always been a passion of mine. I ended up going to school on the GI Bill. I went to art school and then IU at South Bend and Fort Wayne. Art would become my vocation, thanks to my Dad's encouragement and the GI Bill. I have often wondered what my life would have been if it had not been for the marines."[4]

Robert Whitehouse also found his return to Indiana an adjustment. "I came back to Evansville after the war and took a job at an aircraft factory, which made wings for planes. The first day in, I was down by an assembly line with my tie and white shirt on when someone let lose with a rivet," Whitehouse remembered. "I got down on the filthy floor and rolled under a bench—shirt, tie, and all. This made a hell of a noise, and everyone started laughing when an old buddy of mine who'd been in the navy during World War II came over and offered a hand. He said 'Come on Bobby. It's going to take time. Take it from me.' I looked at my soiled shirt and tie and then at him and said, 'I'm suppose to be a white-collar guy—some white collar.' He said 'Don't worry about it.' When the other workers continued to laugh, my old buddy turned around and told them, 'I can tell none of you guys have been through it or you wouldn't laugh.'"⁵

Andy Jacobs, Jr., traveled by train to Indianapolis and "saw a dream come true. [My] mother, father and sisters were there at the station. God had seen fit to let [me] live on, and this *was* living. For most of America, the return of Korean veterans amounted to two things, ho and hum, but that didn't matter to [me]. [I] was too busy counting my blessings. [My] deliverance was delicious. It was time to get back to the business of hitting the books and delivering concrete blocks to help pay for them." His first visit to a barbershop made for an interesting encounter: "Referring to the negotiations pointing toward a long-term truce roughly along the thirty-eighth parallel, a well-fed couch potato asked in a horatory tone, 'You left the job half done, didn't you?' 'Well,' I replied, 'if you mean completely wiping out my company, you're right. We took fifty percent casualties in just one night.' The smiles around the shop were reassuring. This spud was not for them either."⁶

Ironically, when President Lyndon B. Johnson called the Marine Reserve to active duty in the 1960s, Indianapolis's reserve unit was again activated, and Jacobs was called upon to make a speech at the unit's departure. Instead of being a departing reservist, Jacobs, now a congressman, was the one giving the going away speech. He attempted to add some humor to the gloomy occasion, telling the marines: "When a Marine lieutenant walked with his wife across the base, she noticed that each time he returned a salute, he mumbled, 'same to you.' When she asked why, the lieutenant explained that since he was once an enlisted man himself, he knew exactly what each Marine was saying under his breath. Fifteen years ago, as a young Marine member of the Sixteenth, I stood where you are standing now. And as I more or less listened to the speeches of political big shots, I was saying under my breath just about what you are saying now. So, let me begin by quoting that lieutenant, 'Same to you.'" Although the congressman's humor was a crowd pleaser, he could not override the occasion's somber weight. "My heart was both broken and not in it," he recalled.[7]

In late 1969 Jacobs, shaped by his difficult experiences as a marine reservist called to serve in Korea, helped organize an all-night debate in the House of Representatives on President Richard M. Nixon's war policies. The *Washington Post* noted, "Rep. Andrew Jacobs, Jr. (D-Ind.), an organizer of the debate, set the tone as leadoff speaker, saying the purpose was 'not to stir up hatred for the President; we have too much hatred in this country,' but to discuss Vietnam. . . . Despite the Republican reluctance to let it happen, they soon became involved in a lively back-and-forth discussion that was polite and intelligent and provided the most illuminating debate the House has had on the war."[8]

Sometimes Korean War experiences changed Hoosier servicemen's previous views of the world and of home. Ira Neal, an African American who eventually settled in Evansville, arrived on furlough in Memphis, Tennessee, after he left Korea in 1952. He noted:

> I was riding a public bus from the east side of Memphis one day, sitting there in the back of the bus in uniform, proud of having served my country. The ride started in south Memphis—a heavily populated black area—and as it came across town there were fewer blacks and more whites on board. When the bus first started, blacks would sit wherever they wanted, but as the bus moved northward, blacks would move toward the back of the bus as more whites

came aboard. The more whites come on, the more black folks kept moving back. Anyway, I was sitting behind the line where blacks could sit, thinking I was okay. Soon, however, there were many more whites than blacks on the bus, and whites were telling blacks to give up their seats even in the black seat area. This, of course, was an unwritten rule. Whites could do this—take black people's seats whenever they wanted. Finally, this white lady comes up to me and asked me if I'd mind to give her my seat. For some reason I said, 'Yes, I would mind.' I guess I suddenly realized that here I had served my country only to come back to this. Finally a police officer came on the bus and told me to move. I said I'd move, but I wouldn't sit on the seat over the motor—the hot seat. All the while this black lady was tugging on my uniform saying, 'Don't cause trouble' and 'where are you from?' I told her 'I'm from right here lady.' I guess I'd just had it with the system.

Neal ran into the same racism on the army bases after the war. "I was a sergeant first class. A white guy came up to me one day and said, 'Hey you.' I said, 'See these stripes, you will address me by rank or as soldier.' He wouldn't do it, and I got in trouble for not responding."[9]

A case in Terre Haute, shortly after the war ended, demonstrated that the Hoosier State was not immune to episodes of racism. The *Indianapolis Recorder* in an editorial noted the particulars of the episode. The newspaper reported:

> The Board of Public Works and Safety of the city of Terre Haute now has under advisement the case of Police Lieut. William Kuykendall, charged with manhandling and false arrest of a Negro minister. . . . Lieutenant Kuykendall is accused of threatening Rev. Alfred Robbs, president of the Interdenominational Ministerial Alliance; of manhandling him and ripping buttons from his shirt

while shoving him into the police car; and of arresting him and taking him to police headquarters, for no reason at all except that he was a Negro.

If the facts are as stated—and there seem to be plenty of witnesses to them—the course to be taken is clear. The Safety Board should consider what action would be appropriate if the victim were the MOST PROMINENT WHITE MINISTER IN TOWN; and then it should act accordingly. Police abuse of citizens because of their color cannot and will not be tolerated.[10]

Another group of Hoosiers who suffered in the aftermath of the war were family members whose relatives were listed as missing in action. Often a family's struggle for closure would be passed down to younger generations. Charlene Cox of Solsberry, for example, never met her uncle, Donald Hamilton, who was listed for many years as missing in action before being declared dead; the family never really accepted the latter ruling. "When my mother would clean rooms, she'd let me go through this big wooden box which contained all Uncle Donald's letters," said Cox. "Sometimes we would read them aloud. No matter how many times we'd read them, each time seemed fresh and new." Donald's father, Oval Hamilton, never gave up hope that his son would return. Charlene Cox remembered how her grandfather always hoped he'd live long enough for the day his son came home. "I remember Uncle

The family of MIA Donald Hamilton, of Greene County, seeks some closure at the Korean War dedication.

Donald's grave said missing in action on it. My grandfather never let us put flowers on it because he said his son could still be alive. Both of my grandparents also left the porch light on at night and the back door unlocked in case Donald came home unexpectedly. My grandfather always said to the authorities 'Send me just one bone of my son, and I'll accept his death.' On the day before Grandfather passed away at ninety-six, he told me, 'Maybe Donald will get to come home before I die.' He just never gave up hope."[11] More recently, a new generation of family members continue to carry the memory of their relative. Charlene's son Devon, for example, recently drew a picture of his Uncle Donald for a class assignment.

Some closure did occur for Hoosier families who lost loved ones when the state dedicated a memorial for Hoosier Korean War and Vietnam War dead in 1996. Jacobs, a thirty-year member of Congress from Indiana's tenth district, was one of the speakers. Jacobs noted in his address, "We gather here not in triumph, not in glory, not in arrogance, but in sorrow, in gratitude and admiration and in love. To die for one's country is love and that which can be no greater. These memorials, that are dedicated here today, will be here today, tomorrow and till the end of time to remind us to remember, and not to forget, once there were laughing, loving, breathing, young Americans who sacrificed supremely, that we might live as we live."[12] Among those attending were members of the Hamilton family.

Representative Andy Jacobs, Jr., thirty-year member of Congress from Indiana's tenth district, spoke on behalf of veterans of the Korean War at the dedication of the memorial for Hoosiers killed in the Korean and Vietnam Wars.

Courtesy of Andy Jacobs, Jr.

Hobert Young of Oakland City carried with him the memory of the death of a small Korean child his army unit had adopted. Fifty years later this tough survivor broke down and cried as he told the story. "All his people were gone—killed in the war—and so we took care of him. The little boy was killed in an artillery barrage—died in our arms."[13] Stanley Nelson, who lost a leg in the siege at Chipyong-ni, and who had been left for dead in a frozen rice paddy, was saved by a Chinese corpsman. Fifty years later Nelson noted, "Every day when I attach my artificial leg, I am reminded that I was the lucky one. I was plucked alive from a mountain that was littered with my dead comrades. And that Chinese corpsman turned out to be the Good Samaritan who saved my life."[14]

Donald Mayville, one of eight survivors out of his company of ninety-six men on the east side of the Chosin, struggled for many years with what he had seen in Korea. Even after serving three tours of duty in Vietnam, Mayville noted, "I was never the same after coming out of Chosin. When I got home my Mother was disappointed that I wasn't the boy that left home, and she shied away from me for the rest of my life. However, my father and I grew much closer because he went through the same thing with my older brother who was a medic in WWII in the Pacific for three years." Mayville eventually came to understand that talking about his experiences brought him some level of peace. "I feel that talking about the war keeps it out of my mind. I had nightmares for eight years after coming back. But after talking to everybody about it, that stopped," Mayville said.[15]

As the twenty-first century advances, surviving Hoosier veterans of the Korean War are becoming fewer in number. Their experiences and memories of those experiences, however, represent a priceless part of American and Indiana history. Hopefully, future generations of Hoosiers will make strong efforts to preserve the stories of the service of these Hoosier men and of the sacrifice of their families to ensure that in Indiana the Korean conflict will never be the forgotten war.

APPENDIX
Medal of Honor Citation for Donald C. Faith, Jr.

Rank and organization: Lieutenant Colonel, U.S. Army, commanding officer, 1st Battalion, 32nd Infantry Regiment, 7th Infantry Division. *Place and date:* Vicinity Hagaru-ri, Northern Korea, 27 November to 1 December 1950. *Entered service at:* Washington, Ind. *Born:* 26 August 1918, Washington, Ind. *G.O. No.:* 59, 2 August 1951. *Citation:* Lt. Col. Faith, commanding 1st Battalion, distinguished himself conspicuously by gallantry and intrepidity in action above and beyond the call of duty in the area of the Chosin Reservoir. When the enemy launched a fanatical attack against his battalion, Lt. Col. Faith unhesitatingly exposed himself to heavy enemy fire as he moved about directing action. When the enemy penetrated the positions, Lt. Col. Faith personally led counterattacks to restore the position. During an attack by his battalion to effect a junction with another U.S. unit, Lt. Col. Faith reconnoitered the route for, and personally directed, the first elements of his command across the ice-covered reservoir and then directed the movement of his vehicles which were loaded with wounded until all of his command had passed through the enemy fire. Having completed this . . . he crossed the reservoir himself. Assuming command of the force his unit had joined, he was given the mission of attacking to join friendly elements to the south. Lt. Col. Faith, although physically exhausted in the bitter cold, organized and launched an attack which was soon stopped by enemy fire. He ran forward under enemy small-arms and automatic weapons fire, got his men on their feet and personally led the fire attack as it blasted its way through the enemy ring. As they came to a hairpin curve, enemy fire from a roadblock again pinned the column down. Lt. Col. Faith organized a group of men and directed their attack on the enemy positions on the right flank. He then placed himself at the head of another group of men and in the face of direct enemy fire led an attack on the enemy roadblock, firing his pistol and throwing grenades. When he had reached a position approximately 30 yards from the roadblock, he was mortally wounded, but continued to direct the attack until the roadblock was overrun. Throughout the five days of action Lt. Col. Faith gave no thought to his safety and did not spare himself. His presence each time in the position of greatest danger was an inspiration to his men. Also, the damage he personally inflicted firing from his position at the head of his men was of material assistance on several occasions. Lt. Col. Faith's outstanding gallantry and noble self-sacrifice above and beyond the call of duty reflect the highest honor on him and are in keeping with the highest traditions of the U.S. Army. (This award supersedes the prior award of the Silver Star (First Oak Leaf Cluster) as announced in G.O. No. 32, Headquarters X Corps, dated 23 February 1951, for gallantry in action on 27 November 1950.

NOTES

Introduction

1. James R. Hetherington, *Indiana Remembers: Veterans of Korean and Vietnam Wars Honored with Twin Memorials* (Tolono, Ill.: Phoenix Publishing, 1996), 27.

2. Robert "Bud" Fitch correspondence with family. Original letters are in the possession of Gordon Fitch, Lawrence, Kans.

3. Of the 54,246 who died during the conflict, 33,629 were killed in action while 20,617 died of injuries or disease.

4. Roy E. Appleman, *East of Chosin: Entrapment and Breakout in Korea, 1950* (College Station: Texas A&M University Press, 1987), detailed, for example, the harsh environment of the Chosin campaign.

5. Ibid., xii.

6. Larry Zellers, *In Enemy Hands: A Prisoner in North Korea* (Lexington: University Press of Kentucky, 1991), 94.

7. Harold "Sonny" Bender correspondence with family. Original letters are in the possession of June Bender Ettensohn, Boonville, Ind.

8. Gordon Greene correspondence with Rada Mason. Original letters are in the possession of Marynelle Greene, Lincoln, Neb.

9. Fitch correspondence.

10. Greene correspondence.

11. Raleigh McGary correspondence. Original letters are in the possession of Raleigh McGary, Newburgh, Ind.

12. Zellers, *In Enemy Hands,* 99.

13. Fitch correspondence.

14. Ibid.

15. Bender correspondence.

16. Bonnie Eberle scrapbook, copy in the possession of the author.

17. Donald Hamilton correspondence with family. Original letters are in the possession of Charlene Cox, Solsberry, Ind.

18. Bender correspondence.

19. Ralph Steele correspondence to family. Original letters are in the possession of Ralph Steele, Jasper, Ind.

20. Fitch correspondence.

21. Bender correspondence.

22. John Toland, *In Mortal Combat: Korea, 1950–1953* (New York: William Morrow, 1991, 483.

Chapter One

1. Arthur Herman, *Joseph McCarthy: Reexamining the Life and Legacy of America's Most Hated Senator* (New York: Free Press, 2000), 35.
2. Michael Barone, *Our Country: The Shaping of America from Roosevelt to Reagan* (New York: Free Press, 1990), 155.
3. Kenneth P. McCutchan, *At the Bend in the River: The Story of Evansville* (Woodland Hills, Calif.: Windsor Publications, 1982), 89–91.
4. John Bartlow Martin, *Indiana: An Interpretation* (New York: Alfred A. Knopf, 1947), 255.
5. *U.S. News and World Report,* 6 Jan. 1950.
6. *Newsweek,* 2 Jan. 1950.
7. *Lafayette Courier and Journal,* 10 July 1950.
8. *Indianapolis Star,* 23 June 1950.
9. Ibid., 4 June 1950.
10. Ibid., 2 June 1950.
11. Ibid., 4 June 1950.
12. *Fort Wayne Journal-Gazette,* 11, 14 June 1950.
13. Ibid., 23 June 1950.
14. *Indiana Daily Student,* 9 May 1950.
15. Ibid., 6 June 1950.
16. Ibid., 23, 24 June 1950.
17. *Evansville Courier*, 22 June 1950.
18. Ibid., 23 June 1950.
19. *Indianapolis Recorder,* 8 Apr. 1950.
20. Ibid., 10 June 1950.
21. Ibid.
22. A copy of this letter is in the possession of the author. The letter was dated 18 Sept. 1950.
23. Martin, *Indiana,* 274.
24. Ibid., 275.
25. David Halberstam, *The Fifties* (New York: Villard Books, 1993), 17.
26. David Caute, *The Great Fear: The Anti-Communist Purge under Truman and Eisenhower* (New York: Simon and Schuster, 1978), 163, 417.
27. William Marshall, interview with author.
28. *Newsweek,* 22 May 1950.
29. Hobert Young, interview with author.
30. Robert Doane, interview with author.
31. Samuel Muncy, interview with author.
32. Stanley Nelson, interview with author.
33. Delores Beeson, interview with author.
34. Military service records of Charles Garrigus, Jr., Department of the Army, 5 July 1954. Original records are in the possession of Delores Beeson.
35. Edward F. Murphy, *Korean War Heroes* (Novato, Calif.: Presidio Press, 1992), 109.

36. Roy E. Appleman, *East of Chosin: Entrapment and Breakout in Korea, 1950* (College Station: Texas A&M University Press, 1987), 20.

37. Donald Mayville correspondence with author. Original correspondence is in the possession of the author.

38. Ira Neal, interview with author.

39. Herbert Crowe, interview with author.

40. Donald Hamilton correspondence with family. Original letters are in the possession of Ralph Steele, Jasper, Ind.

41. Everett Wayne Leffler correspondence and Barnett/Leffler interviews. Original letters are in the possession of Bettie Leffler Barnett.

42. *Time,* 8 May 1950.

43. Thomas Chappell correspondence with author. For an assessment of the call-up of army reservists, see Bevin Alexander, *Korea: The First War We Lost* (New York: Hippocrene Books, 1986), 49.

44. William Chappell, interview with author.

45. Gary A. Donaldson, *Truman Defeats Dewey* (Lexington: University Press of Kentucky, 1999), 14.

46. *Time,* 19 June 1950.

47. *The Marine Corps Reserve: A History* (Washington, D.C.: Division of Reserve Headquarters, U.S. Marine Corps, 1966), 102.

48. Ibid., 113–25.

49. Paul Torian, interview with author.

50. Ralph Steele, interview with author.

51. David Graham, interview with author.

52. Henry Orth, Jr., interview with author.

53. Andy Jacobs, Jr., interview with author.

54. Howard Suttmiller, interview with author.

55. *Devil Dog,* 29 June 1950.

56. Torian interview.

57. *Marine Corps Reserve,* 119.

58. Ibid., 133.

59. Gordon Greene correspondence with Rada Mason. Original letters are in the possession of Marynelle Greene, Lincoln, Neb.

60. J. Robert Moskin, *The U.S. Marine Corps Story* (New York: McGraw-Hill, 1977), 468.

61. *The Leatherneck,* Mar. 1950.

Chapter Two

1. *U.S. News and World Report,* 6 Jan. 1950.

2. *Newsweek,* 3 July 1950.

3. *Time,* 10 July 1950.

4. Ibid., 31 July 1950.

5. William B. Breuer, *Shadow Warriors: The Covert War in Korea* (New York: John Wiley and Sons, 1996), 18, 37, 49–50.

6. Samuel Muncy, interview with author.
7. Donald Hamilton correspondence with family. Original letters are in the possession of Charlene Cox, Solsberry, Ind.
8. Stanley Nelson, interview with author.
9. Robert Doane, interview with author.
10. David Graham, interview with author.
11. Andy Jacobs, Jr., interview with author.
12. Ralph Steele, interview with author.
13. Mrs. Homer H. McAtee correspondence. The original letters are in the possession of William Marshall of Oakland City, Ind.
14. Ibid.
15. Ibid.
16. *Indianapolis Star,* 20 July 1950.
17. John Toland, *In Mortal Combat: Korea, 1950–1953* (New York: William Morrow, 1991), 77.
18. Nelson interview.
19. *Time,* 31 July 1950.
20. Nelson interview.
21. In Joseph C. Goulden, *Korea: The Untold Story of the War* (New York: Times Books, 1982), 139–40.
22. Hobert Young, interview with author.
23. *Oakland City Journal,* 3 Aug. 1950.
24. Toland, *Mortal Combat,* 162.
25. Doane interview.
26. Carl Spencer, interview with author.
27. Larry Zellers, *In Enemy Hands: A Prisoner in North Korea* (Lexington: University Press of Kentucky, 1991), 56.
28. Ibid., 159–60.
29. Hamilton correspondence.
30. Thomas Chappell correspondence with author.
31. *The Marine Corps Reserve: A History* (Washington, D.C.: Division of Reserve Headquarters, U.S. Marine Corps, 1966), 167.
32. *Evansville Press,* 28 Aug. 1950.
33. Charles "Barney" Barnard correspondence. Original letters in the possession of Betty Ann Risley, Oakland City, Ind.
34. Graham interview.
35. Ralph Steele correspondence to family. Original letters in the possession of Ralph Steele, Jasper, Ind.
36. David Graham correspondence with author.
37. *U.S. News and World Report,* 20 Oct. 1950.
38. Ibid., 9 Jan. 1951.
39. *Indianapolis Star,* 1 Aug. 1950.
40. Ibid., 4 Dec. 1950.

Notes

41. Ibid., 6 Dec. 1950.
42. Ibid., 28 Aug. 1950.
43. Bevin Alexander, *Korea: The First War We Lost* (New York: Hippocrene, 1986), 49.
44. William Hasselbrinck, interview with author.
45. *Indianapolis Star,* 20 July 1950.
46. Gordon Greene correspondence with Rada Mason. Original letters are in the possession of Marynelle Greene, Lincoln, Neb.
47. *Indianapolis Star,* 27 June 1950.
48. Ibid., 1 Aug. 1950.
49. *Evansville Courier,* 25 Oct. 1950.
50. *Indianapolis Star,* 27 June 1950.
51. Ibid., 1 July 1950.
52. Ibid., 1 Aug. 1950.
53. *Lafayette Journal and Courier,* 12 July 1950.
54. *Evansville Courier,* 27 June 1950.
55. *Evansville Press,* 28 June 1950.
56. *Evansville Sunday Courier and Press,* 2 July 1950.
57. *Fort Wayne Journal-Gazette,* 28 June 1950.
58. *Dubois County Daily Herald,* 7 July 1950.
59. Ibid., 31 July 1950.
60. *Terre Haute Tribune,* 26 June 1950.
61. Ibid., 26 June 1950.
62. Ibid., 28 June 1950.
63. Ibid., 29 June 1950.
64. Ibid., 30 June 1950.
65. Ibid., 6 July 1950.
66. *Indiana Daily Student,* 27 June 1950.
67. Ibid., 28 June 1950.
68. Ibid., 6 July 1950.
69. Ibid., 13 July 1950.
70. Ibid., 25 July 1950.
71. Ibid., 18 July 1950.
72. Ibid., 22 July 1950.
73. *Indianapolis Recorder,* 22 July 1950.
74. Ibid., 8 July 1950.
75. Ibid., 29 July 1950.
76. Ibid., 5 Aug. 1950.
77. *Time,* 31 July 1950.
78. *Lafayette Journal and Courier,* 12 July 1950.
79. *Indianapolis Star,* 21 July 1950.
80. Clay Blair, *The Forgotten War: America in Korea* (New York: Times Books, 1988), 262.

Chapter Three

1. Roy E. Appleman, *East of Chosin: Entrapment and Breakout in Korea, 1950* (College Station: Texas A&M University Press, 1987), xii–xv.
2. *Indiana Daily Student,* 2 Aug. 1950.
3. *Fort Wayne Journal-Gazette,* 27 July 1950.
4. Ibid., 30 July 1950.
5. Ibid.
6. Ibid., 26 Aug. 1950.
7. *Evansville Press,* 21 July 1950.
8. Ibid.
9. *Indianapolis Star,* 21 July 1950.
10. Ibid., 27 Aug. 1950.
11. Andy Jacobs, Jr., interview with author.
12. *Indianapolis Star,* 29 Aug. 1950.
13. Ibid., 28 Aug. 1950.
14. *Evansville Courier,* 29 Aug. 1950.
15. Ibid., 31 Aug. 1950.
16. Ibid., 29 Aug. 1950.
17. *Evansville Sunday Courier and Press,* 24 Sept. 1950.
18. Joseph R. Owen, *Colder than Hell: A Marine Rifle Company at Chosin Reservoir* (New York: Ivy Books, 1997), 16.
19. Gordon Greene correspondence with Rada Mason. Original letters are in the possession of Marynelle Greene, Lincoln, Neb.
20. Ibid.
21. Donald Burton, interview with author.
22. Andy Jacobs, Jr., *The 1600 Killers: A Wake-up Call for Congress* (Greenwood, Ind.: Alistair Press, 1999), 8.
23. Robert "Bud" Fitch correspondence with family. Original letters are in the possession of Gordon Fitch, Lawrence, Kans.
24. Ralph Steele, interview with author.
25. Greene correspondence.
26. *Time,* 28 Aug. 1950.
27. *U.S. News and World Report,* 1 Sept. 1950.
28. Greene correspondence.
29. Stanley Sandler, *The Korean War: No Victors, No Vanquished* (Lexington: University Press of Kentucky, 1999), 194.
30. James L. Stokesbury, *A Short History of the Korean War* (New York: William Morrow, 1988), 208.
31. William Chappell, interview with author.
32. John Toland, *In Mortal Combat: Korea, 1950–1953* (New York: William Morrow, 1991), 192.
33. William Chappell interview.
34. Presidential Citation 25 Sept. 1951. The original copy of one of the citations used in this work is in the possession of William Chappell of Huntingburg, Ind.

35. Samuel Muncy interview with author.
36. Donald Hamilton correspondence with family. Original letters are in the possession of Charlene Cox, Solsberry, Ind.
37. Charles "Barney" Barnard correspondence. Original letters are in the possession of Betty Ann Risley, Oakland City, Ind.
38. Jess Thurman, interview with author.
39. Hamilton correspondence.
40. William Chappell interview.
41. Stanley Nelson, interview with author.
42. *Dubois County Daily Herald,* 14, 19 Oct. 1950.
43. Nelson interview.
44. Carl Spencer, interview with author.
45. Raleigh McGary correspondence. Original letters are in the possession of Raleigh McGary, Newburgh, Ind.
46. Nelson interview.
47. Thomas Chappell correspondence with author.
48. Eliot A. Cohen and John Gooch, *Military Misfortunes: The Anatomy of Failure in War* (New York: Vintage Books, 1991), 185.
49. S. L. A. Marshall, *The River and the Gauntlet* (New York: Time, 1953), 1.
50. Russell Spurr, *Enter the Dragon: China's Undeclared War against the U.S. in Korea, 1950–51* (New York: Newmarket Press, 1988), 191.
51. Marshall, *River and the Gauntlet,* 275.
52. Spurr, *Enter the Dragon,* 201, 212–13.
53. Spencer interview.
54. Everett Wayne Leffler correspondence and Barnett/Leffler interviews. Original letters are in the possession of Bettie Leffler Barnett.
55. Marshall, *River and the Gauntlet,* 333–35.
56. Nelson interview.
57. Spencer interview.

Chapter Four
1. *Time,* 4 Dec. 1950.
2. Clay Blair, *The Forgotten War: America in Korea* (New York: Times Books, 1988), 459.
3. Delores Beeson, interview with author.
4. Donald Hamilton correspondence with family. Original letters are in the possession of Charlene Cox, Solsberry, Ind.
5. Edward F. Murphy, *Korean War Heroes* (Novato, Calif.: Presidio, 1992), 89.
6. Alan Cork correspondence. Copy in the possession of the author.
7. Roy E. Appleman, *East of Chosin: Entrapment and Breakout in Korea, 1950* (College Station: Texas A&M University Press, 1987), 12.
8. Raleigh McGary correspondence. Original letters are in the possession of Raleigh McGary, Newburgh, Ind.

9. David McCullough, "Truman Fires MacArthur," *The Quarterly Journal of Military History* 1, no. 1 (1992): 13.
10. *New York Times,* 28 Nov. 1950.
11. *Evansville Courier,* 30 Nov. 1950.
12. Ibid., 1 Dec. 1950.
13. Paul McDaniel, interview with author.
14. Donald Burton, interview with author.
15. Howard Suttmiller, interview with author.
16. David Graham, correspondence with author.
17. Lynn Montross and Nicholas Canzona, *The Chosin Campaign*, vol. 3 of *U.S. Marine Operations in Korea, 1950–1953* (Washington, D.C.: Government Printing Office, 1957), 351.
18. Samuel Muncy, interview with author.
19. Blair, *Forgotten War*, 459.
20. Ibid.,160.
21. Alan Cork, interview with author.
22. Blair, *Forgotten War*, 462.
23. Russell A. Gugeler, *Combat Actions in Korea* (Washington, D.C.: Combat Forces Press, 1954), 70.
24. Distinguished Service Cross Citation for Charles Garrigus, Jr., General orders No. 201, 7 Aug. 1951.
25. There are several accounts of Colonel MacLean's disappearance. The most accurate is probably in Appleman, *East of Chosin*, 141–47.
26. Cork interview.
27. Appleman, *East of Chosin*, 176.
28. Ibid., 187.
29. Murphy, *Korean War Heroes*, 112–13.
30. Appleman, *East of Chosin*, 194.
31. Ibid., 199.
32. Garrigus Distinguished Service Cross citation.
33. Appleman, *East of Chosin*, 269–70.
34. Muncy interview.
35. Cork correspondence.
36. Charlene Cox, interview with author.
37. Appleman, *East of Chosin*, 228.
38. Garrigus Distinguished Service Cross citation.
39. Cork correspondence.
40. Eric M. Hammel, *Chosin: Heroic Ordeal of the Korean War* (Novato, Calif.: Presidio, 1990), 236.
41. Louis Joseph Grappo correspondence.
42. Muncy interview.
43. Murphy, *Korean War Heroes*, 114.
44. Appleman, *East of Chosin*, 269–70.
45. Garrigus Distinguished Service Cross citation.

Notes

46. Muncy interview.
47. Cork interview.
48. Donald Mayville correspondence with author. Original correspondence is in the possession of the author.
49. Appleman, *East of Chosin*, 274.
50. Ibid., 320.
51. Gen. Douglas MacArthur, letter to Gladys Garrigus, 3 Apr. 1951.
52. Garrigus Distinguished Service Cross citation.
53. *Indianapolis Star,* 5 Dec. 1950.
54. *Terre Haute Tribune,* 7 Dec. 1950.
55. *Evansville Courier,* 8 Dec. 1950.
56. *Indiana Daily Student*, 3 Nov., 6 Dec. 1950.
57. Ibid., 15 Nov. 1950.
58. Ibid., 29 Nov. 1950.
59. Ibid., 7 Dec. 1950.
60. *Dubois County Daily Herald,* 16, 17 Jan. 1951.
61. *Indianapolis Star,* 3 Dec. 1950.
62. *Evansville Courier,* 7 Dec. 1950.
63. *Evansville Sunday Courier and Press,* 10 Dec. 1950.
64. *Indianapolis Star,* 6 Dec. 1950.
65. Ibid., 2 Dec. 1950.
66. Ibid., 6 Dec. 1950.
67. Ibid., 8 Dec. 1950.
68. *Evansville Press,* 10 Dec. 1950.
69. *Evansville Courier*, 11, 12 Dec. 1950.
70. Charles "Barney" Barnard correspondence. Original letters are in the possession of Betty Ann Risley, Oakland City, Ind.
71. Hamilton correspondence.

Chapter Five

1. James L. Stokesbury, *A Short History of the Korean War* (New York: William Morrow, 1988), 114.
2. Gordon Greene correspondence with Rada Mason. Original letters are in the possession of Marynelle Greene, Lincoln, Neb.
3. Lynn Montross, Hubbard D. Kuokka, and Norman Hicks, *The East-Central Front*, vol. 4 of *U.S. Marine Operations in Korea, 1950–1953* (Washington, D.C.: Government Printing Office, 1962).
4. Robert Whitehouse, interview with author.
5. Carl Spencer, interview with author.
6. Stokesbury, *Short History of the Korean War,* 55, 207–8.
7. Spencer interview.
8. William Cunningham, interview with author.
9. Marvin Boeglin, interview with author.

10. Marvin Boeglin correspondence. Original letters are in the possession of Marvin Boeglin, Huntingburg, Ind.
11. Dexter Crane, interview with author.
12. Harold "Sonny" Bender correspondence with family. Original letters are in the possession of June Bender Ettensohn, Boonville, Ind.
13. Spencer interview.
14. Stanley Nelson, interview with author.
15. Silver Star citation for Stanley Nelson.
16. Greene correspondence.
17. Clay Blair, *The Forgotten War: America in Korea* (New York: Times Books, 1988), 710, 711.
18. Greene correspondence.
19. Robert "Bud" Fitch correspondence with family. Original letters are in the possession of Gordon Fitch, Lawrence, Kans.
20. Donald Burton, interview with author.
21. Andy Jacobs, Jr., *The 1600 Killers: A Wake-up Call for Congress* (Greenwood, Ind.: Alistair Press, 1999), 11–13, 15.
22. Bender correspondence.
23. Edward F. Murphy, *Korean War Heroes* (Novato, Calif.: Presidio, 1992), 172.
24. D. Clayton James, *Refighting the Last War: Command and Crisis in Korea, 1950–1953* (New York: Free Press, 1993), 7.
25. Ira Neal, interview with author.
26. Herbert Crowe, interview with author.
27. *Indianapolis Recorder,* 15 Aug. 1953.
28. Greene correspondence.
29. Ralph Steele, interview with author.
30. Whitehouse interview.
31. Kenneth Dougan, interview with author.
32. David Graham correspondence with author.
33. Boeglin interview.
34. Crane interview.

Chapter Six
1. Richard Polenberg, *War and Society: The United States, 1941–1945* (New York: J. B. Lippincott Co., 1972).
2. Gordon Greene, *A Star for Buster* (Huntington, W.Va.: University Editions, 1994), 83.
3. *U.S. News and World Report,* 7 July 1950.
4. Ibid., 28 July 1950.
5. *Indianapolis Star*, 1 July 1950.
6. *Terre Haute Tribune*, 3 July 1950.
7. *Indianapolis Star,* 27 Aug. 1950.

8. *Evansville Sunday Courier and Press*, 23 July 1950.
9. *Fort Wayne Journal-Gazette*, 28 July 1950.
10. *Indianapolis Star*, 2 July 1950.
11. *Indiana Daily Student*, 6 Sept. 1950.
12. Ibid., 28 July 1950.
13. Ibid., 29 July 1950.
14. Ibid., 11 July 1950.
15. Ibid., 6 Dec. 1950.
16. Ibid., 2 Sept. 1950.
17. *Evansville Press*, 28 June 1950.
18. *Indianapolis Star*, 20 July 1950.
19. Ibid., 21 July 1950.
20. Ibid., 1 July 1950.
21. *Dubois County Daily Herald*, 29 July 1950.
22. *Indianapolis Star*, 22 July 1950.
23. *Terre Haute Tribune*, 6 July 1950.
24. *Evansville Courier*, 8 Aug. 1950,
25. *Indianapolis Star*, 20 July 1950.
26. Ibid., 21 July 1950.
27. Ibid., 4 Aug. 1950.
28. *Lafayette Journal and Courier*, 12 July 1950.
29. *Evansville Press*, 22 July 1950.
30. William Marshall correspondence. Original letters are in the possession of William Marshall, Oakland City, Ind.
31. *Indiana Daily Student*, 27 July 1950.
32. *Oakland City Journal*, 27 July 1950.
33. *Time*, 7 Aug. 1950.
34. *Indianapolis Star*, 19 July 1950.
35. Ibid., 27 Aug. 1950.
36. Ibid.
37. *Evansville Sunday Courier and Press*, 2 July 1950.
38. *Indianapolis Star*, 27 Aug. 1950.
39. Ibid., 18 July 1950.
40. Ibid., 29 June 1950.
41. Douglas T. Miller and Marion Nowak, *The Fifties: The Way We Really Were* (Garden City, N.Y.: Doubleday, 1977), 49, 50.
42. *Evansville Sunday Courier and Press*, 13 Aug. 1950.
43. *Evansville Press*, 8 Aug. 1950.
44. *Evansville Sunday Courier and Press*, 2 July 1950.
45. *Terre Haute Tribune*, 6 July 1950.
46. *Indiana Daily Student*, 21 Sept. 1950.
47. *Indianapolis Star*, 2 Aug. 1950.
48. Ibid., 6 Dec. 1950.
49. Ibid., 19 Aug. 1950.

50. Ibid., 5 Dec. 1950.
51. Ibid., 29 June 1950.
52. Ibid., 27 Aug. 1950.
53. Ibid., 20 July 1950.
54. Bonnie Eberle scrapbook, copy in the possession of the author.
55. Ibid., 15 Sept. 1950.
56. *Indianapolis Star,* 22 July 1950.
57. *Time,* 28 Aug. 1950.
58. *Indianapolis Star,* 1 July 1950.
59. Ibid., 29 June 1950.
60. *Evansville Sunday Courier and Press,* 24 Sept. 1950.
61. Robert "Bud" Fitch correspondence with family. Original letters are in the possession of Gordon Fitch, Lawrence, Kans.
62. *Evansville Press,* 28 Aug. 1950.
63. Gordon Greene correspondence with Rada Mason. Original letters are in the possession of Marynelle Greene, Lincoln, Neb.
64. Paul McDaniel correspondence.
65. Marshall correspondence.
66. Charles "Barney" Barnard correspondence. Original letters are in the possession of Betty Ann Risley, Oakland City, Ind.
67. Fitch correspondence.
68. Barnard correspondence.
69. Marshall correspondence.
70. Stanley Nelson correspondence. Original letters are in the possession of Stanley Nelson, Otwell, Ind.
71. Ralph Steele correspondence, Original letters are in the possession of Ralph Steele, Jasper, Ind.
72. Marvin Boeglin correspondence. Original letters are in the possession of Marvin Boeglin, Huntingburg, Ind.
73. Harold "Sonny" Bender correspondence with family. Original letters are in the possession of June Bender Ettensohn, Boonville, Ind.
74. Fitch correspondence.
75. Walter Etheridge correspondence with family. Original letters are in the possession of William Etheridge, Evansville, Ind.
76. Barnard correspondence.
77. Greene correspondence.
78. Steele correspondence.
79. Fitch correspondence.
80. Nelson correspondence.
81. Martin Brizius family interview with author.
82. Western Union telegram to Mr. and Mrs. Martin C. Brizius, 11 Mar. 1950.
83. Brizius family interview.
84. Karl F. Bowling, telegram to Mr. and Mrs. Joseph Bowling, 8 Dec. 1950.
85. Western Union telegram to Mr. and Mrs. Joseph Bowling, 9 June 1951.

86. Maj. Gen. William Bergin, telegram to Mr. and Mrs. Joseph Bowling, 15 June 1951.

87. Maj. Gen. William Bergin, letter to Mrs. Joseph Bowling, 21 June 1951.

88. Joseph Haag, interview with author.

89. Maj. Burgess P. Riddle, letter to Nellie [Mrs. Joseph] Bowling, 29 June 1951.

90. Haag interview.

91. Robert Doane, interview with author.

92. William Barnard, interview with author.

93. Greene correspondence.

94. Barnard correspondence.

95. Greene correspondence.

96. Sydney Greenwood correspondence with Fitch family. Original letters are in the possession of Gordon Fitch, Lawrence, Kans.

97. Everett Wayne Leffler correspondence, Bettie Leffler Barnett correspondence, and Barnett/Leffler interviews. Original letters are in the possession of Bettie Leffler Barnett.

98. Maj. Gen. Edward Witsell, letter to Mr. and Mrs. Everett Leffler, 17 Dec. 1950, ibid.

99. Ibid., 11 May 1951.

100. Bettie Leffler Barnett correspondence.

101. *Dubois County Daily Herald,* 28 July 1953.

102. *Indiana Daily Student,* 28 July 1953.

103. *Indianapolis Star,* 27 July 1953.

104. *Indianapolis Recorder,* 8 Aug. 1953.

105. Ibid.

106. *Indianapolis Star,* 27 July 1953.

107. Greene, *Star for Buster,* 303.

Chapter Seven

1. *Indianapolis Star,* 27 July 1953.
2. Ibid., 28 July 1953.
3. William Hyde, interview with author.
4. Ralph Steele, interview with author.
5. Robert Whitehouse, interview with author.
6. Andy Jacobs, Jr., *The 1600 Killers: A Wake-up Call for Congress* (Greenwood, Ind.: Alistair Press, 1999), 29.
7. Ibid., 58–59.
8. Ibid., 80.
9. Ira Neal, interview with author.
10. *Indianapolis Recorder,* 8 Aug. 1953.
11. Charlene Cox, interview with author.

12. James R. Hetherington, *Indiana Remembers: Veterans of Korean and Vietnam Wars Honored with Twin Memorials* (Tolono, Ill.: Phoenix Publishing, 1996), 23.
13. Hobert Young, interview with author.
14. Stanley Nelson, interview with author.
15. Donald Mayville correspondence with author. Original correspondence is in the possession of the author.

BIBLIOGRAPHY

Alexander, Bevin. *Korea: The First War We Lost*. New York: Hippocrene, 1986.

Appleman, Roy E. *East of Chosin: Entrapment and Breakout in Korea, 1950*. College Station: Texas A&M University Press, 1987.

Barone, Michael. *Our Country: The Shaping of America from Roosevelt to Reagan*. New York: Free Press, 1990.

Blair, Clay. *The Forgotten War: America in Korea*. New York: Times Books, 1988.

Breuer, William B. *Shadow Warriors: The Covert War in Korea*. New York: John Wiley and Sons, 1996.

Caute, David. *The Great Fear: The Anti-Communist Purge under Truman and Eisenhower*. New York: Simon and Schuster, 1978.

Cohen, Eliot A., and John Gooch. *Military Misfortunes: The Anatomy of Failure in War*. New York: Vintage Books, 1991.

Committee on Veterans' Affairs. *Medal of Honor Recipients, 1863–1978*. United States Government Printing Office, 1979.

Devil Dog. C Company, Sixteenth Infantry Battalion, Evansville, Indiana, July 1950.

Donaldson, Gary A. *Truman Defeats Dewey*. Lexington: University Press of Kentucky, 1999.

Faux, William. *Memorable Days in America, 1819–1820*. In *Early Western Travels*, edited by Reuben Gold Thwaites. Cleveland: Arthur H. Clark, 1905.

Goulden, Joseph C. *Korea: The Untold Story of the War.* New York: Times Books, 1982.

Greene, Gordon. *The 38th Parallel Revisited.* Lincoln: Department of Nebraska Marine Corps League, 1990.

———. "Boondockers." Unpublished novel, 1972.

———. *A Star for Buster.* Huntington, W.Va.: University Editions, 1994.

Gugeler, Russell A. *Combat Actions in Korea.* Washington, D.C.: Combat Forces Press, 1954.

Halberstam, David. *The Fifties.* New York: Villard Books, 1993.

Hammel, Eric M. *Chosin: Heroic Ordeal of the Korean War.* Novato, Calif.: Presidio, 1990.

Herman, Arthur. *Joseph McCarthy: Rexamining the Life and Legacy of America's Most Hated Senator.* New York: Free Press, 2000.

Hetherington, James R. *Indiana Remembers: Veterans of Korean and Vietnam Wars Honored with Twin Memorials.* Tolono, Ill.: Phoenix Publishing, 1996.

Jacobs, Andy, Jr. *The 1600 Killers: A Wake-up Call for Congress.* Greenwood, Ind.: Alistair Press, 1999.

James, D. Clayton. *Refighting the Last War: Command and Crisis in Korea, 1950–1953.* New York: Free Press, 1993.

McCutchan, Kenneth P. *At the Bend in the River: The Story of Evansville.* Woodland Hills, Calif.: Windsor Publications, 1982.

The Marine Corps Reserve: A History. Washington, D.C.: Division of Reserve Headquarters, U.S. Marine Corps, 1966.

Marshall, S. L. A. *The River and the Gauntlet.* New York: Time, 1953.

Martin, John Bartlow. *Indiana: An Interpretation.* New York: Alfred A. Knopf, 1947.

Miller, Douglas T., and Marion Nowak. *The Fifties: The Way We Really Were.* Garden City, N.Y.: Doubleday, 1977.

Montross, Lynn, and Nicholas A. Canzona. *The Chosin Campaign.* Vol. 3 of *U.S. Marine Operations in Korea, 1950–1953.* Washington, D.C.: Government Printing Office, 1957.

Montross, Lynn, Hubard D. Kuokka, and Norman Hicks. *The East-Central Front*. Vol. 4 of *U.S. Marine Operations in Korea, 1950–1953*. Washington, D.C.: Government Printing Office, 1962.
Moskin, J. Robert. *The U.S. Marine Corps Story*. New York: McGraw-Hill, 1977.
Murphy, Edward F. *Korean War Heroes*. Novato, Calif.: Presidio, 1992.
Owen, Joseph R. *Colder than Hell: A Marine Rifle Company at Chosin Reservoir*. New York: Ivy Books, 1997.
Polenberg, Richard. *War and Society: The United States, 1941–1945*. New York: J. B. Lippincott Co., 1972.
Sandler, Stanley. *The Korean War: No Victors, No Vanquished*. Lexington: University Press of Kentucky, 1999.
Spurr, Russell, *Enter the Dragon: China's Undeclared War against the U.S. in Korea, 1950–51*. New York: Newmarket Press, 1988.
Stokesbury, James L. *A Short History of the Korean War*. New York: William Morrow, 1988.
Toland, John. *In Mortal Combat: Korea, 1950–1953*. New York: William Morrow, 1991.
Zellers, Larry. *In Enemy Hands: A Prisoner in North Korea*. Lexington: University Press of Kentucky, 1991.

INDEX

Able Company (marines), 227, 228; and Chinese spring offensive, 177
Acheson, Dean, 69
Adams, _____, 142
African Americans, 18–19, 77; serve in Korea, xx, 76; and discrimination, 7, 237–39; in armed forces, 8, 19–20; and segregation of armed forces, 20, 182; and response to Korean War, 75–76, 183; and desegregation of armed services, 180–81
Alexander, Bevin, xiv
Allotments, 212, 213
American Association of University Professors, 9
American Red Cross, 179, 207
Ammunition, 46; production of, 3; lack of, 106, 141, 143, 155, 165, 185
Andong, 154
Appleman, Roy E., xiv, 81, 118, 144
Armed forces: and lack of preparedness, xix, 15, 26–27, 38–39; discrimination in, 8, 20, 238; financial hardships encourage young men to enlist in, 12, 13, 15, 16; African-American quotas in, 19–20; reduction of, 26, 27, 28; poor performance of, 77–78; desegregation of, 180–81, 229–30
Atomic bomb, 77, 146, 148, 149, 204, 207, 208, 209

B-26 Invader (bomber), 158, 159
Barnard, Mrs. _____, 226
Barnard, Charles "Barney," 33; complains about lack of training, 60; writes about savage fighting and capture of Seoul, 97; and escape from Chosin, 150; injured, 216; writes of Bud Fitch's death, 227; illus., 59
Barnard, William, 224, 225, 226, 227
Barr, David, 123, 126
Bayh, Evan, xiii
Bender, Alan, 179
Bender, Harold "Sonny": describes Korean landscape, xvii; drafted, 65; letters home, 78–79, 160–63, 215; hospitalized, 178; killed, 180; illus., 180
Blair, Clay, xiv, 78, 114, 170
Bloomfield Evening World, 13
Boeglin, Marvin: and bombing missions, 158–59, 192; letters to wife, 214–15
Boonville, 20
Boot camp, 28, 33, 60, 90–91, 214
Bosse High School (Evansville), 28, 29
Bowling, Joseph, 220
Bowling, Mrs. Joseph, 220, 222
Bowling, Karl, 220, 223; killed, 221; funeral of, 222; illus., 221
Bowling family, 221, 222
Boyer, _____, 143

Branning, Henry E., Jr., 5
Branstetter, Bill, 41
"Brave Hero" (poem), 224
Breakouts, 133; Colonel Faith plans, 132; lack of organization in, 134, 135; becomes fight for survival, 134, 136; survivors of, 144–45
Breuer, William, 38
Brizius, Jackie, 218, 219
Brizius, Margaret, 220
Brizius, Mrs. Martin C., 218, 219, 220
Brizius, Martin Craig, 218; killed, 219; funeral of, 220
Brizius, Robert, 218
Brizius family, 220
Bugout, 48
Burton, Donald: and marine reserve training, 90; Chosin campaign and his narrow escape, 122–23; and Chinese spring offensive, 175
Buyher, Tom, 33

C Company (army), 115
C Company, Sixteenth Infantry Battalion (marines), 32; training of, 60
C-47 (airplane), 187
C-119 (cargo plane), 160
C rations, 46, 49, 118–19, 129, 144
Camp Atterbury (Ind.), 70
Camp Breckenridge (Ky.), 107
Camp Drake (Japan), 15
Camp Pendleton (Calif.), 43, 45, 60, 83, 84, 85, 87, 88, 89, 91–92, 225
Camp Stoneman (Calif.), 59
Campbell, Denning: illus., 86
Capehart, Homer E., 5, 9, 10, 67, 150, 212
Casualties, xv, 52, 53–54, 57, 58, 73, 78, 96, 97, 98, 99, 105, 117, 122, 132, 133, 134, 135, 137, 138, 139, 142, 143, 150, 157, 159, 160, 163, 166, 177, 180, 181, 182, 184, 185, 186, 198, 201, 216, 217, 219, 220, 221, 222, 223, 225, 227, 229, 230, 233; civilians, 100, 101, 241; MIA, 110, 126, 228, 239, 240; Chinese, 126, 156, 162, 165, 170, 172, 175, 180
Cates, Clifton B., 45
Central High School (Evansville), 28
Chappell, Thomas, 62, 78, 94, 100; joins army reserve, 24, 25; reserve unit activated, 58, 59; describes winter combat in Korea, 102–4
Chappell, William, 100; joins navy, 26; and Inchon invasion, 94, 95
Cherrington, George, 159
Chin hung-ni, 122
China: troops fight in Korea, xix, xvi, xx, 72, 81, 156, 174, 175, 215, 233; troops at Chosin Reservoir, 96, 115, 220; threats, concerns, and rumors about troops entering war, 99, 102, 113; enters war, 104, 122; troops attack at "The Gauntlet," 105, 106, 107, 109; troops pushed back across thirty-eighth parallel, 107; troops pursue retreating forces, 110; troops trap American forces, 121, 122–23, 126, 127, 129, 145; ambushes by troops, 122, 188; and dead troops, 123; troops attack at night, 131–32, 156; troops attack convoys, 134, 138, 139, 143; troops capture weapons, 141; and treatment of U.S. dead and wounded, 141, 143, 166, 167; troops detained by Task Force Faith, 144; fears of war with, 145–46, 147; and inability of troops to pursue UN forces, 153; troops begin to move south, 154; number of troops, 161; forces halted by UN troops, 170–71; troops launch spring offensive, 171, 174, 175, 176, 178, 179, 180, 187; condition of troops and equipment, 173;

Index

attempt to indoctrinate African-American prisoners, 183; troops bring up artillery, 183, 184; forces taunt U.S. troops, 185; and end of Korean War, 234
Chipyong-ni, battle at, xvi, 162–63, 164–71, 178, 241
Chosin: Heroic Ordeal of the Korean War, xiv
Chosin Reservoir, xix, 81, 96, 113, 114, 115, 142, 143; battle at, xv, xvi, 18, 127–29, 130–50, 154, 187, 213, 220, 226, 241; marines retreat from, 122–23, 126
Chrysler-Plymouth (Evansville), 3
Chunchon, 174
Civil defense, 206, 207, 208, 209
Civil rights, 77
Civilian Defense Organization, 208
Cockrum family, 224
Cold war, 38
Combat, 46, 47–49, 50–53, 78, 96, 98, 106, 107, 128, 129, 142, 143, 163, 165, 176, 177, 178; African Americans in, 8–9; fatigue in, 49, 132; naval, 94, 95; and Korean weather, 103, 117–18, 121, 130, 133; and inexperienced officers, 104; fear in, 144–45, 185; hand-to-hand, 165; sleep during, 178; and friendly fire, 186; and superstitions, 188; nightmares after, 241
Communism, 9, 38, 66, 69, 70, 71, 73, 77, 147, 183, 193, 202, 234
Communist party, 209, 210
Communist sympathizers, 179
Company A (army), 135, 136
Company B, 18th Infantry Battalion, U.S. Marine Corps Reserve, call-up of, 83–84
Congressional Medal of Honor, xvi, 139
Congressional Record, 31

Cork, Alan: and Korean weather, 117–18; and battle at Chosin, 127–29; and Chinese night attacks, 131–32; and breakout, 135–36, 137–38; wounded, 137; and his extraordinary escape, 141; illus., 127
Corn, Donald: illus., 59
Cox, Charlene, 239, 240
Cox, Devon, 240
Cox, Kenneth Ray, 52, 78, 224; enlists, 12, 13; home on leave, 40–41; as tank gunner, 53; death, 53, 223; illus., 223
Cox, Lois, 52, 53
Cox, William M., 203
Crane, Dexter, 158, 159; serves in air force, 160; stationed in Japan, 192; secretly sent to Hanoi, 193; illus., 192
Crockett, Lem, 205
Croix de querre, 170
Crossland, Dorothy, 7
Crowe, Herbert, 181; enlistment, 20; experiences racial prejudice, 20–21; reflects on war experiences, 181–82; segregated training, 182
Cunningham, William, 158; illus., 66
Cutting, _____, 142

D Company (army), 128
Davis, Bill, 84
Denton, Winfield K., 67, 150, 212
Dickson, Albert: illus., 59, 66
Distinguished Service Cross, xvi, 144
Doane, Bill, 41
Doane, Robert, 12, 13, 40, 41, 53, 223, 224
Dougan, Kenneth, 189
Draft, 5, 57, 65, 72, 100, 175, 179, 199, 200, 206, 213
Dubois County Daily Herald, 70, 100, 147, 202
Dunkirk, xix, 145
Dunn, John, 55

Early, Maurice, 208
East of Chosin: Entrapment and Breakout in Korea, 1950, xiv, 81
Egan, Robert, 122
Eighth bomb squadron, 192
Eighth Engineering Combat Battalion, First Cavalry Division (army), 15
Eisenhower, Dwight D., 46
Elkhart High School, 28
Elliott, John, 60
Ellis, William J., 89
Employment: young men have difficulty finding, 10, 12, 13
Etheridge, Margie, 216
Etheridge, Walter: writes of injury in war, 216; illus., 216
Etheridge, William, 216
Ettensohn, June, 215
Evansville, 201, 202; World War II boom changes, 3; baseball team, 6; oil boom, 6–7; site of marine reserve unit, 27, 28, 29, 32, 43; reserve unit activated, 41–42, 60, 85, 225; marine reserve unit sent to Korea, 85–86; departure of marine reserve unit, 88; economic impact of Korean War on, 201; and preparedness for atomic bomb attack, 207
Evansville College, 9
Evansville Courier, 6, 7, 88, 122, 148, 150
Evansville Press, 7, 69, 149, 201
Evansville Sunday Courier and Press, 69, 148, 207

F-84 (jet), 158
F-86 (airplane), 234, 235
Faith, Donald C., Jr., xvi, 17, 18, 81, 82, 115, 127, 129, 142, 143; receives Silver Star, 130; takes command of task force, 131; leads breakout attempt, 132; death, 134, 139, 143, 144; illus., 131

Falls, Clifford, 84
Federal Bureau of Investigation, 203, 209, 210
Feeney, Al, 86
Fifth Regiment (marines), 172; positions of, 114
First Battalion, Twenty-first Regiment, Twenty-fourth Infantry Division (army), 46
First Cavalry Division (army), 40, 46, 47, 54, 94, 100; enters Pyongyang, 102; trapped by Chinese, 146; sent to break siege at Chipyong-ni, 163
First Marine Division, xix, 100, 118, 148; and World War II, 83; as element of Tenth Corps, 113; establishes supply bases, 113–14; inflicts casualties on Chinese troops, 126; recuperates, 154; and Chinese spring offensive, 175; surrounded at Chosin, 225–26. *See also* United States Marine Corps; United States Marine Corps Reserve
Fitch, Mrs. _____, 226
Fitch, Gordon, 227
Fitch, Henry, 227, 228
Fitch, Robert "Bud," xiv, 173, 230; describes Korea, xviii; letters, 90–91, 171–75; death, 177, 224, 226, 227, 228; celebrates end of World War II, 197–98; joins marine reserve, 225; illus., 59, 66
Flaugher, Laurel, 84
Forgotten War: America in Korea, The, xiv
Formosa, 146
Fort Dix (N.J.), 20
Fort Hood (Tex.), 12
Fort Jackson (S.C.), 13
Fort Knox (Ky.), 12, 15, 20, 24
Fort Lewis (Wash.), 23–24, 107, 181
Fort Riley (Kans.), 18
Fort Wayne: site of marine reserve unit, 27; reserve unit activated, 42,

INDEX 267

83–84, 85; and parade for departing reservists, 84
Fort Wayne Journal-Gazette, 5, 70
Fox Company, 106
France: troops in Korea, 162, 163, 170; troops in Indochina, 193
Frostbite, 123, 133, 144, 168, 182

Garrigus, Charles, Jr., xvi, 18, 81, 82, 117, 118, 121, 129, 142, 143, 144; serves in World War II, 16–17; reenlists, 17; writes of conditions in Korea, 114; listed as MIA, 126; leads convoy of wounded, 133, 134; and acts of heroism at battle of Chosin, 130, 131, 134, 135–36, 139–40; stays with convoy, 139; awarded Distinguished Service Cross, 145; illus., 140
Garrigus, Charles, Sr., 16, 145
Garrigus, Delores, 16
Garrigus, Gladys, 16, 114, 145
Garrigus family, 122, 126
"The Gauntlet," 105, 106, 109
Geneva Convention, 167
George Company (marines), 176, 177
GI Bill, 56, 199–200, 235
Goshen, xviii
Goulden, Joseph C., xiv, 49
Graham, David, 62; joins marine reserve, 29–30; activation of, 41–42; concerns about training, 60; guard duty, 60–61; cold weather and securing a sleeping bag, 125–26; and Korean honey pot, 190–91
Grapes of Wrath, 16
Grappo, Louis Joseph, 136
Great Depression, 4, 16
Green, _____, 128
Greene, Gordon, 170; and training, 32–33, 89; and combat, 66; hopes only to serve occupation duty in Korea, 93–94; and diminished numbers in his company, 183–84; and World War II home front efforts, 197; celebrates end of World War II, 197–98; and allotment to mother, 212; wounded, 217; writes of Bud Fitch's death, 227; returns home, 230; illus., 59, 66
Greenwood, Sydney, 227, 228
Guadalcanal, 83
Guerrillas, 116, 154, 155, 156, 161
Gustin, Ralph C., 201

Haag, Joe, 222, 223
Hagaru/Hagaru-ri, 114, 122, 129, 132, 133, 136, 140, 143, 144
Hale, John, 142
Hamhung, 118
Hamilton, Donald, 121, 150; stationed in Japan, 21–22; hopes for discharge, 22–23, 40, 55, 56, 57, 115; and start of war, 39–40; writes of U.S. troops sent from Japan to Korea, 55–56; sent to Korea, 58; and expectation of short war, 96; writes of combat experience at Inchon and Seoul, 98; writes of unreliability of South Korean troops in combat, 115–16; and Chosin Reservoir, 116–17; disappears, 136; listed MIA, 239, 240; illus., 21
Hamilton, Oval, 40, 57, 58, 115, 116, 117, 239, 240
Hamilton family, 150, 240; illus., 239
Hammel, Eric, xiv
Hammerstein, Gerald, 149
Han River, 234
Hanoi, 193
Harper, Joe, 142
Hasselbrinck, William, 65
Hensel, R. H., 83
Hill 55, p. 189
Hill 189, p. 54
Hill 749, p. 185

Hill Nine-O-Two, 176, 177
Hill 1081, p. 123
Hill 1221, pp. 143, 144
Hitchcock, Robinson, 199
Hitler, Adolf, 7, 75
Hoarding, 201, 202, 203, 206, 210
Home front, 197–230; and media, 62, 64, 67, 68–78; and hopes for short war, 71, 73, 74; families deal with activation of reserve units, 85, 87; optimism over early success of troops, 100; and support of troops, 149; and Communist sympathizers, 179; and World War II, 197
Hongchon, 172
Hope, Bob, 102
Hungnam, 118, 143, 144
Hyde, William, 234–35
Hygiene, 97, 119, 121, 173

In Mortal Combat: Korea, 1950–1953, xiv, 95
Inchon, xix, 58, 78, 82, 86, 88, 94, 95, 96, 98, 142
Indiana: and Korean War casualties, xv, 230, 233; postwar prosperity, 4; patriotism, 10; and racial discrimination, 7–8, 238–39; and post–World War II ambivalence, 9; national media uses to gauge feelings on Korean War, 77; and wartime production, 198–99; communists in, 202, 209, 210; and general mistrust of federal government, 205, 206; and civil defense, 206–7, 208
Indiana Business Review, 4
Indiana Daily Student, 5, 6, 72, 73, 74, 83, 146, 199, 200, 201, 204, 208, 229
Indiana Fair Employment Practice Act, 7
Indiana Girls' School, 7
Indiana National Guard, Thirty-eighth Infantry Division, 70

Indiana State Fair, 199, 209
Indiana State Police, 207
Indiana University, 6, 201
Indianapolis, 202; revival of manufacturing during World War II, 3–4; marine reserve unit in, 27, 31; marine reserve unit activated, 42, 85–87, 236; and send-off for marine reserve unit, 86; and preparedness for atomic bomb attack, 208, 209
Indianapolis Newsboys Band, 86
Indianapolis Public Schools, 198
Indianapolis Recorder, 7, 8, 75, 76, 183, 229; reports episode of racism, 238–39
Indianapolis Star, 4, 5, 62, 64, 67, 68, 77, 85, 87, 145, 148, 201, 202, 203, 205, 208, 209, 229, 233, 234
Indochina, 193
Inflation, 203, 204
Integration, 229–30
Intelligence and Reconnaissance (I & R), 14
Iron Curtain, 147
Item Company, Third Battalion, Fifth Marine Regiment, 122
Iwo/Iwon, 100, 116

Jacobs, Andy, Jr., 46, 193; joins marine reserves, 31; activation and send-off of marine reserve unit, 42, 86–87; boot camp, 90; and Chinese spring offensive, 176–77; wounded, 177; poem, 177; returns home, 236; speech, 236–37, 240; organizes congressional debate on Vietnam, 237; illus., 30, 240
Jacobs, Andy, Sr., 5, 31, 46; quoted, 193; illus., 30
Japan, 31, 94; compared to Korea, xviii, 101; post–World War II occupation of, xix; U.S. forces in, 13, 14, 15, 17, 18, 20, 21, 40, 55;

U.S. garrisons from sent to Korea, 46
Jenner, William E., 9, 10, 45, 67, 150
Jessup, Philip C., 6, 72
Johnson, Louis A., 38, 46
Johnson, Lyndon B., 236
Jones, Robert E., 82

Keiser, Laurence, 52
Kimpo Airfield, 98, 187, 234, 235; falls to American forces, 96
King, _____, 128
Kodijo Island, 182
Korea, 88; weather in, xvi–xvii, 51, 54, 78, 103–4, 108, 109, 116, 117, 118, 120, 123, 125, 126, 127, 133, 156, 157, 160, 161, 164, 171, 172, 215; terrain, xvii, xviii, 51, 92, 176, 179, 189; people and customs, xvii, xviii, 156, 190, 191; post–World War II occupation force in, 13–14; reunification of, 38, 99, 153; description of landscape, 51, 184; U.S. ground troops sent to, 67, 68; troops remain in, 234, 235. *See also* North Korea; South Korea
Korea: The First War We Lost, xiv
Korea: The Untold Story, xiv
Korean War: and memorial for, xiii, xv, 240; veterans of, xiii, 235, 241; as forgotten war, xv; casualties, xv, 171, 180, 184, 229, 230, 233; stages of, xix–xx, 153; home front, xx, 74, 75, 149, 197–230; becomes static, xx, 171, 180, 184, 185, 189; and African-American response to, 8, 75–76, 183; and fear will begin World War III, 37, 67, 70–71, 75, 145, 147, 198, 208; beginning of, 37–38, 71; U.S. sends troops to, 38, 72, 73; U.S. supplies South Koreans, 40; retreats, 48, 81, 122–23, 126, 145, 148, 162, 180; and intelligence, 55, 163; U.S. troops unprepared for, 58, 64, 67; and media support of, 62, 64, 67, 68–78, 198, 199; veterans of World War II serve in, 62, 65, 97; hope for end of, 73, 121, 171, 173; China enters, 81, 104, 121, 122–23, 127, 145, 146, 215; swings back in favor of UN forces, 82; and difference from World War II, 88; and hopes for short war, 90, 93, 96, 119, 120; conduct of North and South Korean troops, 97; optimism about, 99, 100; Chinese threaten entry, 99, 102; U.S. forces cross thirty-eighth parallel, 100; and civilian casualties, 100, 101, 241; and refugees, 100–101, 179; and "The Gauntlet," 105, 106, 107, 109; and MIAs, 112, 126, 228, 239, 240; and guerrillas, 116, 154, 155, 156, 161; weather as factor in, 117–18, 121, 126, 127, 130, 133, 145, 156; media paint grim picture of fighting, 121–22, 145–48; and battle at Chosin Reservoir, 122–23, 126, 127–29, 130–50, 187, 213, 220, 226; and air support, 129, 157, 158–59, 160, 172, 173, 176, 191–92; and Chinese night attacks, 131–32; and Seventh Division breakout attempt, 132–44; and Chinese treatment of dead and wounded enemies, 141, 143, 166, 167; use of atomic bomb in, 147, 148; and wartime production, 149; sniper attacks, 154–55; France sends troops to, 162, 163, 170; and battle at Chipyong-ni, 162–63, 164–71; and prisoners, 163, 182, 183; and Chinese spring offensive, 171, 174, 175, 176, 178, 179, 180, 187; and ROK troops, 179, 180; accelerates desegregation of armed services, 181; becomes war of

attrition, 183; and truce agreement, 191, 192, 233, 234; concerns about rationing and price controls, 198, 201, 203–4, 205; economic impact of, 201; and hoarding, 201, 202, 203, 206, 210; and inflation, 203, 204; and taxes, 204, 205; and fears of government misuse of power during, 205, 206; and civil defense, 206–7, 208, 209; and apathy toward, 210–11, 230, 236; compared to World War II, 211; and financial hardships on families of servicemen, 212–13; and how servicemen inform relatives of wounds, 216–17; and activation of reserve units, 225, 233–34; marines save center of UN line, 228; and integration of armed forces, 229–30; end of, 229–30; lack of memorial for, 230; and number of Hoosiers who served in, 233; and closure for families of missing and killed, 239, 240

Korean War memorial, xiii, xv

Koto-ri, 114

Kroger, 18

Kunson, 158

Kuykendall, William, 238

Lackland Air Force Base (San Antonio, Tex.), 160

Lafayette Journal and Courier, 68, 77, 204

Leatherneck, The, 228

Leffler, Bettie Lou, 107, 229

Leffler, Everett Wayne, Jr.: poem about service at Fort Lewis, 23–24; joins army, 107; and letters home, 107–9; declared MIA, 110; change in status of, 228–29; illus., 25, 107

Leffler, Everett, Sr., 228

Leffler family, 228, 229

Les Brown's Band, 102

Liberty Squadron (air force), 192

Life magazine, xvii

Little Creek (Va.), 90

LST (landing ship, tank), 3

M 1 rifle, 48, 51, 54–55, 89, 97

MacArthur, Douglas, xix, 78, 82, 94, 99, 104, 113, 120, 121, 145, 181; assumes command of UN forces, 38

McAtee, Mrs. Homer, 43, 45

McCarthy, Joseph, 9

McCracken, Branch, 6

McCray, William, 67

McDaniel, Mrs. _____, 212–13

McDaniel, Paul: and retreat from Chosin Reservoir, 122; and allotment for dependents, 212, 213

McGary, Raleigh: describes North Korean people, 101; and weather and conditions in the field, 118–21; hopes to be home soon, 120; illus., 119

MacLean, Allan, 114, 115, 126, 130, 131, 132

Madden, _____, 128

Maddox, Edward F., 77

MaGill, _____, 143

Maginot complex, 68

Manchuria, xix, 72, 100, 104, 110, 115, 220

Marine Corsairs (airplanes), 95

Marine Hospital (Evansville), 85

Marshall, S. L. A., xiv, 109

Marshall, William: recalls World War II patriotism, 10; joins reserves, 43; efforts to prevent activation of, 43–45; leaves for marine reserves, 45; and boot camp, 214; illus., 59, 66

Martin, John Bartlow, 9

MASH, 187

Maxwell, Marilyn, 102

Maynard, _____, 142

Index

Mayville, Donald: enlists, 17–18; and breakout attempt, 142–44; and loss of officers and noncoms, 142, 144; returns home, 241
Media: predicts economic stability, 4; reports on situation of reservists, 60–65; paints grim picture of war, 121–22, 145–48; and support of Korean War, 198; warns against hoarding, 201, 202, 203
Medical aid, 98, 102, 136, 142, 144, 157, 168, 169, 186, 187, 217; Chinese, 241
Medical supplies, 133
Memorial High School (Evansville), 28
Memphis (Tenn.), 237
MIG-15 (airplane), 234
Milburn, Frank, 100
Miller, Col. ____, 14
Miller, Cosby, 82, 139, 140
Miller, Forrest: illus., 59, 66
Monclar, ____, 170
Montagne, Ed, 138
Morale, 55–56, 84, 85, 89, 90, 93, 102, 110, 131, 153
Mulvihill, Tom, 138
Muncy, Samuel: enlists, 13; serves in Japan, 14; recalls start of Korean War, 39; participation in Inchon landing, 96; recalls weather and Chinese attack, 126–27; and breakout at the Chosin, 134–35, 140–41; pinned down by Chinese fire, 139; illus., 96

Naval Armory (Indianapolis), 86, 87
Neal, Ira, 18; enlists, 19; and desegregation of army, 181; and Korean experiences, 182; and discrimination following his return from the war, 237–38; illus., 19
Nelson, Mrs. Paul, 217
Nelson, Stanley, 78, 241; enlists, 15; and start of Korean War, 40; arrives in Korea, 46–47; and combat, 47–48, 49; and jubilation of crossing thirty-eighth parallel, 100; relates effects of war on Korean population, 100–101; capture of and retreat from Pyongyang, 102, 110; and battle of Chipyong-ni, 163–70; wounded, 165, 166, 168, 217–18; aided by Chinese medic, 168–69; rescued, 169; receives awards, 169–70; letters to family, 214; illus., 15, 168
New York Times, 122
Newark Common School (Greene County), 12
Newsweek, 4, 37
Ninth Regiment (army), 179
Nixon, Richard M., 237
Noland, Edward, 45
North Korea, 70; and control of power plants, 13; invades South Korea, 17, 38, 39, 40, 43, 46, 71, 73; troops attack U.S. forces, 46, 47, 48–49, 52; weapons, 47, 183, 184; troops continue to advance, 49; troops attack after sunset, 53; U.S. Air Force strafes troops, 54; troops trap American forces at Osan, 72; army pushed back by UN forces, 82; bombardment of, 94, 95; UN forces land behind lines of, 94, 95; and mines and booby traps, 94, 155; troops cut and run, 96, 99; conduct of troops, 97; navy shells troops, 100; description of people, 101; and treatment of prisoners, 102, 183; troops hit UN line, 148, 171, 180; lack of air force or artillery, 161

O'Connor, Paul R., 84
O'Keefe, Bob, 217
Oakland City: celebrates end of World War II, 197–98; "Roll of Honor" in, 230

Oakland City College, 224
Oakland City Journal, 52, 205
Oceanside (Calif.), 83
Okinawa, 12, 31, 49, 50
Orth, Henry, Jr., 30
Osan, 72

P-47 (airplane), 3
Pace, Frank, 27
Parris Island (S.C.), 91
Patriotism, 27, 62, 64, 66, 210, 211
Pearl Harbor, 71
Pohong, 171, 172
Pohong-Dong, 171
Poole, Wayne: illus., 86
Pope, Mrs. Fred, 198
Potential Leadership School (PLS), 13
Presidential citation, 215
Price-and-wage controls, 198, 201, 203, 204, 205
Prisoners of war (POW), xvi, 49, 97, 117, 163, 167, 182; report poor performance of weapons, 54–55; treatment of, 102; African-American, 183
Purple Heart, 216
Pusan, xviii, xix, 46, 50, 52, 53, 77, 78, 82, 99, 145, 153, 154, 157, 185
Pyongyang, 99, 100, 110; U.S. troops capture, 102

Racial discrimination, 7–8, 20–21, 75–76, 77, 182, 183, 237–39
Ramsey, Andrew W., 75, 77
Refugees, 100–101, 179
Reilly, William, 142
Reitz High School (Evansville), 28
Republic Aviation Corporation (Evansville), 3
Republic of Korea. *See* South Korea
Reserves: reasons to join, 24, 27; training of, 28, 29, 31, 32, 33; and attendance, 31–32; media reports situation of, 60–65; and loss of civilian jobs and wages, 62, 63, 64–65; families complain about call-up of, 62–63; lack of preparation and training of, 63–64, 93; veterans in, 83. *See also* United States Marine Corps Reserve
Retreats, 106–7, 109–10, 121, 122, 145, 148, 162, 180
Reynolds, Warren C., 84
Rhee, Syngman, 95
Ridgway, Matthew, 153, 154, 156
River and the Gauntlet, The, xiv
Riverside Amusement Park (Indianapolis): discrimination at, 7–8
Robbins, Hugh W., 136
Robbs, Alfred, 238–39
Rogers, Dwight L., 200
Roop, James B., 84
Russia. *See* Soviet Union

Sabotage, 206
Sadako, 150
Saipan, 31
Sands of Iwo Jima (movie), 27
Saudi Arabia, 26
Schmidt, George C., 85
Schricker, Henry F., 5, 87, 206
Scott, Bernard, 77
Second Division (army), xvi, 12, 23, 52, 53, 161, 180; caught in surprise Chinese attack, 104; and "The Gauntlet," 105, 106
Segregation, 180, 182
Selective Service Board, 45
Seoul, 82, 98, 160, 217; marine and army forces march toward, 96; capture of, 97, 99; U.S. forces begin withdrawal toward, 103
Seventh Division (army), xv–xvi, xix, 17, 21, 39, 56, 100, 114; serves in Japan, 14; and Inchon landing, 96; participates in Inchon/Seoul campaign, 98; attempts to trap

INDEX 273

North Korean army, 99; as element of Tenth Corps, 113; moves toward Chosin Reservoir, 115; and opinion of enemy troops, 121; trapped by Chinese, 126; attempts to break out of Chinese trap, 132–44; retreat to coast and evacuation of, 144; reaches Manchurian border, 220
Seventh Regiment (marines), 171, 172
Seventy-second Tank Battalion (army), 12, 52
Sheetz, Garold: illus., 59, 66
Shortridge High School (Indianapolis), 31
Silver Star, 130, 144, 169
1600 Killers: A Wake-up Call for Congress, The, 176
Sixteenth Infantry Battalion (marines), 86, 87
Smith, Clyde, 6
Smith, Margaret Chase, 43, 45
Smith, O. P., 113, 114
Sniper attacks, 154–55
South Bend: marine reserve unit in, 27, 28, 29, 42
South Korea, 48, 70, 95; invasion of, 17, 43, 46, 71, 73; maintains a constabulary force, 38; U.S. supplies planes and ammunition to, 40; troops outmatched, 46, 68, 180; unreliability of troops in combat, 72, 115–16, 179; American forces hope to keep foothold in, 83; conduct of troops, 97; and customs, 162
South to the Naktong, North to the Yalu, xiv
Soviet Union, 37, 67, 71, 72, 77, 146, 202, 205; fears of World War III with, xix, 198; supports North Korea, 38; fears of nuclear attack from, 207
Spencer, Carl, 78; and combat experiences, 53–54, 156, 157; and effects of war on Korean population, 101; and "The Gauntlet," 106–7; and air support, 157, 158; and battle at Chipyong-ni, 163; illus., 54
Spurr, Russell, 104, 105
Stalin, Joseph, 67, 68
Star for Buster, A, 197
Stars and Stripes, 57
State Civil Defense Organization, 208
Steele, Ralph, 62; joins marine reserve, 28–29; activated, 42–43, 60; and boot camp, 91–93; and static war, 184–87; wounded, 185–86, 217; letters, 214; returns home, 235; illus., 187
Steinbeck, John, 16
Stillwell, John, 26
Storms, Harvey, 143
Strait, Lawrence, 84
Sunbeam Electric Company (Evansville), 3
Suttmiller, Howard: joins marine reserve, 31; and Hill 1081, p. 123; recalls cold weather, 123, 125; illus., 124

T-34 (tank), 38, 55, 110
Task Force Crombex, 170
Task Force Faith, 132, 133, 143; efforts detain Chinese troops, 144
Task Force MacLean, 126, 130; and lack of organization in, 114; trapped by overwhelming number of Chinese forces, 121, 126, 127
Task Force Ninety-Five, 94, 95
Task Force Smith, 46
Tawara, 31
Taxes, 204, 205
Tenth Corps, 117, 118, 129, 130, 148, 153; marches toward Chosin Reservoir, 100; vulnerability of, 113; trapped by Chinese troops, 121, 122, 126; escape of, 145, 150; North Korean forces hit, 180

Terre Haute, 238–39
Terre Haute Tribune, 70, 71, 145, 198, 202, 208
336th Fighter Interceptor Squadron (air force), 234
Third Battalion, Thirty-first Regiment (army), 142
Third Battalion, Twenty-ninth Infantry (army), 49, 50
Third Marine Battalion, 177
Thirty-eighth Field Artillery Battalion (army), 107, 109
Thirty-eighth parallel, xix, xx, 13, 72–73, 77, 107, 154, 161, 171, 172, 178, 215; North Korean Army flees across, 99; U.S. troops cross, 100, 174; Chinese tempted to cross, 153; UN forces reach, 173; most fighting occurs along, 180
Thirty-eighth Regiment (army), 179
Thirty-first Regiment (army), 129, 130, 179; stationed in Japan, 14; at Chosin Reservoir, 114; surrounded by Chinese troops, 122; attacked by Chinese, 127
Thirty-second Regiment, 17, 21, 39, 129, 138; leaves for Korea, 56–57; at Chosin Reservoir, 114, 116; surrounded by Chinese troops, 122, 127; survivors of recall breakout, 145
Thurman, Jess, 97
Thurston, Arthur M., 207
Time magazine, 37, 47, 77, 93, 205, 210, 211
Toland, John, xiv, xx, 95
Torian, Paul, 28, 41
Training, 14, 19–20, 27, 49, 58, 59, 83, 96; and African Americans, 8; basic, 12, 15; reserve, 28, 29, 30, 31, 32, 33, 85, 86, 90, 91–93, 94; boot camp, 28, 33, 60, 90, 214; concern about short duration of, 88–89

Truman, Harry S., 46, 67, 69, 70, 71–72, 73, 149, 150, 213; cuts military spending, 26, 27; sends ground troops to Korea, 38; confers with MacArthur, 113; desegregates armed forces, 180, 181
Tulagi, 83
Turkey: troops fight in Korea, 106
Twenty-fifth Division (army), 58
Twenty-fourth Division (army), 46, 58; leaves for Korea, 55–56
Twenty-fourth Infantry Regiment (army): performance in Korea, 76, 81
Twenty-ninth Regiment (army), 12, 51, 52; sent to Korea, 49
Twenty-seventh Regiment: casualties in, 52
Twenty-third Regiment (army), 160, 170, 179; at Chipyong-ni, 162, 163, 171

United Nations, 69, 71, 72, 74; forces in Korea, xix, xx, 38, 46, 82, 93, 117, 146, 148, 153, 156, 178; and pursuit of fleeing North Korean troops, 99; forces take Seoul, 99; MacArthur divides forces, 99; forces at Chosin Reservoir, 115; ineffective in Korea, 147; air forces of control skies, 157, 158, 191; forces unable to take prisoners, 163; forces halt Chinese drive, 170–71; forces attacked by North Koreans, 180; forces form static front, 183; line saved, 228; and end of Korean War, 234
United States Air Force, 157, 158, 160, 191, 192, 233, 234; training, 19; bombing and strafing runs, 47, 164, 172, 173, 192; Chinese fear, 129; drops supplies, 160, 163
United States Army: recruitment efforts, 10; size of, 38; weapons of

not fit for combat, 38–39; lack of preparedness, 49, 50, 58; retreats in Korea, 50; poor performance of in Korea, 54; receives inadequate intelligence, 55; troops deployed from Japan to Korea, 55–56; failure to adequately train reserves, 63–64; trapped at Chosin, 220; racism on bases, 238
    Eighth Army, 99, 157, 174; and casualties, 78; charged with taking Pyongyang, 99; moves toward Yalu River, 102; threatened with entrapment, 102, 103; retreat of, 110, 121, 145, 153, 162; extended beyond main supply lines, 113; at Chosin Reservoir, 114; and effects of victory at Chipyong-ni, 171
    See also Second Division; Seventh Division
United States Department of Defense, 45
United States Department of the Army, 45
United States Marine Corps, xv, 28, 45, 81, 120, 132, 136, 141, 143, 144, 176, 184, 185, 218, 233; demobilization of, 27; uniform, 29, 30, 31, 84; holds Pusan perimeter, 82; and Inchon landing, 96; at Chosin Reservoir, 122, 150, 213; air support by, 132, 138; clear out guerrilla bands, 156; enable UN line to hold, 178, 228. *See also* First Marine Division
United States Marine Corps Reserve, 26, 31, 212; and training of, 27, 30, 32, 33, 59–60, 83, 84, 85, 86, 88, 90, 91–93, 94, 225; recruitment, 28, 29; and low attendance of meetings, 32; activation of, 41–46, 58, 59–60, 83–88, 91, 225, 233–34, 236; lack of preparedness of, 83; and expectations for in combat, 89; concerns about short duration of training, 88–89; land at Kimpo Airfield, 97

United States Navy, 233; supports landings in Korea, 94–95, 96; shells fleeing North Korean troops, 100
U.S. News and World Report, 4, 62, 93, 198
USS *Toledo,* 94, 95, 100

Veterans, xiii–xiv, xv, xvi, 62, 84, 241; join reserves, 24, 83; treatment of, 31; serve in Korean War, 48, 91, 97; and training, 92; and education, 200; warn against hoarding, 202; disappointment of, 235
Veterans of Foreign Wars (VFW), 202, 210
Vietnam War, xv, 87, 193, 237, 241; and memorial for, 240

Wake Island, 113
Walker, Walton H., 114, 153
Wallace, Henry, 9
Washington Post, 237
Weapons, 38–39, 48, 49, 94, 95, 97, 98, 102, 103, 110, 116, 132, 142, 156, 157, 158, 159, 160, 161, 163, 164, 168, 173, 183, 184, 185, 234, 235; atomic, xix, 37, 77, 146, 148, 204, 207, 208, 209; production of, 3, 149; missiles and rockets, 27; poor performance of, 46, 51, 53, 54–55; napalm, 54; North Korean, 55, 183, 184; Chinese, 127, 165; mines and minefields, 143, 165; booby traps, 155
Western Union, 18
Whitehouse, Robert: patrol experiences, 154–56, 187–89; wounded, 189; returns home, 235–36; illus., 155